George Gissing
A Biography

George Gissing
A Biography

MICHAEL COLLIE

ARCHON BOOKS

First published in 1977
© Michael Collie 1977

Wm Dawson & Sons Ltd, Cannon House
Folkestone, Kent, England

Archon Books, The Shoe String Press, Inc
995 Sherman Avenue, Hamden, Connecticut 06514 USA

British Library Cataloguing in Publication Data

Collie, Michael
  George Gissing, a biography.
  1. Gissing, George   2. Novelists,
  English – 19th century – Biography
  I. Title
  823'.8   PR4717
  ISBN 0 7129 0770 X

  Archon ISBN 0 208 01700 3
  LC 77 30190

Printed in Great Britain
by W & J Mackay Limited, Chatham

Contents

Acknowledgements

It is a pleasure to thank the following libraries for permission to quote from the unpublished autographed letters of Gissing in their collections; Yale University Library for the letters in the Beinecke Rare Book Room and Manuscript Library; the Carl and Lily Pforzheimer Foundation Inc., for the letters in the Pforzheimer Library; the Henry W. and Albert A. Berg Collection in the New York Public Library, Astor Lenox and Tilden Foundations, for the letters and diaries in the Berg Collection; and the University of Virginia Library for the letters in the McGregor Collection.

In preparing to write this book I was helped in countless ways by Dawn Hirschler and Margaret Bowman. It is a pleasure now to be able to thank them warmly for their assistance.

Mme Le Mallier's hospitality and generous help, several years ago, is remembered with warm appreciation, while Alfred Gissing's kindness in allowing me to use the family papers is also gratefully acknowledged.

1

The Bourgeois Bohemian

ON 13 July 1895, the Omar Khayyam Club had a dinner in honour of George Meredith at the Burford Bridge Hotel, half a mile away from his tiny house at the foot of Box Hill and about an hour's run by train from London. The club had been formed in 1892 by a group of friends led by Clement Shorter, a literary entrepreneur who was busy establishing himself as one of London's principal editors. The club's practice was to invite established literary figures – people from all walks of life with a known and genuine interest in literature – to periodic, informal meetings over dinner. Sometimes they met in London; sometimes in the country. In helping to organize agreeable social encounters of this kind, Clement Shorter was a little less than disinterested (much more of a Jasper Milvain than an Edwin Reardon, in terms of Gissing's characters) in that he wanted to encourage well-known writers to contribute articles and short stories to the type of magazine they would not previously have taken seriously. At the same time, the primary interest of the group was literary, not commercial (a distinction they were still sure it was important to maintain), so that when they met at the Burford Bridge Hotel on this occasion it was for the exchange of news, for literary gossip, for professional talk between writers of experience, as well as to honour the acknowledged giant amongst them, the writer who had lived by the pen alone without any sacrifice of principle. Meredith in 1895 was at the height of his reputation, the homage was genuine and there was distinction in the mere fact of being invited.

At least on this occasion the dinner was a success, even for George Gissing. Few of those present would readily have associated the man whom Clement Shorter introduced to them with the author of the novels most of them had read. His physical appearance was dominated by his strong features, dark hair and heavy moustache. A man of letters in the nineteenth century sense (a person of broad literary

interests but not a dilettante), Gissing was invariably happy in the
company of men who shared his passionate, overriding interest in
books and his wide knowledge of contemporary European writing.
And they were happy in his, for there existed a bond between such
people, the bond of a classical education combined with an awareness
of European culture and a deep-rooted affection for words, literacy,
literature, a bond which gave them the assurance that goes with
exclusiveness and allowed them the luxury of not having to question
the social role of a writer, like Gissing, however critical of society he
might be. The then remote country hostelry at the foot of Box Hill,
with its orchards and farm buildings, and inside its easy comfort, to
an extent characterized this exclusiveness. It was an atmosphere in
which Gissing, the most private, secretive, elitist of them all, could
feel perfectly at home. He was exactly the type of cosmopolitan,
travelled, cynically aloof but energetic and educated Englishman with
whom they, the members of the Omar Khayyam Club, could identify.
And he could identify with them, because at least superficially they
subscribed to the Victorian convention that a man's private life was
his own business. It mattered little, as they walked up Box Hill after
dinner and enjoyed their cigars in the cool of the evening, that Gissing
the writer was poised as usual between financial failure and brilliant
literary success, and that Gissing the man was, as usual, haunted by
the possibility but depressed by the actuality of marriage. By character
and achievement he was, in the most natural way possible, one of the
company.

In 1895, Gissing was a gaunt but still handsome thirty-seven. During the previous eight or ten years he had alternately sold and re-
purchased, pawned and redeemed his dinner jacket, either according
to the state of his purse or because of his erratic feelings about his
ability to overcome a generally pervasive sense of social alienation.
At Burford Bridge he looked well in his 'uniform'. His figure was an
athletic one. He shared with many of his dinner companions acceptance of what for them was a fact of life that his appearance, his
essential presentability, were designed to conceal, or permitted the
concealment of other aspects of his existence, which had nothing to
do with books, and he was not alone in supposing, creature of the
time that he was, that the life one lived need not at all be confused
with how one contrived to live it. Behind the appearance of a conventionally dressed Victorian 'gentleman' who happened to be a
writer, he was ill almost to the point of breakdown, estranged from
his second wife, bewildered by having to be responsible for her and
their two children, and worn out by domestic and financial problems,
real and imaginary. Yet he was also a well-established writer, was
known both for early naturalistic books like *Demos* and *The Nether
World* – which an archdeacon had called 'so sombre and earnest in its

terrible realism that it will be forgotten easily by any serious thinkers'
– and by more recent novels like *New Grub Street* and *The Odd
Women*. Furthermore he was associated with the increasingly urgent
'movement' towards the professional freedom that was represented
both by the Society of Authors and by the emergence of new publishers like Lawrence & Bullen, publishers committed to publishing
relatively inexpensive, accessible, single volume novels that would
free both writer and public from the circulating libraries. His recent
work had been reasonably well reviewed. The *Athenaeum*, for instance, in welcoming *In the Year of Jubilee* as 'impressive', had said
that 'this remarkable book is greatly enhanced by the admirable style
in which it is written – always direct, forcible, and free from manner-
ism',[1] an opinion that was then widely shared. So Gissing was
received warmly by his fellow writers and enjoyed himself. Away
from his home and in the company of men, he was cheerful, a good
talker and full of stories. Indeed, whenever he could escape from his
house in Brixton with his dinner jacket and two or three books in his
suitcase, he was perfectly happy. And why, he thought, should he not
escape from such a wife?

Gissing even made a speech at the Burford Bridge dinner, recording that remarkable event in his diary. Clodd had toasted Meredith,
Meredith had replied, and L. F. Austin (who had himself, incidentally,
reviewed Gissing's *In the Year of Jubilee* earlier in the year in the
Sketch) gave a 'capital speech' in honour of the guests. 'Then my
name was shouted, and there was nothing for it. I told the story of
Meredith accepting *The Unclassed* for Chapman, and my interview
with him, when I did not know who he was.' By this time, of course,
the commercial failure of *The Unclassed* in 1884 was past history. In
any case, in such a company the commercial failure of serious fiction
was a fact of life. Its not selling suggested to them that it was probably
a good book. Though Gissing had had to steel himself, in 1884, to
'read very calmly these adverse reviews' (like the one in the *Academy*,
for instance) even then, at that early date, he had been recognized as a
writer who had the ability and courage to deal with difficult subjects
outside other people's range. Few authors had the 'daring', to use a
word from another contemporary review – an unsigned one in the
Evening News – to take seriously the friendship of a bohemian young
man and a London prostitute as he had done in *The Unclassed*, and
few had the ability to do so without 'pruriency or prudery'. Meredith
had recognized this immediately, though Gissing's admiration for
him dated not so much from these early days when Meredith had
helped to shape *The Unclassed*, as from his first enthusiastic reading
of Meredith's *Diana of the Crossways* in the important collected
edition of 1885, a reading which may well have helped him on his
way from social realism and satire to a more deeply conceived type

of psychological fiction. (As a matter of fact, Meredith may have influenced *The Unclassed* twice, on the second occasion in just as significant a way as the first, since in September 1895, a few months after the meeting at Burford Bridge, Gissing revised the novel for the second edition proposed by Lawrence & Bullen.) Gissing recognized Meredith as the strongest of allies in the fight of the serious author to be allowed to write and publish freely (Meredith became President of the Society of Authors when Tennyson died), and for this reason was all the more willing to contribute to the after-dinner talk which in other circumstances he would have despised. Partly as a consequence of his speech *The Chronicle*, in its report of the occasion, grouped Gissing, Hardy and Meredith as the 'three most important novelists of the day', as indeed they were.

The achievement of the three men during the early nineties had been formidable. Meredith, astonishingly, had recovered his health and written *One of Our Conquerors* (1891), *Lord Ormont and his Aminta* (1894) and *The Amazing Marriage* (1895). Hardy had ended his novel-writing career with *Tess of the d'Urbervilles* (1892) and *Jude the Obscure* (1894). And Gissing had followed *New Grub Street* (1891) and *Born in Exile* (1892) with *Denzil Quarrier* (1892), *The Odd Women* (1893) and *In the Year of Jubilee* (1894). No wonder they felt they had, and were seen to have, so much in common. Gissing, the younger man – Meredith was sixty seven and Hardy fifty five, – was embarrassed by this report in *The Chronicle*, fearing that what he called 'the exaggeration' might do him more harm than good. Nonetheless, the friendly talk with Meredith and Hardy at the Burford Bridge Hotel did Gissing good. It brought him more into the public eye and it resulted in invitations from them both. In the literary world of London where he desired to be accepted and respected he was in every sense an established and important writer.

During the next few years, until Gissing went to live in France, he visited Meredith frequently at Box Hill, sometimes going for dinner, sometimes accepting the open invitation and turning up unannounced. Guarded by his gardener, Frank Cole, and tended by his nurse, Miss Nicholls, Meredith was always glad to see such visitors – as Paul Valéry, for example, so charmingly related. And invitations to meet the great man in Box Hill were not to be taken lightly, for Meredith was scarcely known for his tolerance of fools and conformists. As Chapman & Hall's manuscript reader he had customarily dismissed manuscripts in single-sentence reports with phrases like 'shambling work, with none of the merits of roughness' (on 'Jack Straw's Castle') and 'close on imbecile' (on 'Agnostia Huckstone'). But he recognized Gissing's qualities and accepted him as a writer of integrity, a fact which resulted in Gissing settling in Dorking a couple of years later.

Gissing also visited Hardy at Max Gate in September 1895 just before he revised *The Unclassed*. From his point of view, perhaps from Hardy's also, the visit was less than a complete success. He found that Hardy retained 'a peasant's view of life', that he did not read very much (for Gissing, the worst of sins) and that he was 'unsettled' and 'discontented', probably because of 'his long association with that paltry woman'. If he did not read much, Hardy had at least read Gissing's books. They responded to each other's books with the critical spirit that can and with them did accompany profound understanding. There were strong similarities between their works, for example between Tess in *Tess of the d'Urbervilles* and Clara Hewett in *The Nether World*, and between the dance in the barn and the dance at Crystal Palace in the same novels, of which they could not help but be aware, whether or not there was any question of influence. They shared an insight into the eccentric and the pathological and from their own books knew this. Perhaps Gissing felt closer to Meredith than to Hardy because, whereas Hardy was withdrawn, gloomy, superficially domestic and tame, Meredith was still aggressively masculine and independent. Furthermore their literary talk was not interrupted, Meredith's wife having died ten years earlier. Sitting by the fireside in the tiny sitting room at Box Hill, or in Meredith's 'chalet' at the end of the garden, smoking and talking books, was simply more enjoyable than observing the proprieties with Mrs. Hardy at Max Gate. All the same, the Omar Khayyam dinner significantly confirmed a tacit literary alliance between the three men, an understanding of a kind which Hardy and Meredith could perhaps take for granted but which for George Gissing was at least as important as popular success.

How can this picture of Gissing in 1895 be reconciled with the popular view of him in 1975? Up to the First World War, Gissing's achievement was clearly recognized by people like Arnold Bennett, Henry James and Virginia Woolf, who did not doubt it was worth taking him seriously, despite their reservations about his conception of the novel. Then for a while his books were allowed to go out of print, for roughly a fifty-year period until in the early sixties literary critics again became interested in his work and began to be sceptical about the standard accounts of the writer. During the period of neglect, he had been known for the wrong reasons. Unsubstantiated anecdote about the cause of his supposed failure as a serious artist had somehow ruined his reputation. There have been thieves, pedants, scholars, sensualists, puritans, escapists who have avoided being written off in the casual way in which some people used to dismiss Gissing. Other writers have failed to be wealthy, without being dismissed to oblivion. Why, then, in this case were the man and work confused? Partly, perhaps, because the repeated republication of unrevised or shoddily edited texts affected his literary reputation as adversely as anecdote and literary gossip ruined his personal reputation. Old stories die hard. Even now, he tends to be remembered as a mainly autobiographical writer, whereas he was, at least for part of his career, a deliberate naturalist of the continental type; remembered as a novelist who invariably wrote the same, rather dull, kind of book, whereas he was in point of fact experimental and varied. He is seen as a writer whose view of life was conditioned, some said conditioned absolutely, by his own experiences in prison, in exile, in poverty and in unhappy marriages, whereas it is more useful to realize that he was clinically detached and as such a perceptive, if somewhat cold and remorseless critic of contemporary life. So it seems; yet which view is really right? Was Gissing an important, late nineteenth-century novelist (an experimental *writer* of interest as well as a social critic)? His contemporaries, many of them, believed so. Or was he, as is often said, and as Angus Wilson recently said yet once again, a writer who, though determined, lacked the basic skills to succeed? This new account of Gissing is an attempt to answer the question.

It will be a new account of the facts of Gissing's life as it is possible to determine them, a new biography of a writer who happened to have a sensationally fascinating life, and not yet another pseudo-interpretation of the novels, or some of them, on the assumption that they provide the type of directly autobiographical evidence which would make it impossible to take Gissing seriously. What above all becomes clear as one reads through once again both the published and unpublished correspondence, as well as the diaries, notebooks and fiction manuscripts, is the huge difficulty of reconciling the emerging figure of the wholly devoted writer, who for whatever his reasons spent his life creating novels, with the image of puzzling, rather shifty late Victorian nihilist who never discovered a coherence of thought and action and perhaps never believed such coherence possible. And this, though important, is not the only problem. A special snag is that because he led such a quiet, even furtive, life there are few contemporary accounts of him, a situation which is compounded by the fact that it seems wisest not to take entirely on trust (as others have done) what Gissing said about himself, since Gissing's own evasive half-truths are part of the mystery that has to be unravelled.

And mystery, in the first instance, there certainly is – not least in the discrepancy between many contemporary accounts and the picture that later critics built up. George Moore, retrospectively, called him 'a man of medium talent, who would have done much better if he had lived in any other time than the one in which he did live', an odd thing to say about a man who devoted his whole life to the contemporary scene. Frank Swinnerton went much further towards the distortion that was soon to become fashionable. For Swinnerton Gissing was 'an egotist of a particular kind', a man 'at war with life' whose introspection involved 'a hatred' and a 'distaste' for his fellow men and whose books appealed to the mediocre reader because they were 'capable of flattering a sense of superiority in mis-cultured readers'; a man whose 'interest in ideas and in books had been cultivated to the ruin of his purely human sympathies'; and a novelist whose work was 'the rather querulous, random self- expression of the serious egotist'.[2] As for the masochism, it was Professor Korg who proposed that something dark in Gissing's nature made him search out situations, indeed create situations, which by being unbearably painful would justify, as it were, a deeply felt desire for self-mortification and self-pity.

These are theories that are not inconsistent with folk-lore accounts of Gissing's life, which was indeed so extraordinary in its main outline as to need an explanation of some kind. Yet they do not represent the full truth. The mystery of Gissing's life lies in the extreme eccentricity of his own reactions to his own experiences and in the almost horrifying discrepancies between his public and his private life. If George Moore was right, if Gissing would have done much better in another age, it would not have been because of his writing – which essentially consists of an attempt to write about contemporary life without recourse to social theory, and about people, without the knowledge of human motivation that post-dated Freud – but because, at the very least, he would not nowadays have had to conceal his cynical, sensual, passionate, irrational nature. He could have lived with that freedom which his nature always desired but which he was too deeply inhibited to visualize fully. Whether freedom from Victorian restraint would have made a more fundamental difference, would have allowed him to be a different person, is another matter, a speculation only just within the scope of a biography. It has made that difference for others; probably it would have for him.

In any case, Gissing was not remembered as a dreary pessimist by everyone. Rebecca West correctly observed forty years ago that the spell Gissing 'exerted on his friends was obviously due to his extreme personal charm',[3] while W. M. Colles, the novelist's first real literary agent, remembered him as 'one of the most loveable men and the brightest of companions. His laughter was whole-hearted. His sensibility was reflected in his refined face, and as he spoke his eyes lighted up with rare brilliancy giving a glimpse of a rare and beautiful soul'.[4] A newspaper photograph of 'Mr. Gissing being seen off at Victoria Station' by a group of his friends shows a man with a jaunty, relaxed expression on his face, his Homburg pushed up from his brow, and the sparkle of gaiety and happiness in his eyes. So he often was with his friends. They did not know, nor did he ever tell them, that before catching the train at Victoria Station at the beginning of his journey to Siena, he had engineered, and not for the first time, the type of rupture in domestic life that for another person would have been traumatic, totally destructive, totally incapacitating. On the contrary, the man they knew under that rakishly angled Homburg was the successful writer who was setting out for a winter in Italy to write what they vaguely understood to be a critical book on Dickens and no doubt a novel as well – for was he not one of the country's leading novelists? Male friendship, such as Gissing's with H. G. Wells, Meredith, Hardy or Clement Shorter, did not necessarily involve domestic familiarity and this ordinary fact of Victorian existence suited Gissing down to the ground, because it meant that he did not need to be troubled by the inconsistency between the eminently civilized attitude to human relationships expressed in his novels and the eminently barbaric attitude he often adopted towards his wives and the people closest to him. Convention did not require that he should be 'one of the most loveable men and the brightest of companions' to them. Besides, throughout his life he had preferred the security of seeing himself misunderstood to the psychological perils of autobiographical honesty.

In fact it was a certain perversity of mind that provided for him the necessary security of soul. For example, when Gabrielle Fleury first visited him in Dorking he craved love, friendship, sex, intelligent talk. The whole of his correspondence with this French woman who became his mistress, his last companion, his third 'wife', shows how deeply he needed her affection and friendship. Yet he noted in his diary that, when he went to meet her at Dorking Station, though he recognized her first, he instinctively, compulsively, turned his back on her, forcing her to make the first move, wanting to be wanted and refusing to take the responsibility for the moment of recognition. This perversity was almost equalled by his immense secretiveness – a secretiveness which in a sense is the real subject of this biography. He himself tended to conceal his own best characteristics, his intelligence, his learning, his desires, as well as the satanic side of his nature and the dark corners of emotional immaturity.

In particular, Gissing concealed his bohemian 'real-self'. Bohemian? Not an extravagant word for a man who was indifferent to possession and place, was pragmatic and cynical in relationships with other people, and was able to live for weeks out of a suitcase without a sense of deprivation. This bohemianism was probably literary in origin: he read Henri Murger's *Scènes de la vie Bohème* at an impressionable age and as the *Commonplace Book* shows, took its 'morality' seriously. But it was also thought out and deeply felt. Throughout his life Gissing was a professed agnostic, a positivist when positivism was briefly fashionable and at all times a determinist, a man who took from popular, post-Darwinian theory not a sense of possible social amelioration but a bitter insight into the relative meaninglessness of individual experience. From the beginning to the end of his life he was consistently anti-bourgeois, attacking directly or ironically middle-class institutions – marriage, war, the church – and middle-class attitudes, especially middle-class moral attitudes. Moreover, he was willing to write about subjects others avoided: like poverty, prostitution, urban conditions, acts of bad faith, matrimonial estrangements, lovelessness, failure. His bohemian nature did not express itself in frivolity, iconoclastic behaviour, non-conformity, but in a detachment from society that was concealed beneath an apparent conformity, in a loneliness which left him free to write, and in sets of nihilistic rejections which he never reconciled with his own unwillingly acknowledged needs and desires. He was a repressed bohemian. He did not stand apart from Victorian society with the panache of the *fin-de-siècle* dandy, the assertiveness of the radical, or the mere *joie de vivre* of the non-conformist. Rather, he stood apart from Victorian society secretly, furtively, as though unsure of himself, often appearing to live by double standards, often appearing to be in a muddle on matters on which he was perfectly clear. Recognized for what he was, a British version of a conventional nineteenth-century type, a bohemian, a decadent, his utterly bizarre life makes some sort of sense. But this character he maintained for himself by not being recognized for what he was. By this strategy an extremely determined and often brilliant writer reserved for himself the absolute freedom he needed for his work. In this lies the special enigma of his hectic and troubled life.

2
Youth, Education, Prison and Exile

GEORGE Robert Gissing was born on 22 November 1857, lived at home in Wakefield until his father died in 1870, was then sent, at the age of thirteen, to a Quaker boarding school at Alderley Edge in Cheshire and, in 1872, earned a three-year stay for himself at Owens College (now Manchester University) by obtaining distinguished results in the Oxford Local Examinations. He followed the conventional route of someone who had to make his own way in the world and could reasonably be expected to do so on the strength of his own intelligence. In this he at first succeeded, then failed.

No-one who had known him as an intense, overserious child in Wakefield, or as a precocious, hard-working adolescent at Alderley Edge, or as a quick-witted, gifted undergraduate at Manchester, could possibly have anticipated what was to come: imprisonment, exile, sensationally inept marriages and a long, painful breakdown in health. Nor could such a person have anticipated that the classicist would become one of the first students of the Victorian city, committing his life to the writing of types of social realism that were opposed in spirit to the ancient writers he most revered. Gissing dismissed his own childhood out of hand, as well as his early formal education: 'The indelible impressions which other men receive in their earliest years seem in my case to have been postponed until after I was twenty. My childhood is of no practical use to me; it was passed in mere comfort.'[1] Gissing's life bears out what he says here, for of the indelible impressions received in childhood he remained unconscious. The deep base of his pride, his sexuality and his creative determination remained a mystery to him and he grew up as a strangely dislocated man who either had no sense of the connection between childhood experience and the development of adult attitudes or, if he had such a sense, repressed it and remained silent about it.

Gissing was the eldest son of a Wakefield chemist, Thomas Waller

Gissing, and of Margaret Bedford, the daughter of a Droitwich solicitor. Their other children were William, who was to die at the age of twenty, Algernon, who was destined to have an extremely unsettled career as a never quite successful novelist, and Madge and Ellen, who never married but who lived in Wakefield and in nearby Yorkshire villages for the whole of their lives. Thomas had his shop on one of the main streets at what was then 55 Westgate. The house is still standing and can easily be identified by the plaque placed there by Gissing enthusiasts a few years ago. Indeed it is structurally unaltered, for until very recently Boots the Chemist used the downstairs front room as the shop (just as Gissing's father had done) whilst the back rooms and upstairs (once meagre accommodation for the family of six), were used as storage space. As in many north of England towns the back, or in this case the side door opens into a closed yard separated from the streets by an archway and surrounded by workshops and store houses. Shop and archway were barriers between the children and the outside world, and with the father always on the premises the children, before they went to school, were never free from his influence, which was strict. It was a bastion of privacy, this home in which minor disobedience was rare because it was difficult to achieve and to know a book, curled up by oneself by an upstairs window, was easier than to know a person. Later in life Gissing himself commented on this when he noted in his *Commonplace Book* that his 'childhood was somewhat solitary', recollecting that 'the Hicks were the only *family* with whom we habitually associated'.[2] Furthermore the quiet, guarded, confined life had other, typically Victorian consequences.

> When I read in a French novel of the intimacy existing between members of a family, – mothers, brothers, sisters, – I reflect with astonishment at my own experiences. I never in my life exchanged a serious confidence with any relative, – I mean concerning the inner things of one's heart and mind. This may in part be a personal characteristic of our family; in part, I feel it is due to the innate puritanism which also forbids us to hint at anything like sexual relations.[3]

Certainly it was a characteristic of the family and one against which Gissing reacted with extreme vigour once he was away from home. The protected atmosphere of the Wakefield house left him vulnerable to the type of personal disaster that a brilliant intellect will frequently fail to comprehend even in retrospect.

Yet Gissing always remembered his father, who died in 1870 when Gissing was thirteen, with great affection albeit an affection mixed with quirky memories. Fourteen years later, for instance, he was sufficiently moved to recollect and note down the apparently trivial fact that his father's breakfast had always been 'a captain's biscuit that had lain on top of milk all night' so that it soaked up the cream. In a similar note, he recalled his first visit to London, which was in 1867. His father asked him what he would most like to see and, when he replied 'The Houses of Parliament', took him instead to the Zoological Gardens at Kew and to the Crystal Palace. These were the almost random notes of a man who always loved his father and who knew that his influence had been great, despite the fact that he found it impossible to determine what precisely that influence had been. Gissing also recalled having been teased by his father (something which few other people in George's overly serious life were ever allowed to do) for reading Milton one Sunday evening. In *The Private Papers of Henry Ryecroft*, Gissing has Henry Ryecroft indulge in a memory which fairly clearly was his own. At Christmas Ryecroft says that he cannot associate with the multitude of Christian people: 'It is better to hear the long-silent voices, and to smile at happy things which I alone can remember.' Nearly every happy thing that Gissing could remember was associated with his father. 'When I was scarce old enough to understand, I heard read by the fireside the Christmas stanzas of "In Memoriam". Tonight I have taken down the volume, and the voice of so long ago has read to me once again – read as no other ever did, that voice which taught me to know poetry, the voice which never spoke to me but of good and noble things.'[4] Books became the powerful and exclusive bond between father and son. In early childhood these were not children's books but the English classics in the glass fronted bookcase in the upstairs sitting room. It was the father who in the course of evening and Sunday readings instilled in his son, George, a reverence of the printed page and of the great writers of the past, like Charlotte Brontë. Could you love a person, then, who did not also love books?

Were there other ways of loving? In George Gissing's childhood this question never arose since literacy was the key to success and education almost the guarantee of it. George was so intelligent that it was the most natural thing in the world for him to identify his love for his father with his love of books, especially as it was not shared by other members of the family. For the rest of his life Gissing never entertained any doubts about the superiority of the male intellect and only late in life abandoned the prejudice that men and woman could not share intellectual interests under the one roof. Nevertheless, his affection for his father was of a very secure kind, and was life-long.

In this same unpublished notebook, which Gissing himself entitled 'Reminiscences of my Father', are other hints of Gissing's relationship with his father. 'We children did not associate with the children of any other shopkeepers in Wakefield', he recorded in 1884. 'Of the other chemists my father had the poorest – even a contemptuous – opinion.' Children of people who are contemptuous of others are not, of course, likely to have a full social life. 'We *never* came in contact with families of other shopkeepers', Gissing wrote in his *Commonplace Book*; 'so we hung between two grades of society, – as I have done ever since in practical life.'[5] Yet Gissing does not seem to have resisted his father's influence in this respect. Another note in 'Reminiscences of my Father', this one written in 1896 when Gissing made an even more deliberate attempt to remember as much as he could of his early life, reads as follows: 'When the shop caught fire, and we ran a risk of being burnt out, father said afterward that the mob would have stood in the streets and "cheered as each floor fell through". I don't know the cause of this feeling.' This, too, speaks of an enclosed world and of an aspect of provincial life that Gissing carried with him into later years. Evidently his father had encouraged the idea that other people were the 'mob', had justified the enclosed world he created for his family and made it secure, and had encouraged Gissing's propensity for study in ways which tended to separate him from other people. Gissing did not retain a single childhood friendship. Nor did he ever recall childhood experiences, except those he had shared with his father. When he left home, he was already, intellectually, very much by himself and in a class of his own, brilliant in anything academic but in other ways more or less ignorant. 'The world frightens me,' he has Ryecroft say, 'and a frightened man is no good for anything'.[6]

Ellen Gissing said that her brother's 'pre-occupied air was not attractive to other boys'. In fact he seemed something of a prig. Ellen wrote:

> We must remember, that in his younger days he possessed great physical strength, sufficient to enable him to endure enormous hardships, as was proved later. For his physical well-being a great amount of exercise, much fresh air, and games of all kinds were imperative; but from these he always completely withdrew himself. All such things he looked upon as a waste of time. Although he delighted in long rambles in the country, all his time was needed for study, and in his early days he was usually so placed that the unspoiled country was quite beyond his reach.[7]

Not completely, of course. There were expeditions into the immediate countryside, especially with his father. M. B. Hicks remembered the family as 'always grubbing in hedge bottoms', and this was because Thomas Waller Gissing was an amateur botanist whose enthusiasm resulted in two publications: *Ferns and Fern Allies of Wakefield* (1863) and *Materials for a Flora of Wakefield and Its Neighbourhood* (1867). From the Gissings' vantage point on top of the hill in Wakefield the enclosing folds of the fields and open countryside of the nearby Pennines were visible at all times. A childhood picture that has been preserved with its caption 'Vote for no walks' means, of course, that the children walked frequently and not, as Jacob Korg surmised, the opposite. In fact, like most of their contemporaries, they rarely went anywhere except on foot. At holiday time, though, the family went further afield sometimes to the east and sometimes to the west coast of northern England, Seascale in Cumberland being one of their favourite resorts. Then, as now, the tiny unobtrusive seaside town could be reached by rail and once there the family, or George anyway, enjoyed its remoteness and austere beauty. In an early letter, George Gissing who, as eldest child, had the job of walking to Gosforth three miles away for the mail from Wakefield, recorded his excitement when his father allowed them one year to stay an extra week: he ran all the way back to Seascale, he said, and almost knocked his mother down in his excitement. For Henry Ryecroft the aromatic scent of the rest-harrow conjured up the hours by the seaside at Seascale, 'the shore of Cumberland running north to St. Bee's Head', the faint shape of the Isle of Man out to sea and the mountains inland. Gissing later celebrated the area in memory when, in *The Odd Women*, he had Everard Barfoot take Rhoda Nunn on an excursion from Seascale down the coast to Ravenglass, from Ravenglass inland by miniature railway to the village of Boot where Algernon was to live for a while, from Boot to Burnmoor on foot, and finally down to Wasdale Head, an expedition that Gissing had made himself on more than one occasion during his childhood. The unpublished romantic and adolescent poem 'On Wast Water' dates from one of these, and though he visited Algernon at Boot later in life, the childhood memory of the inspiring austerity of Wasdale stayed with him. Similar memories of family excursions on the Northumberland coast crop up in a number of stories. Gissing was susceptible to place, associated pleasant places with his family, and throughout his life searched out the beautiful and idyllic whenever he could. Yet the two sides of him were in conflict. The claustrophobic urban world of work and books were never reconciled with the expansive world of the countryside. Throughout his life when he had one he wanted the other. This, though, is to anticipate. Gissing, throughout his early life, was confined for the most part to Wakefield, his immediate family habits, the upper rooms of the house in Westgate and his books, in an existence supervised but also lovingly shared by his father.

A chilly entry in one of Gissing's notebooks perhaps reveals something, by implication, of his relationship with his mother: 'Occurs to me now as very strange that he [his father] did not exercise more intellectual influence over mother. In my memory he had clearly accepted the difference between their points of view, and was content to enter a protest now and then.' This is reminiscent of the unequal marriage of the Yules in *New Grub Street*. Whereas Gissing's father sympathized with his intellectual interests, his mother did not, or was incapable of understanding or sharing them. A preference for lucidity of thought and expression, for precise observation and for the exercise of controlled intellectual curiosity were encouraged by this chemist-cum-botanist father. The mother, on the other hand, so strongly insisted on an orderly household that Gissing remained in awe of her for many years after leaving Wakefield, sometimes feeling compelled to tell her everything, so great was her moral influence, sometimes concealing from her his transgressions – that is, his independent actions. When Mrs. Gissing criticized the housekeeping of Algernon's wife, Katie, in 1888, Gissing wrote a cutting letter to his sister, Nelly, which was clearly based on a long-established understanding between the brothers and sisters about their mother's ability to 'sacrifice human progress and peace' for the sake of cleanliness in the kitchen. 'It is sad, sad to think that anyone would be rendered incapable of spiritual activity by ceaseless regard for kitchen-ware & the back-door steps.'[8] She never in any sense had a life of her own, but simply filled, and filled well, the role of the Victorian housewife who did not need an existence beyond that defined by domestic duty. Gissing had little experience of other households. He therefore became convinced that housework and stupidity went together and that women could only be emancipated by not being married. Otherwise they would be like his mother.

Were it not for the strong possibility that Gissing's relations with his father and mother were the direct cause of his own domestic troubles later on in life, in as far as he was conditioned to suppose no other relationship but that of authority and subservience was possible, and no other expression of conjugal love genuine except the performance of conjugal duties, his prim recollections of his own youth would just be amusing. His advice to Katie was that 'the inhabitants of a house must unite in recognizing that the mind is of more account than the body. Mother would grant you that, hypothetically; but we know sadly enough that her practise is in precisely the opposite direction'.[9] The irony of these mind and body remarks seems to have escaped him. On another occasion he tried to describe the unsatisfactory relationship he had with his mother to someone whose relationship with her own mother was particularly close.

The relations between my mother and myself would seem to you rather strange. We are excellent friends, but – as is so often the case in England – we have very little in common, mentally or morally, and *never* talk in a confidential way. My mother has lived a very narrow life in a little provincial town; she is purely domestic, and religious in a very formal way. Often I have lamented the lack of sympathy between us. But it does not cause her any suffering – of which I am glad.[10]

Because ordinary, day by day accounts of Gissing's secluded child-hood have not survived and because there is not the possibility of constructing or re-constructing the series of events that gave direction to his first years, if direction they in any sense had, it must be supposed that Margaret Gissing's puritanical though kindly way of running a house in fact dominated those years just as Gissing supposed he remembered. If so, she was responsible for more than she could ever have imagined. Although he later said that his mother had played such an insignificant part in his life that he could not remember what she looked like, he never in fact reached the point at which it was no longer important to react against her opinions.

Indeed, were it true to say that Gissing was intellectually emanci-pated but morally enslaved, it would be his father who was res-ponsible for the first and his mother for the second. The father was remembered with affection, his mother with something approaching fear. Besides, his father was ambitious for his son and spent a great deal of time with him. Gissing revered his father, as Ellen his sister was to attest after his death.

> He had one lode-star, and that was his father. To him he looked for guidance in all matters; for not only had he a deep devotion to him, but he also felt that his father was the only person who really understood him, whose words, therefore, were worth listening to, and the only person whose learning was such that he could trust him for guidance along the path which even at that early age allured him – the path of knowledge. His one desire was to pursue all kinds of learning, up to the point which he felt few ever reached.[11]

Eloquent testimony from a sister. One is at least not surprised by the masculine attitudes that pervade many of Gissing's works! While there is no doubt that Gissing's attitude to his father affected the whole family, particularly to the extent that he shared responsibility for them all as eldest son, his own remarks sometimes come closer to the bone. Twenty years after the death of his father he wrote:

> Twice or thrice a year I dream of my Father, & always with one circum-stance characterizing the dream. Though he appears to me in different places, & under very different conditions, he is invariably, for a reason unknown, held beyond the possibility of intimate association. Thus, last night, I dreamt I was just leaving, with a company, the dining room of some hotel, having dined, when lo! my Father comes in, & I exclaim to myself 'How unfortunate that he did not come before, & dine with us!' – I remember one dream in which he seemed to be living in the same house, but hopelessly shut away. At times I have felt a passionate desire to approach him, & have even done so with words of affection, but he never responded; his manner was always abstracted, unconscious, at best coldly aware of me.[12]

Interestingly, there are very few father and son relationships in Gissing's novels, perhaps because relationships of any stability call in question the *fin-de-siècle* attitudes of the 'unclassed' intellectuals Gissing habitually wrote about and perhaps because he unknowingly suppressed one of the root causes of his own inadequacy with other people.

Whatever intellectual guidance Gissing may have received from his father, his boyhood was confined within strict physical limits: the upstairs parlour with its glass-fronted bookshelves from which the Gissing 'men' would take appropriate volumes for their Sunday reading, ending frequently with recitations from Tennyson; the walled garden, detached and a little distant from the house, as described in *A Life's Morning*, in which Gissing and his father would sit and read on summer evenings; the Mechanics Library on which they absolutely depended both for books and for practical information about the outside world; and the Back Lane School with its Palladian front and tiny rooms in which Gissing obtained his first instruction. Experience outside these safe, North of England confines was denied Gissing until he went away to school at the age of thirteen, which meant that his academic habits of mind were deeply ingrained well before he knew much about how others lived. In Wakefield, in the eighteen-sixties and seventies, life was necessarily confined and confining. How else escape the full horror of English provincial Philistine life except through books, except by family readings of Virgil, except by denying the life of the street and by seeing Life and Art as a vast opposition?

In 1871, after the death of his father, Gissing and his brothers, William and Algernon, were sent to the Quaker boarding school at Alderley Edge in Cheshire. In his little book, *George Gissing at Alderley Edge*, Pierre Coustillas brought together all the information he had culled from a miscellany of documents on Lindow Grove School at the time Gissing was there and before it had been moved to Colwyn Bay. Amongst these is the prospectus by James Wood, owner and principal. There were workshops, a chemical laboratory, a covered playroom, bathrooms and dormitories 'numerous, lofty and well-ventilated'. Friends of Thomas Gissing helped his widow find this school after his death, whether influenced or not by the prospectus, which concluded: 'Parents who have had their sons educated at Lindow Grove, professors and others interested in Education, will, it is believed, bear willing testimony to the satisfactory results of the training of the boys, whether tested by their sound scholarship or by their general development and refinement of character.' All three Gissing boys went to Lindow Grove at the same time and, though George Gissing started work at Owens College two years later, he in fact lived at Alderley Edge until 1875, when he moved to lodgings near the college. Of these years T. T. Sykes, an old school friend said in obituary reminiscences in the *Cheshire Daily Echo* and other local papers, 'At school he was from the first a perfect glutton for work – the ordinary lessons were not enough for him, and he very soon outstripped the rest of the boys.'[13] But he of course also engaged in the activities of the school in a more ordinary sense: storytelling through the night, tilting in the school yard, and revelling in the long, cross-country expeditions when they were allowed out of bounds, and sometimes when they were not.

He immediately distinguished himself. More than thirty years later Arthur Bowes, another of his school-fellows recorded his impression of Gissing at the age of thirteen or fourteen: 'Energy of character, self-reliance, and an exorbitant passion for study were his chief characteristics at this time. Into whatever task he entered he threw his whole soul. On the great "speech night" it was Gissing who mouthed the most brilliant Greek and Latin orations, and who filled the most important parts in the French plays.'[14] Only three years after his arrival at the school he passed his matriculation examinations for the London University BA; in the following spring (1875) he passed the Intermediate Examinations for the same degree and began, with his future assured, to attend Owens College. At first he remained as a boarder at Lindow Grove School in Alderley Edge, though later in 1875 he took lodgings near the College, probably at 43 Grafton Street, where he certainly lived later on. He took the transition from school to college in his stride, responded positively to the challenge of university work, and was soon part of a circle of self-consciously intellectual friends similar to the male characters in *Born in Exile*. Owens College moved into new buildings during Gissing's time and was already an important institution, in fact was probably the most important academic institution in the north of England. Whatever might have been the imaginative process by which Gissing transposed his own departure from Owens College, into Godwin Peak's departure from Whitelaw College in *Born in Exile* for flagrantly snobbish reasons that had much to do with his ill-spoken uncle's buying a restaurant outside the gates, it seems fair to speculate that Gissing's attitude to college was similar in its intensity to that of the characters in the novel: they were in competition for academic honours and attached immense importance to academic success, which for them justified feelings of superiority because the success was a function of native ability and hard work. This was an atmosphere which the young Gissing liked, and he did well. So much more tragic, then, were the events which suddenly brought his education to an end, after he had been living by himself in lodgings for less than a year.

Gissing's career at Owens College was terminated abruptly when he was arrested, convicted and sent to prison. It was alleged that there had been several instances of theft from a cloakroom during 1876, which were eventually reported to the police. On 30 May 1876 police who had concealed themselves in a section of the cloakroom, caught Gissing taking money from an overcoat and on 6 June he appeared in court, where he pleaded guilty to the charge that was brought against him: 'For that the said George Robert Gissing on the thirteenth day of May, in the year of our Lord aforesaid, at the said City of Manchester, did feloniously steal, take, and carry away five shillings and two pence in money the property of Samuel Robinson contrary to the statute in that case made and provided.'[15] On conviction he was sentenced to one month's imprisonment with hard labour.

Why Gissing stole the money is not completely clear. For many years it was held that Gissing had stolen it so that he could help a girl friend and that he had done such things for her before, even to the extent according to one account of buying her a sewing machine so that she would not need to take to the streets like her friends; but there is no firm evidence to corroborate this. The story remained current because of the lack of any other explanation. Putting two and two together, Morley Roberts claimed that Gissing had been supporting the girl he later married and therefore needed much more money than he received from home. Again, there is little evidence. Nonetheless, with a speed not altogether uncharacteristic of a certain type of university administration, Gissing's disgrace was quickly and implausibly related to the life of dissipation he had allegedly been leading. Gissing had been leading in the eighteen-seventies a type of free personal and sexual life that in the nineteen-seventies would be considered not in the least unusual. He had a desire for the companionship of women, which was never satisfied and which in fact never could be satisfied, at least not by one person, since it derived from a deep hunger for affection which had been denied in youth and against which his intellect provided such a formidable barrier. At college, this was simply expressed as an interest in girls, which is normal enough. But in 1876 it was unlikely that adventures outside the college walls would be condoned and Gissing's adventures were mainly sexual. Events showed that he got to know not just one but a good number of girls during his first year at Owens College and that he had a well-established reputation for philandering. Willingly or unwillingly, his fellow students testified to this effect when Gissing got himself into trouble. The Owens College staff soon knew too. The minutes of the Owens College Senate meeting of 13 June 1876 refer to the Principal's report on the affair.

The Principal further stated that Gissing had also been leading a life of immorality and dissipation. The Principal added that Gissing had

entered the College as an Oxford Local Exhibitioner in 1872 and had held
that Exhibition for the usual term of three years and was now in the
fourth year of scholarship; that he had obtained an Exhibition in Latin
of forty pounds per annum tenable for two years and another in English
of thirty pounds tenable for two years in 1875 in the University of
London, and that in the same year he had gained the Shakespeare
Scholarship in the College of the annual value of forty pounds tenable
for two years. RESOLVED: That the Senate be advised to recommend
the Council to formally expel Mr. Gissing from the college and that the
Shakespeare Scholarship which he holds be declared forfeited.[16]

What, then, had Gissing been doing that led the Principal to talk
of 'a life of immorality and dissipation'?

For an account of what happened to Gissing at Owens College one
almost of necessity turns first to Morley Roberts' *The Private Life of
Henry Maitland*, the thinly disguised attempt at a biography which
he cast in fictional form after Gissing's executors had refused access
to or use of the surviving letters, diaries and manuscripts. Because
Roberts was a college friend whose acquaintance Gissing renewed
during his years in London, it is certainly reasonable to expect that
his testimony will be trustworthy and illuminating. Unfortunately the
expectation is to a large extent ill-founded.

One month younger than Gissing, Roberts had come to Owens
College from Bedford Grammar School. During a long life in which
he worked variously as civil servant, Indian Office clerk, shepherd in
Texas, railroad navvy in Minnesota, lumberman in Oregon, and vine-
yard worker in California, travelled widely throughout the world, and
wrote some forty-five novels as well as many other books, he was to
see Gissing from time to time, whenever they were in London together, and in fact often showed himself to be a staunch, or at least
well intentioned friend, helping Gissing when his first wife died and
going immediately to his bedside when Gissing himself was dying in
the south of France. Roberts was the kind of man Gissing portrayed
as Jasper Milvain in *New Grub Street*, clubbable, worldly, somewhat
superficial and a successful hack. Whether Roberts, who was in a
different year, knew Gissing well in college is doubtful, except in the
sense that everyone knew him because of his academic brilliance. It
was much later that the two men became friends. Nevertheless he
was at Owens College when Gissing was expelled and so Roberts'
testimony, despite its tone, has to be taken seriously. The whole
college, he said, was in 'a most extraordinary ferment', and he himself
came close to being implicated in the affair. 'I have often imagined a
certain suspicion, in the minds of some of those who are given to
suspicion, that I had myself been leading the same kind of life as
Henry Maitland.'[17] This was because the police found in Gissing's
rooms, so it was alleged, letters from Roberts to Gissing in which

there was mention of a girl to whom Roberts, in *The Private Life of Henry Maitland*, gives the fictional name of Marion Hilton.

Of this girl, Roberts gives a brief, but characteristic portrait; characteristic of him, that is:

> One day [Gissing] showed me a photograph. It was that of a young girl, aged perhaps seventeen – he at the time being very little more – with her hair down her back. She was not beautiful, but had a certain prettiness of youth, and she was undoubtedly not a lady. After some interrogation on my part he told me that she was a young prostitute whom he knew, and it will not be exaggerating my own feelings to say that I recognized instinctively and at once if his relations with her were not put an end to some kind of disaster was in front of him.[18]

Good for Morley Roberts! Most biographical sketches and much criticism have derived from this crucial, much-quoted passage. Roberts said that he extricated himself from the situation, for rumours were rife that many others at the college were also suspected of extra-mural activity, by telling the Principal everything he knew 'with the utmost frankness' and indeed preserved his spotless character by emigrating to Australia on 23 September, after a very 'serious dis-agreement' with his father. It is from Roberts and from Roberts only that we get the story of Gissing's being expelled from college after he had had an affair with a 'prostitute,' and since he was evidently attempting to save his own skin what he says can be taken with a grain of salt.

A few letters have survived in the Owens College archives that have a bearing upon the case. These are not letters from Morley Roberts to Gissing but from John George Black to Gissing. Black, like Gissing, was expelled or rather, to put it more precisely, the Senate approved the Principal's recommendation 'that he be requested to write to Mr. Black's father recommending him not to offer his son for readmission to the College in October next'. The relevant part of the Senate proceedings for 23 June 1876 reads as follows:

> The Principal stated that the friends of G. R. Gissing, the student who had recently been expelled, had forwarded to him certain letters found by them among his effects, which they considered ought to be seen by the Principal, in order to a fuller knowledge of the circumstances which had led to Gissing's expulsion from the College: The Principal further stated that among these letters were four written to Gissing by J. G. Black, a student of the College, and that it appeared from them beyond question –
> (1) that Black had been privy to, and abettor of the profligate courses of Gissing, and
> (2) that he had himself been guilty of profligate conduct of a kind and under circumstances such as render it necessary that he should not continue a student of the College. That he had therefore in virtue of the power vested in him suspended Black from the College and all privileges

of studentship involving forfeiture of any honours that might have been
won at the June examinations, subject of course to confirmation by
Senate. Finally, he stated that there had not been time for summoning
the Discipline Committee, but that he had laid the letters before Professor Ward, whose judgement had entirely concurred with his own on
the inferences to be drawn from the letters, and on the course which
should be adopted.[19]

Some of the circumstances of the case point to the possibility that
Gissing was unlucky: he just happened to be the person caught and
punished for activities that others were involved in as well. Morley
Roberts fled the country while Gissing was in prison. Gissing's
'friends' forwarded to the Principal Gissing's letters which incriminated yet another student, one who had not yet been implicated. The
Principal did not have time to convene the Discipline Committee.The
Samuel Robinson from whose overcoat Gissing was accused of stealing marked money was not a student, in fact was probably working
for the police, and there is, therefore, at least the possibility that a
trap had been laid for Gissing in that student cloakroom which had
nothing to do with the 'habit' of theft alleged by Morley Roberts.
Finally, although John Black's letters were kept on file to support the
Senate's action, the letters which were supposed to have incriminated
Gissing a few months earlier were not. In fact, no documentary
evidence relating to Gissing's expulsion was kept except the Senate
minutes already referred to. An embarrassing affair which discredited
the College had come to light and the College expeditiously made an
example of Gissing, whose opinions on the matter remain unknown.
John Black's father, however, appeared before Senate and succeeded
in having him readmitted.

The girls outside the College walls were as interesting to the
students then as now. Not much imagination is needed for anyone
to visualize both the students' escapades and assignations, and their
subsequent meetings and talks when boasting about sexual success
was almost as enjoyable as the experience of sex itself. Black's letters
show that some of the students were involved with the same set, went
to the same houses, saw the same girls and that Gissing, more head-
strong and daring than the others, became more thoroughly committed. He knew from his reading, after all, how a real bohemian was
supposed to behave! Obviously it would be unfair, either at the time
or retrospectively, to use letters Gissing received from someone else
as evidence of 'immorality and dissipation' in Gissing. On the other
hand, Black's letters are not only, in the eyes of a College Principal,
alarmingly frank, but are also facetious. It was wrong to be explicit
about sexual matters. If you were facetiously explicit you could only
be described as an 'abettor of a profligate course'.

At all events, the first letter, dated 30 February 1876, is about

Black's inadvertently spending time with a girl with whom Gissing was in love.

> My Dear Gissing,
> My dear fellow, I feel wretched at receiving your letter – you saw me on Tuesday 'smiling' bitterly when we were talking of this poor girl; what do you suppose are my feelings when I know the real case! How could you expect me to think that all you said of her was said in good earnest? I believed everything, except that you had really fallen in love with her. Then, why – can you imagine me so base, if I had known your affection for her, to wish to cut you out! My dear fellow, you don't know me yet, you don't know how I have felt towards you. Gradually we have come together, and gradually an affection has sprung up in me such as I never felt for any other; and that this affair should cause any difference between us gives me at the thought infinite sorrow. I would never have spoken so openly on a matter like this that should be hidden, and have been felt by you. Hitherto I have had no friend; I have been a solitary creature consuming my own reflections; and, though surrounded by the happiest home that ever any one had, there has been a blank in my life. Do not, pray, think bitterly on this; I have done you, it is clear, a gross wrong, – forget it; and as you see I was not at all aware that you were so attached to her, – forgive me. Hear the real circumstances.
> In an unlucky hour I walked to the Free Library with Shelley, and as I was coming back at about seven, I thought I would go and see if you were in Water St. They told me there she had gone out with a young person, and would be back for tea; I supposed you had gone with her to have her portrait taken; I felt unusually miserable and ill, (you will hear more of this) and determined to wait for you. At eight o'clock I went again and asked for her, I thought you possibly might be inside as you were not in the first room: Mrs. B. showed me into the second room – empty, you could not be in the house then; and then the devilish thought came across me that I would stop with her. She came up – said she had expected me before; was glad I had come, for she had been crying for the last half hour and then we went into the other room. I asked her if you were not here on Sunday night; she said Mr. Gregory had been. It afterwards came out that you had told her you were of Owen's College. It struck me you could not have known what you were doing – so I denied it instantly.
> Now, I had not the least idea she was so ill, and I could not imagine she was drunk; she did not want me to go now – I had no desire for her, – I never felt so peculiar in my life; my head swam, and I hardly knew what I was doing.
> I am not saying this in excuse, for I saw no reason then why you should care in the least. I had great difficulty in leaving her: and as I was going, she made me promise I would say nothing to you.[20]

The rest of the letter is about Black's state of health – 'I fear I have caught some disease' – and his anguish that they have somehow misunderstood each other. Evidently Gissing then asked Black, though why by letter is a mystery, where holiday or weekend lodgings could be found in Southport or the vicinity, and Black, addressing Gissing as 'Il mio caro Adonis,' gave him the names of four landladies who would not be expected to fatigue students with questions about their companions. Gissing obviously selected one of them, for Black's next letter is addressed to G. R. Gissing Esq., at Mrs. Walpole's, 33 Tulketh Street, Southport. On the envelope Black wrote: 'Important. Will Mrs. Walpole kindly forward this to G.R.G.'

Important or not, it was a letter designed to have a forceful effect on any college principal in 1876.

> Cleveland Villas
> High Crumpsall
> 26 March 1876
>
> Dear G.,
> The irritation continued growing worse, and on examination, I found the prepuce swollen, and on turning it down, I found the whole of the inside salmon-coloured, as you called it, only little spots as though the skin had been eaten away so as to show the flesh and it almost looked as though it was bleeding. I applied a little of the subtilissimus, but the end continues to be irritated. The prepuce is a little hard as well; and there was a drop or two of yellow matter near the red spots.
>
> I don't know what an ulcer should look like. Are these anything like the symptoms of soft chancre? Or is it like your inflammation? Or do you think it is only balanitis?
>
> Please answer by return – I hope this will find you – and excuse me thrusting this frightful communication on you in a time of felicity. But answer instanter, for I tremblingly await my doom!!!
>
> Give me Wahltuch's private address.
>   Yours, non hilariter
>   J.G.B.
> Quoth the raven, 'Never more'.
> Should the subtilissimus go a bright green after being applied?[21]

If Black thought Gissing was spending a long weekend in South-port with 'Marion Hilton', this is perhaps a somewhat odd letter to write, dated as it is 26 March, three days after he had given Gissing the Southport addresses. Evidently the two friends were in the habit of sharing with each other sexual intimacies about which they were partly serious and partly not serious, though on this occasion Black was being absurdly indiscreet. Two cloistered Victorian students discover sex, joke with each other and exchange information. One of them needs the address of a discreet landlady. The other catches syphilis, or thinks he has caught it, and reasonably enough consults his friend who is the son of a chemist. Gissing and Black and their friends were young bucks looking for excitement and some relief from lectures on Ancient History and the behaviour of German verbs, and believing that these escapades away from home were nothing more than that, entered lightly into them.

Gissing was, of course, caught out but certainly the tone of the fourth and final letter does not give the impression that any great crisis had arisen.

Cleveland Villas
11 April 1876

Dear Gissing,

What art thou doing? My soul desireth thee as the bird doth the mountain. There is an uncertainty in thy peregrinations which passeth understanding. Heute warst du hier, morgen bist du da, und jetzt du bist ich weiss nicht wo. Teufelsdruck? quo tendis! Anxious questionings on every side – Lugubrious murmurs of fearful meaning – hanging prussic acid – damnation – judgment of Minos, whilom King of Crete.

Art thou lapped in luxury's delight? Thinkst thou the sun will ever shine? Nay verily, the day will come, has come when the sun shall shine no more and all thy glory shall depart.

The following queries were made in the course of the week. Ward loguitur 'Any-body-seen-any-thing of Mr. Gissing?' Wilkins, vir ad unguem factus, fastidiosus, et bellus homo – 'Dew yeowe know what has become of Mr. Gissing, Ei have no observed his presence heah lately?'

Signor Tollero, homo fantastico e jocoso; loquitur quasi per nasuk – 'Know where Gissing is?' 'Out of town.' 'Ah, looked very seedy – great many people died this winter.' 'Why you don't think he looks cadaverous, do you?' 'No, but he wd do well to take opportunity of enjoying the sun.' 'In fact, I am surprised to see you here.' 'Well, we left off with Holofernes under the table, will you go on?' So Tollero and I continued the divine history of Judith.[22]

And in this vein it continues, Black ending somewhat coyly: 'Delicacy forbids me to commend myself to anyone but yourself, I suppose.'[23] It has been said that Gissing was toying with fire to be away from Owens College during the period in which he had been stealing money from the college cloakroom, but it is easier to suppose that Gissing simply extended his stay away from college during the Easter vacation without feeling the need to explain himself to his friend. He may not have been completely gratified by Black's third letter.

Professor Greenwood, Principal of the College, was certainly not gratified by it, for he reported to the Owens College Senate: 'I trust Black had been privy to, and an abetter of, the profligate conduct of a kind and under circumstances such as to render it necessary that he should not continue a student of the College.' He could hardly have said less, since Black had obviously been leading the same life as Gissing, and had inadvertently slept with the same girl. At least he said it was inadvertent.

Gissing never wrote about the month he spent in gaol. Nor are there prisons in any of his novels. Very rarely, as a matter of fact, did he depict criminal actions of any kind, perhaps because the very idea of criminality would imply a set of moral standards that would be

inconsistent with the neutral or 'realistic' attempt to show things as
they were without the prejudice of a point of view. Or perhaps it was
the other way around. Perhaps he so much needed to suppress any
recollection of his own experience in gaol that he was incapable of
including criminality in his work even though it was so obviously
part of the fabric of the life he was writing about. According to A. C.
Young Henry Hick's father helped him to get a job when he came out
of prison, one which he could only have held for a brief period, however, since in the fall of 1876 Gissing emigrated to America departing
from Liverpool on 5 October bound for Boston. Gissing's formal
education had come to an abrupt end and he never in later years
referred to the episode. He probably never absorbed it, for in a
repressed man one gets the measure of his traumas and their effects
as much from his silences as from his words, and Gissing was completely silent.

That year in America was divided into four periods. At first he
stayed in Boston itself, lodging at 71 Bartlett Street and presumably
living for the most part on the money he had taken with him. Then,
for the first two or three months of 1877, he taught a variety of
subjects, including French and German in the High School at
Waltham, Massachusetts.[24]

Gissing was a person who throughout his life thought strictly in
terms of winter and summer. He customarily tended to end whatever
he had been doing during the winter in March or April and began to
do something else. At all events he abandoned his job at the end of
term in March and travelled with an immigrant's ticket to Chicago
where he managed to survive for a while by selling stories to the
editor of the *Chicago Tribune*.[25] This was the third part of his stay.
Finally, during the summer months, he seems to have wandered
about, mostly in New York State, in the same way as many students
aged twenty or thereabouts do today, eventually returning to England
in the autumn. He reached Liverpool on 3 September 1877 having
completed, as it were, a year's penance. Clearly he had not made the
slightest attempt to settle in North America, though he may at first
have pretended that he was going to do so.

If there were pretence, which is not really a good word for someone
as single-minded as Gissing, it took the form of letters home, those
letters which he had of course promised to write and which mostly
related to everyday things in which he himself had little interest. His
family, then and later, wanted to know how he would manage: the
perennial family questions. Families frequently think that sons ought
to earn a living, safely, in some acceptable, orthodox way. Sons,
frequently, do not agree. Gissing's letters to his family must be seen
in this context, since they obviously preferred hearing that he was
worried about finding a job to hearing that he was exploring North

America as best he could on a shoestring. He would also know something which they would not fully comprehend, that it was impossible for him to stop being a classical scholar and a man of letters just because he had been in prison for theft. So he wrote letters about the Americans' dirty boots, the price of fruit in Boston, the difference between English and American trains and so forth, skating over – at least in the surviving letters – the issues that must have concerned or interested him most. He told his family that he lived in a 'splendid' boarding house, where he had a room and board for ten dollars a week, had the daily breakfast of meat and potatoes with the other nine occupants, and in the evenings read aloud to them from Thackeray. Mr. Garrison, editor of the *Atlantic Monthly*, was his 'principal friend'.

Meanwhile, somewhat compulsively, he was working at his German, translating Heine for publication, writing 'Sketches of Life in a Manufacturing Town' and reading George Eliot. 'We have a glorious library here', he told his brother Algernon in November, 'It is free for all to use and I can assure you it is excellently patronized; for here, you know, everybody reads. There are very few books that one would be at all likely to want that it does not contain.'[26] Gissing's encounter with the Boston Public Library was probably the most significant event of his stay in North America. A more decisive encounter with contemporary French and German fiction was possible in Boston than in Manchester.

After Christmas, Gissing obtained an appointment at the High School in Waltham to teach classics for $800 a year. The appointment was noted in the *Free Waltham Press* for 5 January 1877, and years later G. A. Stearns recalled Gissing's first appearance at the school, as he sat on the platform with the other teachers 'at devotional exercises'. Looking back over a span of more than fifty years, Stearns remembered the young Gissing as a tall broad-shouldered man, with a shock of light brown hair worn rather long, dull light blue eyes, and a full sandy beard that had evidently never known a razor.[27] It is easy to imagine that Gissing enjoyed this job, for he was an excellent teacher – as later events revealed – and at first found the school a satisfactory one. He was the senior of the two newly appointed assistant teachers and reported to Wakefield that his classes were 'orderly, attractive and interesting.' Yet he did not even last a term. Only two months after the beginning of term, the same paper announced that the teacher, one of a staff of four, had 'suddenly left town' giving as the reason that 'a great disappointment had suddenly unsettled his mind'. On the same day (9 March), the *Waltham Sentinel* said that 'he left town without being aware of what he was doing'. Korg's speculations on Gissing's reasons for leaving Waltham seem completely unjustified. He believes he must explain Gissing's 'peculiar self-defeating and self-tormenting quality as obvious in his books as in his actions', which, according to Korg, was partly based on the notion 'that prosperity would have conflicted with the pessimism and sense of injustice that seem to have been part of his nature.'[28] This is nonsense. Korg took over from Roberts the story that Gissing was a congenitally miserable man, masochistically preferring personal disasters throughout his life to the pleasures he might have had if he had modelled an entirely different and more orthodox career for himself. Someone who has just come out of prison can reasonably be depressed without further justification, but in any case there is little evidence one way or the other to show that Gissing enjoyed or did not enjoy his six months or so in Massachusetts. The man who was about to embark upon a career which involved writing more than a novel a year for twenty years may not have been completely satisfied by the life of a teacher in a small school. Because Gissing left the school before the end of term, it seems probable that his employers had discovered the truth about the man they had hired, while in more general terms it is easy to imagine that he would have preferred not to take roots. 'Why did you leave Owens College, Mr Gissing? What made you come to Boston?' would be the first questions of hospitable matrons – ones which Gissing would have found difficult to answer if real friendships began to grow. To leave at all meant leaving abruptly and this he did.

The next three or four months were spent in Chicago. Of this period the only account that exists is that given by Whelpdale in *New Grub Street*, an account which is generally taken to be autobiographical because it is not relevant to the story being told, and because Gissing deleted it together with other autobiographical passages when he revised the novel.[29] Whelpdale recounted to Marion, Dora, Jasper and Maud that he had had the 'brilliant idea' of crossing the Atlantic to see the Centennial Exhibition in Philadelphia, had got into 'perilous straits' financially and had therefore taken an 'emigrant ticket to Chicago', had arrived there with only five dollars in his pocket and, having taken a room in a 'dirty little boarding house, in Wabash Avenue', managed during the next few months to keep alive by selling stories to a friendly newspaper editor. That this is what happened to Gissing himself is further suggested by the fact that at least some of the stories were later identified as contributions to the *Chicago Tribune* and published in the volume called *Sins of the Fathers*. Whelpdale's account goes on:

> For some months I supported myself in Chicago, writing for that same paper, and for others. But at length the flow of my inspiration was checked; I had written myself out. And I began to grow homesick, wanted to get back to England. The result was that I found myself one day in New York again, but without money enough to pay for a passage home.[30]

By chance Whelpdale saw one of his stories reprinted in a news-paper from Troy, New York, as had Gissing himself, and on the spur of the moment went there, travelling by steamer up the Hudson River. 'On landing at Troy I was as badly off as when I reached Chicago: I had less than a dollar. And the worst of it was I had come on a vain errand; the editor treated me with scant courtesy and no work was to be got.'[31]

So Whelpdale stayed alive by buying small quantities of peanuts on the street corners, until – by luck again – he found or was directed to an itinerant portrait photographer who needed an assistant. He worked for this man for a short while until the loan of money he needed for his return passage from Boston to Liverpool arrived from England.

Apart from this fictional account of Whelpdale's travels, there is no record of what happened to Gissing in North America during the second part of his stay. At some point he wrote a story called 'An English Coast-Picture' which appeared in the July 1877 number of *Appleton's Journal* over the pseudonym of 'G. R. Gresham'. There is also a surviving notebook (now in the Beinecke Library) in which he recorded his reading and made notes on literary subjects, such as names and plots for novels. But if he kept a diary, it has not survived. Particular episodes affected him strongly: he dreamed night after night about the Niagara Falls, for example. He seems not to have been profoundly affected though, for he never stayed in one place long enough to put down roots and he clearly longed to be back in England. In this, as in other matters, he kept his own counsel. He had no difficulty in being secretive about his year in North America. The experiences were his and his alone, and he had in any case no one with whom to share them.

3

His First Marriage

WHEN Gissing returned to England from North America in October 1877 he went almost immediately to London. The options open to him were not numerous. He was not expected back in Manchester: he could as well put his foot inside Owens College as become a lyric poet. Nor would an extended visit to Wakefield have been a comfortable experience, given what people knew of him and, worse, what they imagined. He had already, in Waltham, tried the alternative of establishing himself anonymously in a small town: that was obviously incompatible with making a name or a living for himself with his pen. London was the natural place for him to go. There he would have the greatest chance of earning a living, of shaking off his immediate past. Where else but in London would a budding man of letters settle to write his first novel, whatever his background or circumstance? He was drawn almost irresistibly to the Grub Street world of the British Museum, the book-shops, the lending libraries and the reading rooms, and the anonymous, safe world of the boarding house.

Because he had been in prison, obtaining a job of any kind would not have been easy. There was no one in London who could act as reference for him and give him the 'character' that Victorian convention required. The few people, family and friends, whom he might have searched out he at first avoided. He was not yet of age. Indeed, he was not yet twenty, which meant there existed whole sets of awkward situations in which it was legitimate for others to ask him about his background, and some positively difficult and embarrassing situations, in which the word or signature of a parent would be looked for. It was in London that he had the greatest chance of survival despite these complications and until he was of age it was bound to be little more than survival. Thousands of young men and women were already crowding into London and somehow managing

by themselves, but only by doing the type of work that Gissing would
have refused. Gissing had no intention whatsoever of keeping them
company, even had he been capable of doing so. The idea of working
for money so that he could be a part time writer in the modern style
was anathema to him.

Gissing settled to work so rapidly that he had obviously decided to
be a novelist before he arrived in London. 'I am getting on with my
novel', he told his brother Algernon on 28 February 1878, 'which I
hope to be drawing to a conclusion in a little more than a month'.[1]
This confirms that he had started it at, or even before Christmas,
perhaps when he moved lodgings to 22 Colville Place, his first known
London address. But which novel this was remains uncertain. Many
of the statements Gissing made to members of his family, like this
one about his first book, are not completely reliable, because he got
into the habit of writing about what he judged they could understand, so that the surviving mass of letters to brothers and sisters has
to be seen in this light. They wanted the assurance that he was working, that he would make something of his life, that all was not lost.
He gave the assurance by emphasizing his work schedules and the
difficulties he had to overcome. This early mention of work in progress may be a case in point. Naturally he may not have worked
exclusively on the novel which appeared three years later as *Workers
in the Dawn*. Before *Workers in the Dawn* there was at least one major
attempt at a novel, now lost. Passages in later novels, notably *A Life's
Morning*, *New Grub Street* and *Born in Exile*, may be semi-auto-
biographical fossils from this early, hit or miss, experimental period.
No doubt there were many false starts. What is clear, though, is that
he had already made the decision from which he never deviated. At
whatever cost, whatever the difficulty, he would be a writer. To be a
modern writer meant being a novelist.

Gissing's ambition during the winter of 1877–8, his first in London,
was to obtain an advance against royalties sufficient to keep him
alive until his twenty-first birthday on 22 November 1878, when he
expected to receive what was for those days the vast sum of £500 as
his share of a legacy from his father. But this ambition could not be
satisfied immediately. He therefore eked out a living as best he could,
at first by living on the small amount of money he had brought with
him and then by coaching pupils in Latin and Greek, initially at the
miserably low rate of four shillings for a three-hour session. The type
of life he lived during this brief, early period is graphically represented
by the character, Biffin, in *New Grub Street*: Biffin ate his bread and
dripping supper with a knife and fork to make it seem more sub-
stantial and frequently used his huge overcoat to conceal the inadequacy of the rest of his clothes, while he laboured away at his
realist novel, 'Mr Bailey – Grocer', sustaining himself meanwhile

with Greek poetry and tutoring sessions at sixpence an hour. Such
was Gissing's own beginning in London. The discomfort was always
worth it. He was always sustained by his main purpose – to be a
writer. His own reading told him that this involved trials, so in a
sense the austerity, even the hunger, were signs that things were going
well. In the *Commonplace Book* he whimsically noted down some of
the expedients he had adopted during different periods of penury. 'In
Gower Place, it was bread & milk: that starved me. In Wormington
Road, it was German sausage (for weeks): that made me ill. For two
or three months at 7K it was Desiccated Soup: that again pinched my
stomach. Potatoes mashed with dripping – bread soaked in hot water
with dripping or butter, & other such expedients have often served
me'.[2] Youth and youthful idealism combined with a hunger for an
intellectual and literary life made it possible for him to live on next
to nothing, at first enjoying, then enduring it and ultimately dying
from it.

Gissing succeeded in maintaining his independence by tutoring in
Latin and Greek, or at least almost succeeded; for about a year
between September 1878 and September 1879 he worked as a part
time clerk at St. John's Hospital, which is the only time he is known
to have done anything other than write and teach. He was to live in
this way for the next six or seven years until the publication of *Demos*
in 1886, after which he lived solely on the income from his books. Of
course, even when he began to attract pupils, he was paid by the hour
and was always vulnerable to the almost catastrophic loss of income
that resulted from a parent's changing his mind or from a pupil's
illness. London was a dark, dirty and friendless place; the heavily
polluted air soon began to affect his health; everything was alien to
him, particularly the people with attitudes and habits he had never
encountered before; and yet he was determined to manage. His
brother, William, chastised him for living on lentils, and the other,
Algernon, was so shocked by Gissing's lodgings that he insisted on
something better before he would make a second visit. Ryecroft was
allowed to reminisce about *his* years in London, recollecting what he
called 'the dear old horrors' and the 'raging hunger' he had felt as he
looked at the shop windows full of puddings and pies. 'I see that alley
hidden on the west side of Tottenham Court Road, where, after living
in a back bedroom on the top floor, I had to exchange for the front
cellar.'[3] This was to achieve a saving of sixpence a week on the rent.
'The front cellar was stone-floored; its furniture was a table, a chair,
a wash-stand, and a bed; the window, which of course had never
been cleaned since it was put in, received light through a flat grating
in the alley above. Here I lived; here *I wrote*. Yes, "literary work"
was done on that filthy deal table, on which by the bye, lay my
Homer, my Shakespeare, and the few other books I then possessed.'[4]

Gissing, like Ryecroft, preferred deprivation to dependence on another human being. He even preferred to beg than to incur a debt. 'For me, there have always been two entitities – myself and the world, and the normal relation between these two has been hostile.'[5] Gissing's London experiences, especially in the period before his twenty-first birthday, his knowledge of the streets and alleys, his frequent changes of lodgings, his loneliness and suffering inform his early work, not least when he is not writing directly about himself. Gissing said that no one but he had the experience needed for books about the poorer districts of London, which was probably the case. That was later. In 1877 and for most of 1878, he was sustained by his own determination to be a writer, by literary example – most notably Murger's *Scènes de la Vie de Bohème*, and of course by the fact that he would eventually receive his legacy. Real success at first proved elusive and yet, by the autumn of 1878 when he moved to 31 Gower Place, the worst was over.

The Gissing family in Wakefield had to wait a whole decade (1877–87) before it became clear to them that he would succeed in the course he had set himself. During this period he had at least eleven addresses, ten of them between 1877 and 1884 when he moved into a flat just off Baker Street. When he did begin to enjoy a small measure of financial success, he promptly left the country, demonstrating clearly enough that it was not the comfortable, middle-class Wakefield kind of success he wanted. His family obviously thought that he had been hiding himself away because of the episode in Manchester, or because of his marriage, or because of the difficulty he experienced in establishing himself as an author, and were not prepared for the fact that, over and above all these questions about which he had every right to be sensitive, he wanted a very modern type of independence in which he could live in a way that was consistent with his advanced opinions, without responsibility and without having to take anyone else into account.

In 1877 and 1878, however, going anywhere, let alone abroad, was quite beyond his means. His most frequent expedition was to the British Museum – and not just because it was relatively warm as the Gissing denigrators inevitably suggest. He continued to read insatiably. In May of 1878, when he still had only two pupils and was working more or less full time at his first novel, he took the occasion of a letter to Algernon about the legal details of a plot to advise him about keeping notes of his reading, giving in the process a hint of his own practice.

> Do you keep a journal of your reading? It is very interesting to do so and make slight critical notes. I have not had much time for reading lately, and now am grinding up Cicero's *De Officiis* which is the book my new pupil has. I have just been glancing through Dickens' *Uncommercial*

Traveller, a capital series of essays – and reading some French novels by Eugène Sue and Henri Murger. Thank Heaven, the French is just as easy as English for me. I would give something for a good set of German books, for I have absolutely none.[6]

This note, with its earnestness and affectation, is typical of hundreds Gissing was to write throughout his life. Whatever he was up to, he was also reading. Whenever he wrote to anyone, he would mention books. Friendship was through the medium of books and without books there could be no friendship. Meanwhile, alone and almost penniless, he was beginning on foot the exploration of London that lasted for more than a decade. 'It must be very interesting examining the holes of London', wrote his brother William in June 1878, 'as long as you don't catch a fever'.[7]

Gissing's principal London friend, at least until Morley Roberts returned from overseas, was Eduard Bertz, a German a few years older than Gissing who had left Germany when his socialist sympathies and party membership had placed him in danger, had lived for a while in Paris, and had arrived in London in 1878 as a political exile. The two men first met early in 1879, after Gissing had read an advertisement in the personal columns of a London newspaper which requested an English gentleman, eager for scholarly companionship, to reply through the paper's offices.[8] Gissing was to use this episode later in his second published novel, *The Unclassed*, when he has Julian Casti, a lonely but intelligent clerk, respond to the advertisement of Oswald Waymark: 'Wanted, human companionship. A young man of four-and-twenty wishes to find a congenial associate of about his own age. He is a student of ancient and modern literatures, a freethinker in religion, a lover of art in all forms, hater of conventionalism. Would like to correspond in the first instance. Address O.W. City News Room, W.C.' Gissing answered Bertz's advertisement; they met for the first time in January 1879 and soon found that they indeed had similar interests. Their first expedition together was to see Henry Irving in *Hamlet*. 'Last Friday night, according to agreement, I went with Bertz to the Lyceum, and we enjoyed ourselves immensely. He had tea with us here before we went, and supper on returning.'[9] So began a friendship that was to last until Gissing died in 1903, although only for two relatively brief periods were they in London together: from January 1879, the date of their first meeting, to July 1881, when Bertz emigrated to Tennessee; and from the summer of 1883, when he returned to London, to Easter 1884, when he ended his exile and went back to Germany.

Friendship with Eduard Bertz did not constitute any type of emotional strain. Both saw themselves as men of letters. Both were poor. Both wished to earn their living by writing, as they eventually did. Because they were outsiders, newly arrived in London, there was a level on which they could easily share their experiences, talk about books and from time to time concoct a meal together. Bertz helped Gissing with the German chapters of *Workers in the Dawn*. Gissing was to help Bertz to find a publisher for the book that gave him enough money to return to Germany in 1884. When they were not together, they engaged in the calm, unexcited, informative correspondence that adds much to one's knowledge of the shape of Gissing's working life. This was the type of relationship that Gissing liked, one in which the other would not make demands on his time or interrupt unpredictably his self-imposed work schedule. No doubt Bertz did know a good deal about Gissing's circumstances, since there would otherwise have been no point in his holding back or destroying their early correspondence when Gissing died. Yet the friendship was not intense, but was of the kind that Gissing so frequently depicts in his novels. Intelligent, well-read, penniless, uprooted young men got together with a pipe and a bowl of stew to talk about literature, feeling superior in many respects to those who busy themselves with the demands of mere existence.

When the two men first met, Gissing was already living with a girl called Helen Harrison. She it was who made tea and cooked supper for them when they went that night to the theatre together. So it has to be supposed, simply because there is no record of Gissing having lived with anyone else. Later on, Gissing blotted out this period of life as having been too painful to remember. He destroyed his diary of these London years because he wanted to conceal from new friends and a new mistress that Helen Harrison had ever existed. People who had known Helen did likewise. For example, Bertz destroyed Gissing's early letters so that they should not tarnish his memory. So we see Helen only across the barrier of Gissing's deliberate attempt to have her forgotten. No photographs, letters, records, recollections of Helen have survived. Yet Helen was not a person who entered and left Gissing's life lightly. On the contrary, the experience was traumatic. He loved her passionately, probably more than anyone whom he knew later in life, and the breakdown of their relationship almost destroyed him. This we know. But the details of their life together exist now only in hints and possibilities. Of the detail little is known, much less than is often claimed.

The exact time at which Gissing and Marianne Helen Harrison began to live with each other cannot be ascertained with certainty. Some have claimed it was almost as soon as Gissing reached London. In September 1878 George told his brother that 'after friday our address will be 31 Gower Place'[10] so unless Gissing was being coy with the personal pronoun they were already together. Certainly by early 1879 they knew each other well, for there are fairly frequent references to 'we' in the correspondence and before long Gissing was reporting, for him freely, on some of their experiences. In a letter to his brother dated 5 August 1879, he told him,

> We have had such fine weather lately that it has tempted us out a little into the open air. One day last week we had a glorious walk. We went by train to Richmond, walked thence through the Park, past the Star and Garter, all the way down to Kingston, then crossed the river, and back up the other side, through Strawberry Hill and Twickenham (where we saw Pope's Villa), to Richmond again. This was very grand. . . . Another day we went to Kew, and another to Hampstead Heath. There are gloriously fine views from parts of Hampstead. We saw quite a number of painters at work on different scenes. Yesterday, it being Bank Holiday, we carefully shunned the country. However, I was glad it was a fine day, for I dare-say millions of people were out in pursuit of pleasure.[11]

This letter and several others like it, breathe the same spirit as those descriptions of happy, Thames-side expeditions in *The Unclassed* and is consistent with the fact that Gissing was busy, active and confident, even through correcting a translation of a German novel at one shilling for every twelve pages and walking each morning to tutor one of his pupils at 7 a.m. was not a life that would have delighted everybody.

Various accounts of this have been given but none seems completely reliable. A. C. Young says, categorically, that 'when Gissing returned to England in 1877 after his year's exile in America, he travelled directly to Manchester, where his young mistress, Nell Harrison, still lived. Together they moved to London, which offered them anonymity'.[12] At the beginning of Section II of *Letters*, Gissing's brother and sister simply stated: 'In the autumn of 1877 Gissing returned to England and, under the same unsettled circumstances, entered upon his London life. He was now married.'[13] Roberts, who had returned from Australia in 1879 after an absence of three years, met Gissing in a pub during the summer of 1880, having discovered that his old college acquaintance was in London by seeing advertisements for *Workers in the Dawn*. Recalling that reunion he said: 'I asked him as delicately as possible about his domestic circumstances, and he then told me that he was married, and that his wife was with him in London.'[14] Gissing had in fact married Helen Harrison in October 1879, only shortly before Roberts' return to England. There is actually no way of proving that Helen Harrison was the same person as Gissing had previously known in Manchester. Perhaps she was. Roberts assumed she was and maybe Gissing allowed him to make the assumption and maybe he did not. Obviously he allowed his family in Wakefield to believe he was married when he was not. Much, much later, in 1927, Gissing's sister, Ellen, said that 'in marrying one with whom any real companionship was impossible he showed a side of his character which was especially strong – constancy of affection and faithfulness to those who had a right to look to him for help'.[15] What did Ellen mean when she said this? Did she just mean, as most people have assumed, that because Gissing had known Helen Harrison in Manchester she had a moral right to save appearances by rejoining him? The tone of Gissing's letters somewhat belies the idea that he might have married simply because of a sense of duty. 'We only sat up to see the old year out and the new in, and following Father's immemorial practice, I read Tennyson's appropriate poem aloud; then we threw up the window and listened to the bells which sounded finely on a south-west wind. It was a wonderfully warm night, but a little cloudy.'[16]

Roughly at the time of his marriage Gissing wrote about the problem of reputation and about the complications that result from 'our social delicacies and pruderies. The world is so very slow to believe that connections other than of a certain sort can possibly exist between young people of different sex who see each other in private; it is so easy for corrupt imagination to picture situations completely familiar to themselves, so extremely difficult for them to conceive the existence of virtue and self-respect'.[17] These remarks, part of 'A Town Idyl', are applied by the narrator to a fictional situation but they might just have well have been applied to those who created the current image of Gissing and his first wife. The most remarkable of these was also the most influential. When Gissing's literary executors refused Morley Roberts permission to write a biography of Gissing, he circumvented their decision by writing *The Private Life of Henry Maitland*, a fictional biography based upon recollection and not upon the surviving documents. This is well known. In fact, Morley Roberts stressed that he *was* writing from memory and had been unable to check his facts. All the more surprising, then, is the vast influence of his account of Gissing's first marriage.

Roberts said it was 'curious' that he never met Gissing's wife. He never met Helen but he had no difficulty in arriving at a judgment on how the Gissings lived. When he went to see them 'she was usually unfit to be seen because she was intoxicated.' The Gissings had lived at 5 Hanover Square in Islington for about a year and had then moved to 55 Wormington Road in the early spring of 1881 so that Gissing would be closer to his West End pupils, but Roberts 'gathered from him that the habits of his wife were perpetually compelling him to move from one house to another'. The house they lived in was 'certainly in some dull neighbourhood' and 'was full of children of the lower orders playing in the roadway'. It must have been a very trying experience for a person whose tastes were as refined as Roberts'.

The servant who took me upstairs was a poor foul slut, and I do not think the room had been properly cleaned or dusted for a very long time.

The whole of the furniture in it was certainly not worth seven and sixpence from the point of view of the ordinary furniture dealer. There were
signs in it that it had been occupied by a woman, and one without the
common elements of decency and cleanliness. Under a miserably broken
sofa lay a pair of dirty feminine boots. And yet on one set of poor
shelves there were, still shining with gold, the prizes Maitland had won at
Moorhampton College and the painfully acquired stock of books that he
loved so much.[18]

Why Roberts would suppose that Helen, whether she herself had
come from Manchester or not, would want to see one of Gissing's
friends from Manchester is difficult to imagine. If she knew, as she
presumably did, that Roberts had been the student, or one of the
students, who had given Gissing's letters to the Principal of Owens
College, her staying in the next room is understandable.

Roberts said 'we simply sat and smoked and drank a little whis-
key.'[19] Then Gissing asked him if he would mind leaving, but 'a little
afterwards he told me that that very afternoon his wife had gone out,
and obtaining drink in some way had brought it home with her, and
that she was then almost insane with alcohol.' In such a way is a
story begun. There is little evidence to support the allegations and
innuendoes that Roberts made in this notorious chapter. In *The
Private Life of Henry Maitland*, Roberts was writing from memory
about something that occurred thirty years earlier. Not unnaturally
the picture was blurred. Roberts himself had been in London from
late 1879 to the middle of 1884. Gissing lived with Helen after their
marriage only until late in 1881, though they were briefly reunited in
1882. Consequently the period in which Morley Roberts would have
found George Gissing and Helen Harrison together was a brief one,
extending simply from the middle of 1880 to perhaps the autumn of
1881. He makes it seem as though he visited the Gissings in Hanover
Square just after they were married, whereas a more likely 'cul-de-
sac', since he only met Gissing after the publication of *Workers in the
Dawn*, would have been 29 Dorchester Place. There is something disagreeable about Roberts drinking whisky but criticizing Helen for
'obtaining drink in some way', with the implication that only
prostitution would give her the income; and in his patronizing remarks about the furniture, the cleanliness of the room, and the
scandalous fact that there were women's boots under the sofa,
observations so mannered and silly that they cast the whole account
into doubt. Being ill is not a crime. It is not even a crime to avoid your
husband's friends or to take to the bottle when a man like Morley
Roberts decides to pay a visit.

There is an element of unreality in all this, since Roberts did not
derive his information about Helen from his having known Gissing
in London in 1880 and 1881, but from *Workers in the Dawn* and *The*

Unclassed which he later assumed to be autobiographical. On this shaky basis he concocted the story that has dominated most accounts of Gissing's early life since then, a story that is without common understanding, humanity or fact. Nonetheless, it was taken over and embellished by Jacob Korg in *George Gissing A Critical Biography*[20] and it is in this form that it now exerts such a deadly influence on Gissing criticism.

Of the Manchester period Korg stated, following Roberts, that Gissing 'somehow met and fell in love with a young prostitute' and added that it is 'easy to imagine the mixture of idealism, naïveté and infatuation that made up Gissing's devotion to "Nell", as he always called her'.[21] Even in Korg's account, the infatuation was to last three years at least and survive the separation caused by Gissing's year in North America. Then, to explain why Gissing stole money from the college cloakroom in 1877, Korg wrote an influential paragraph based on the folk-lore account of Gissing's life that was still prevalent:

Gissing regarded Helen as a victim of society, and he undertook the mission of redeeming her. In an attempt to supply her with a respectable way of making a living, he bought her a sewing machine. He gave her money and gifts, even selling a watch left him by his father. But he soon found he could not provide enough for her needs, for, as subsequent events clearly show, the facts were that Helen was addicted to drink and had turned to prostitution to get money for it.[22]

When Korg wrote this, he did not know about the letters in the Owens College archives: for 'prostitution' he was therefore depending on Roberts. The 'facts' to which he referred were those retailed by Roberts, reinforced by passages in Gissing's early novels read autobiographically, by the later account of Helen's death and by the assumption that she had been an alcoholic and a prostitute since her Manchester days. In short, it was not a question of fact at all. Perhaps Helen Harrison was a prostitute in 1876–7, at the age of seventeen, but there is no hard evidence, in fact no evidence of any kind.

Of the later period in London, Korg was equally definite.

Whatever illusions may have possessed Gissing when he took Helen back must have been quickly dispelled, for by November of 1879 he had learned enough about her to write the powerfully circumstantial account of a marriage like his own that appears in *Workers in the Dawn*. Helen was continually ill. At different times she had neuralgia, 'rheumatics', an abscess of the arm, an eye condition necessitating an operation, and, most sinister of all, mysterious convulsions followed by comas.[23]

Korg does not explain what is sinister about an abscess or an eye condition. No doubt these were the direct result of prostitution! 'But Helen had worse faults than poor health', we are told. 'She was not merely ignorant, but foolish, wilful and disobedient as well. When he was not distressed at her illness, Gissing was repelled and distracted by her vulgar friends, her foolish conversation and her slovenly habits. Worst of all, however, were her alcoholism and the problems it created.'[24] This inhuman, sensational patronizing story is in turn taken over by Pierre Coustillas who talks of 'Nell's constant ill-health and irresponsibility'.[25] And by others. Yet it cannot be completely right. There is nothing to suggest that Gissing was disillusioned about Helen before they were married or that his reason for marrying her was wrong-headed or perverse. Certainly the passages about Carrie Mitchell in *Workers in the Dawn* would not be used to support such a claim, since Gissing only wrote them after he married. If Gissing became disillusioned, it was because of the marriage itself. And on that subject the two may have been in complete agreement.

Although no record has survived of Gissing's day by day life in 1879, *Workers in the Dawn* was almost certainly written in three stages.[26] The first ended in July 1879 when Gissing completed the early part of the novel with Lizzie Clinkscales still imagined as an important character in a story which hinged upon the conflict between the hero's dedication to art and his commitment to social reform. Carrie Mitchell, who became the principal character, did not at this point exist. The second stage, which extended from August to November, involved the introduction of Carrie Mitchell. Immediately the novel was given a psychological depth and interest that it had previously lacked. A crucial stage had been reached by 20 August when Gissing told his brother that he had completed the twenty-eighth chapter, which the manuscript shows was the point at which Carrie Mitchell was introduced. The third stage was the period in which the novel was completed and revised. The completion involved an extension that would accommodate the story of the hero's relationship with Carrie Mitchell and the revision involved the deletion of passages unacceptable to the publishers who read the book.

The textual and bibliographical evidence which shows that Gissing introduced Carrie Mitchell to *Workers in the Dawn* either immediately before or during the two or three months which followed his marriage is more complicated than this and has been given elsewhere.[27] Gissing undoubtedly found himself able to take up and complete the manuscript over which he had languished in the early part of 1879 because of the excitement of his relationship with Helen. There will be other examples of this. The sexual excitement allowed him to write although the writing often brought an end to the relationship by making the excitement no longer necessary. Gissing found the energy to finish *Workers in the Dawn* during the first months of his marriage with Helen Harrison. The question is: can one take this a stage further and positively identify Carrie Mitchell with Helen Harrison?

Certainly the novel was given a huge emotional impetus, a force that in its first version it completely lacked, because Gissing saw and experienced through his wife things that he had not known before. About half way through *Workers in the Dawn*, Arthur Norman moves to Gower Place and his 'notice' was attracted to one of the other lodgers. 'This was a young girl, of perhaps seventeen or eighteen' who was 'very pretty, if not positively handsome, tall, with dark hair which she arranged in a tasteful way, and dressed in black which seemed to indicate mourning'. The rest of this paragraph is vintage Gissing: on many occasions later in his writing career does he resort to its formulations and explore their implications.

> Though her beauty was of a somewhat sensual type, and her features betrayed no special intelligence or good-humour, Arthur felt strangely attracted to her for all that. To a beautiful female face he was always especially susceptible, and in this case the natural ardour of his years was additionally excited by the occasional and brief glimpses he obtained of her, and by the fact that she resided under the same roof as himself. There was, moreover, a fixed paleness upon the girl's face, and now and then a look of suffering which excited his compassion. As week after week went by, he noticed that these signs increased. He thought she must be ill, and felt his interest in her grow yet stronger.[28]

Arthur discovers that this girl is pregnant, that the father of the child refuses to help her, and that she is wholly dependent upon the charity of the landlady, her aunt. When she has to stop working, Arthur prevents the landlady from throwing her out by secretly paying her rent.

> Now it was the senses that had sway over him. His blood coursed hot through his veins, his pulses throbbed. One moment he burned with vehement anger at the unknown depth of resentful ferocity in his nature, the existence of which he could not have believed; the next, his being seemed to melt with excess of passion, as he thought of Carrie's beautiful face and form, and dwelt with unutterable tenderness upon the vision of her tear-reddened eyes, her pale cheeks, her feeble step. He suffered physically; it was as though some force were straining at his heart-strings, making him pant for breath.[29]

But when Carrie Mitchell discovers that he has been paying the rent, she is overcome by the cruelty of her position and leaves the house. Only by coincidence does Arthur find her again. He comes across her at Christmas time huddled in a church porch with her dead child, takes care of her, arranges for her to spend three weeks in hospital, has someone buy her clothes, establishes her in a room of her own and patiently helps her recover her vitality. He is possessed

by her and almost believes that he possesses her, for when Carrie
first goes out by herself and then lies to conceal the fact, he cannot
contain himself and blurts out: 'you should not go where I do not
wish you, where I *will not have you go* – at least as long as you accept
my help'.[30]

This episode led directly to reconciliation, forgiveness, love. 'All
afternoon . . . did the two wander side by side, absolutely ignorant of
the places they passed; listening to nothing but the sweet utterances
of each other's lips, seeing nothing but the glad looks on each other's
faces'.[31] Within a few weeks they were married in the Registrar's
office. 'Neither of them had a parent or guardian, so the fact that
they were both under age was of no consequence.'[32] In the cramped
quarters in which they make their home, almost immediately there is
tension, disagreement, suspicion. Carrie has nothing to do, begins to
crave excitement, distraction of some kind; Arthur works all day, but
in the evening wants to educate Carrie, to teach her to read, to improve her accent. Almost immediately occurs the paragraph of
explanation that has so impressed so many Gissing readers.

> It is all very well to say that on the second day after his marriage he
> ought to have been as much in love with his wife as to care for nothing
> but listening to her heedless talk and to think everything worthy of
> detestation which caused her the least annoyance. Arthur's nature being
> what it was, such love as this was impossible to him. What he intensely
> loved, he could not but wish intensely to respect. The pity which had
> originated his love was in itself a species of respect; he had convinced
> himself by force of emotion that Carrie could not deserve the suffering
> she endured, and he had almost reverenced her as an instance of un-
> merited misfortune. Then of course her striking personal beauty had
> forced him to look up to her as something superior. He could not believe
> that such outward perfection could exist with a common-place and sterile
> nature. When he openly declared to her his affection, the warmth with
> which she reciprocated it had added another link to his chain by convinc-
> ing him of the strength of her feelings. He felt that an indifferent, passion-
> less woman would have been intolerable to him. But now a vague dread
> began to encroach like an unnatural darkness upon his heart, a terrible
> fear lest he might have deceived himself not only with regard to her
> intelligence, but also as to the extent of her affection for him. He could
> not bear the suspicion. At all costs he must throw it off. Possibly it might
> force itself on him later, gain ground surely and with the pitiless persist-
> ency of fate, but as yet it was too, too early. Why, he had scarcely tasted
> the fulness of his joy, should the cup already be dashed from his lips?[33]

Carrie learns to humour Arthur, pretends to be learning to read,
has his evening meal ready for him when he returns from work and
does all that is required of her. Under cover of this subservient
attitude, she goes out more frequently, makes friends with women to
whom the landlady objects as being too 'flashy' and begins to drink,

attempting to conceal the fact from her husband by eating pepper-mint. Inevitably Arthur discovers signs of her taste for gin and brandy and there is recrimination on both sides, for Carrie finds a drawing of another woman amongst his belongings and challenges him to say that he loves no one else. What follows is the vividly depicted breakdown of the marriage, where the jealousy and frustra-tion of the man match the distraught behaviour of the woman as she grows to depend more and more upon the bottle. This in turn is followed by bouts of prostitution, reformations, reconciliations, and more drunkenness. Carrie eventually gives way and returns to Polly Hemp's brothel, while Arthur emigrates and eventually commits suicide. While it would be tedious to retell in detail something like half of this extremely long novel, it is fair to notice that what gives the Carrie Mitchell/Arthur Golding part of the plot its strength is not just the extremely lively dialogue and wealth of detail evidently based upon observation but also the fact that the whole situation is seen compassionately with a multiple point of view, sometimes Carrie's, sometimes Arthur's, sometimes the narrator's. If the whole book had been written in this way, it would have been one of the most brilliant of first novels.

How closely the story of Carrie Mitchell resembled that of Helen Harrison we shall probably never be able to tell. Like Carrie and Arthur, Gissing and Helen Harrison had lived in the same lodging house until they were married. There is no evidence that Helen Harrison ever had a child, although many people have commented on what Coustillas called the 'belated ceremony'.[34] Infant deaths were not invariably identified by name so there is no way of telling whether a pregnancy provided Gissing with the incentive to get married, something which would have been consistent with Ellen Gissing's saying that Helen had a 'right' to expect Gissing's help and support. Whereas Carrie and Arthur were married in a Registrar's Office, Gissing and Helen Harrison were married (on 27 October 1879) in St. James' Church, Hampstead Road, the marriage certificate giving the bride as Marianne Helen Harrison, aged 20, spinster, daughter of John Harrison, deceased: which means she must have been seventeen years old when Gissing was expelled from Owens College. The parallel is close enough for one to feel that this part of *Workers in the Dawn* must have been autobiographical in some sense, but certainly not in the sense that Gissing retold his own experiences in a direct and scarcely veiled way. The timing makes this impossible. Gissing was married on 27 October 1879 and he sent the finished novel to Chatto & Windus in December, hardly leaving time enough for anything but instantaneous marital disaster. Certainly Gissing's first marriage disintegrated rapidly but not rapidly enough for *Workers in the Dawn* to be completely autobiographical.

The marriage lasted at the most two years, from October 1879 to January 1882, though they were together again for short periods later that year. The cause of the break up from Gissing's point of view was Helen's behaviour. From Helen's point of view it was Gissing's. Never in his life was he able to make compromises for the sake of another person. His work and his private, bookish pleasures always came first. His pleasure was complete personal freedom. Throughout his life he preferred to be able to come and go exactly as he wished without the need to explain himself to anyone, and indeed would opt for considerable privation rather than sacrifice himself in any way. He preferred to be poor than to be dependent. His work, meanwhile, took most of his time. During the spring of 1880, immediately after his marriage, he corrected the proofs of *Workers in the Dawn*, a task which took him longer with this his first book than it was to do in later years. At the same time, he was at work on his next novel and in March told Algernon his working hours: 'I rise at 6.45, walk from 7 to 8, pondering the chapter of the day, which I write from 9 to 2, five hours, you see; about as much writing as one can do well in a day.'[35] This regimen may not have been attractive to a young bride especially when, in addition, Gissing began to spend two evenings a week with Bertz, walking the six miles to Tottenham and returning home by train just before midnight. Important, too, was the fact that he did not tell Helen he had used what was left of his inheritance to pay for the publication of *Workers in the Dawn*. Nor did he tell his brothers and sisters, who in fact never discovered the whole truth. 'I sincerely hope my book will bring me something', he wrote in May. Of course he did. He had gambled, secretly as usual, but without a clear appreciation of the odds. 'Very much depends on the next two or three weeks. I think the reviews of *Workers* will certainly begin next Saturday, and, should they be favourable, I may, of course, hope for some profit from the book. If I am ignored I must think very seriously of some mechanical day-labour.'[36] He had at this point been married for six months. He did not tell his wife that if the venture failed they would be left without any money at all.

To have the book published Gissing had signed a contract by which he agreed to pay Remington £50 at the time of signing, £40 when the first two volumes had been printed and the remaining £35 when the third volume had been printed. The receipts show that the final payment was made on 19 May. Since the book was to be sold at a guinea and since the agreement specified that the author was to receive two-thirds of the profit, Gissing naturally thought that he only had to sell sixty or so copies before he began to receive an income. Remington, however, claimed about a year later that he had only sold forty-nine sets of the 277 that had been made up and, further, that he had spent £24 on advertising. Perhaps it was fortunate for Gissing as an author that he did not learn the full extent of this disaster until he was fully committed to his next book. For Gissing the husband, however, life soon became very difficult indeed and, if Helen had not been prepared for the reversal of fortune and it seems she had not, she must have been shattered by it. She had been rescued from penury by a man who suddenly was reduced to the same condition. Not a pleasant experience for any woman.

Gissing did not, of course 'think seriously of some mechanical day labour' except when justifying himself to his family in Wakefield. He thought chiefly of his writing. Study and intellectual work had nothing to do with bread-winning, he told his brother Will. He was still full of confidence. 'I always *feel* the energy of health, and indeed, considering my haphazard manner of dealing with the matter, it would much surprise me to hear that I had not more than an average constitution.'[37] 'I shall, of course, have no holiday of any kind', he said in the same letter, somewhat misleadingly, since he did in fact go on holiday in August, 'for I have never before been in such mind for productive work'. Yet his marriage began to deteriorate under the stress of the moment. Interestingly, this deterioration was attributed in the *Letters* to both 'temperament' and 'harassing domestic circumstances'.

The marriage deteriorated because, whatever the cause, Helen was mentally as well as physically ill. As early as April 1880 – in a postscript in a letter to Algernon – Gissing spoke of her as having a 'recurrence of very severe fits'.[38] No medical evidence has survived, but to twentieth century ears it sounds as though Helen must have been an epileptic. At first this did not stop them leading a normal life in the sense that they continued to live happily with each other just as they had done before they were married. In the spring they went to the occasional concert – 'Nell and I went to the Albert Hall to hear the organ'[39] – and when it was warm they went on the river, Gissing's favourite sport. 'Nell makes a good sailor', he told his brother, and meanwhile he was getting on 'famously' and 'wonderfully' with his new novel, 'Mrs. Grundy's Enemies'. During those months his letters would be interspersed with remarks like 'Nell much as usual – sends kindest regards.' Only as the summer progressed did the further deterioration of Helen's health begin to wear them down, coinciding as it did with the poor reception of *Workers in the Dawn* and an acute shortage of cash. They went to the seaside for a brief holiday in the hope that her health would improve, but it did not.

By the autumn of that year he came to realize that proper treatment with a period in hospital was inevitable, despite Helen's only too natural unwillingness and despite the cost. 'Getting her into hospital is the only plan,' he told his brother frankly, which was a huge admission, since going to a hospital or even a doctor, was for

him as mysterious, frightening and doubtful a business as opening a
bank account. He simply did not know what to do and looked about
him for help.

   At this time, George and Helen Gissing had taken up with a Paul
Rohart whom Gissing had previously known in Wakefield. The
Roharts opened a shop in Peckham Rye which Gissing sarcastically
said was to be called 'The Noted Little Provision Shop' and during
1880 the Gissings spent a number of 'very hateful' afternoons there.
Though Gissing called him a 'grossly vulgar person' and, in a fine
case of the pot calling the kettle black, told Algernon he thought the
Rohart's marriage would be destroyed by their perpetual quarrelling,
Rohart helped to get Helen into hospital in November. Gissing never
understood that other people formed judgments about his behaviour
that had nothing whatsoever to do with his own explanations of what
he did. Like many other introverts, he thought his inner life was secret
and a mystery. If others formed opinions of him not based on his
own account they must be wrong. On this occasion he told Algernon
how he and Rohart had got Helen into hospital and then said:

> Nell and I both know (now) that the man has systematically calumnated
> us for a long time on every possible occasion, that is he has tried his ut-
> most to make us disagree and that he very nearly succeeded in making
> Nell believe some time ago that he knew Bertz personally (of course a lie)
> and that Bertz was a dissipated scoundrel whose companionship could
> only lead to the gallows! At present he has taken advantage of Nell's
> removal to the hospital to make the authorities there believe that I starve
> and beat her (literally) and to do his best to persuade Nell to go away
> from me and serve in his shop with Maria.[40]

Later in his life, friends on whom he had no sort of claim volunteered
to look after the children of his second marriage and when this
happened Gissing accepted it as an act of generosity without giving
any indication that he understood his friends' action was a scarcely
veiled criticism of his attitude to his family. Of course someone had
to look after the children if his wife would not do so. How else could
he write? Something of the same sort occurred when friends attempted to help Helen; Gissing gave no hint of any realization that it
might be he who was at fault. After all, he did not *choose* to live with
the utmost austerity. It was a condition of his work. He was simply
incapable of appreciating that his wife might legitimately have
desires or needs that were not also his. Elsewhere in the correspondence there are hints that he did in fact beat both wives (he told his
sister on one occasion that he had stopped using the stair rod!).
Whether he did or not, his letter to Algernon about Rohart reveals
more about Gissing himself than Rohart.

   Helen was in and out of hospital throughout the latter part of 1880
and the whole of 1881. Even today an undiagnosed condition, or one

which is only partly understood, can be terrifying. Under strain, Gissing began to say peevish things about his wife's behaviour, making that song and dance about the extent to which it interfered with his work that led some people, later, to sympathise much more with him than with her. Helen has been represented, for example, as having let him down because incapable of entertaining his visitors with intelligent talk. It was sinful of her to have been ill, so inconsiderate. It was only in his letters to his brother, Algernon, which were only in small measure reproduced in *Letters* (the bulk of this correspondence is in the Beinecke Library) that Gissing revealed his worries about her physical condition, as well as the strain of broken nights and constant disturbance of his work routine. Home from hospital in February 1881 she had, twice in one week, a strong attack of delirium lasting each time more than two hours. Later in the spring, she had a similar fit in a chemist's shop and had to be carried home. Neither Helen nor Gissing, living as they were in small rooms in Wormington Road, could stand this for very long. In the early summer Helen left him for a while – worn out not just by her ill health, but by Gissing's attitude to it and by the tensions it created between them. But she soon returned. 'The months and the years go, go', said Gissing, reporting Helen's return to Algernon, 'but always a darker outlook, & perhaps the best years of all are already gone. To look back on a wasted life must be bad, but worse still, I think, to feel the waste actually going on, to know what might be, & to be helpless'.[41]

Gissing was helpless because he was confronted by something he could not understand intellectually: the unkindest experience of all given the kind of person he was. In January 1882, Helen had a serious breakdown or 'fit' in a chandler's shop after Gissing had refused to go out with her and once more had to be carried home. On another occasion she fainted in the street. Since neither Gissing nor Helen knew the real cause of her illness, but only its symptoms, their powerlessness in the face of adversity resulted in estrangement and, on Gissing's side, a desperate attitude. Something was happening to him that disturbed his normally logical and well-ordered universe.

He knew perfectly well that Helen was mentally ill, but he did not know the cause. 'I certainly thought she had gone mad', he told Algernon after the doctors had visited the house during the night. Despite numerous visits to hospital, Helen failed to obtain satisfactory diagnosis or treatment, hardly a surprising fact given how little was known at that time about 'nervous diseases' or nervous breakdown. Gissing tried to understand, read Henry Maudsley's works on mental illness or 'insanity' as Maudsley called it, began to mention Maudsley's symptoms of mental illness in his letters to Algernon, but in the end failed to comprehend what was happening:

a torment which made Gissing fear that he too might break down. Yet Helen herself was really ill; that much at least Gissing understood. In January 1882, when the young couple had endured their agony for more than a year and when Gissing himself was on the point of distraction, he said in a letter to Algernon: 'I do not know if she is to be blamed for all this considering that, without doubt, her mind is affected. Still no-one is called upon to sacrifice everything in life to a weak-minded person's whims.'[42]

The 'whims' were becoming serious. There is no evidence of any kind that Helen drank a lot before her illness, and certainly not a shred of evidence to support the contention made by Korg that her convulsions were the result of her alcoholism. Her symptoms as recorded in the letters were not those of an alcoholic. But Gissing now found a bottle of gin in their rooms and associated her drinking with her mental condition.[43] There were 'scenes' in public places and on one occasion Helen wanted to charge three men with assault. During the spring and summer of 1882 she lived by herself, with friends, but not peacefully. Gissing was called in when a policeman had to break up a brawl involving his wife and 'a couple of drunken women.' They could not live together, yet he was still responsible for her.

A letter to his brother written to Algernon on 18 May 1882 expresses his mood. The period of affection is over. He wrote about Helen not as a person he loved, or had ever loved, but as an inconvenience, and then only in a letter which mostly concerned Algernon's examination results and his own reading. 'In private affairs', he told his brother, 'there is some little prospect of temporary peace'. Helen had returned to London, had briefly lived in a room in Kensington which Gissing had found for her and, soon enough, had returned to her old haunts in Soho Square.

> This is very astonishing, like everything else in the same connection . . . no doubt the truth is that the people there want her money & anxiously persuade her to go. She is very particular in refusing to let me interfere in the matter. Well, I am glad enough to be quit of anxiety at the sum of £1 weekly. I shall not myself go to the Hospital ever; that is understood, & acquiesced in. I only can't understand why she determined ever to leave the place, for I am convinced that the atmosphere of vulgar gossip is essentially congenial to her.[44]

Gissing probably was not exaggerating when he said he was astonished by Helen's preference for the seedy atmosphere of Soho Square, because he was entirely unequipped to understand that another person might not want what he wanted and because never at any time did he acknowledge that Helen's behaviour had anything to do with him. If Helen had announced that since he seemed to wish to write all the time she had decided to make friends of her own, a perfectly natural reaction in the circumstances, Gissing would have been 'astonished'. Yet there would have been a measure of right on his side as well, perhaps a large measure. Though Gissing was criticised by Helen's friends – 'vile people who write me abusive letters for my neglect and cruelty' – there was not really very much he could do about the situation. It was out of control. Her condition had not been diagnosed. Even if they had lived seventy or eighty years later and had been able to benefit from twentieth century treatment and diagnosis, it is not likely that the marriage would have survived the strain Helen's behaviour placed on Gissing, who not merely wanted but absolutely needed to work. In the end, he broke down: 'I wish utterly and absolutely to cease all relations save sending a postal order each week – and to think how well I was getting on with my work.' That was in June 1882.

Having already been separated from Helen for various periods when she stayed with friends, Gissing knew that he had to find some way of having her cared for. She came back to him in the late summer of 1882, when he tried locking her in her room and then, more reasonably, hiring a companion to accompany her when she went out. These were not solutions calculated to help someone as ill as Helen Gissing. In November, Gissing told his brother that she was going into hospital once again:

A step has at last been taken. They have consented to receive Helen into the Westminster Hospital, where in all probability they will operate upon her arm. She goes on Tuesday. This is not a day too soon. For more than a week I have scarcely slept more than a half an hour at a time through the night, & the results are most appreciable. I have, in the meantime, got Mrs. Harrison's help in searching for a permanent home. This will be made use of when she leaves the Hospital.[45]

Gissing had by this time moved from 29 Dorchester Square to 17 Oakley Crescent in Chelsea, which was strictly a residence for himself where he was 'waited upon' and not at all intended as a home for Helen. 'Attendance is arranged upon a most satisfactory footing', he told Algernon when urging him to visit London, making it plain that there was no thought in his mind of preparing for Helen's recovery.

The home found for Helen was in Battersea, but naturally enough she rejected it. To Gissing's astonishment she made it clear that she was leaving him and they in fact never lived with each other again. Gissing reported the separation to Algernon in a characteristically egotistical way. 'Close upon the astonishing intelligence conveyed in my last, I have to send you news of changes. My wife, in brief, has gone to live with some people in Brixton, taking for her own use one half of the furniture, & leaving me the rest.'[46] Gissing's thoughts were for himself. He thought he might have had the 'trouble of removal' but his landlord offered him an even smaller back room for seven shillings a week. Since there was not room for a bed (and in any case Helen had taken it), he had to sleep on his sofa, but the room, though 'very very small' and 'chock full of things,' was – Gissing cared about little else – 'redolent of quiet work'. He was by himself again just as he really desired. 'By Midsummer, I hope to have another novel finished,' he said, without further comment on the loss of his wife except that he was paying her £1 a week. It was his fate to be the kind of person who complained unceasingly about the domestic arrangements when he lived with anyone else, though by himself he derived pleasure from the most trivial domestic contrivance. In the back room of 17 Oakley Crescent, he liked the fact that his 'washing apparatus' could be made to disappear within a convenient little cupboard.

Both Helen and George Gissing had been reduced by the misery of their predicament to an inhuman condition in which each was bitterly suspicious of the other. Gissing said absurdly disloyal things about Helen in order to justify his rejection of her in favour of his work, while Helen, with little money and away from her own home, seems to have degenerated as a character, slipping from bad to worse until she died some six years later. In 1883 Gissing seriously contemplated a divorce action but failed to gather the necessary evidence. Nevertheless the marriage was over: Gissing never lived with his wife again and did not even see her during the last three or four years of her life. She died of chronic laryngitis (according to the death certificate) on 29 February 1889.

Whatever the underlying cause of the illness, which put her in and out of hospital continuously during the two years they lived together, it is likely that Gissing himself did little to improve the situation. Friends of theirs had suggested that Helen should help in their shop. This was unsuitable, Gissing thought. Helen exchanged gifts with Algernon, but Gissing could do nothing about his mother: she opposed the marriage from the beginning and the wound never healed. It is scarcely possible that Helen would have been helped by this. Meanwhile Gissing's self-imposed work schedule was so heavy he had little room for the companionship on which their friendship had originally been based. Helen was expected to share his sacrifices, as were all those people he subsequently knew. Perhaps this would have been tolerable if she had the benefit of home and income, but she had married a professed bohemian, someone who was determined to manage without such things. And one can guess, though this is no more than conjecture, that Gissing's sexual attitudes were somewhat primitive. They were in love when they married. But it would have been just like Gissing to be sexually uninhibited before marriage and convert, after marriage, to being a model Victorian husband who associated sexual abstinence with the right management of domestic life. Gissing, however, remained silent on such matters.

Helen and George Gissing were lovers trapped by a turn of events outside their control and beyond their comprehension. People have written of this period as though Gissing were merely irritated by Helen's 'low' behaviour. It was actually a profoundly tragic period of life for them both, a period in which love and aspiration rapidly deteriorated under pressure from pain and suffering. After their final separation Gissing lived for several years by himself, at first in Chelsea and later in a flat off Baker Street, and when he saw Helen after her death he could not recognize her. Years later, Gissing had Ryecroft comment on the dehumanizing effects of poverty.

You tell me that money cannot buy the things most precious. Your commonplace proves that you have never known the lack of it. When I think of all the sorrow and the barrenness that has been wrought in my life by want of a few more pounds per annum than I was able to earn, I stand aghast at money's significance. What kindly joys have I lost, those simple forms of happiness to which every heart has claim, because of poverty! Meetings with those I loved made impossible year after year; sadness, misunderstanding, nay, cruel alienation, arising from inability to do the things I wished, and which I might have done had a little money helped me; endless instances of homely pleasure and contentment curtailed or forbidden by narrow means. I have lost friends merely through the constraints of my position; friends I might have made have remained strangers to me; solitude of the bitter kind, the solitude which is enforced at times when mind or heart longs for companionship, often cursed my life solely because I was poor.[47]

4

Literary Apprenticeship

WHILE Gissing's relationship with Helen was disintegrating, he spent every spare moment away from his pupils thinking about the question of how to write a modern novel. This he shared with no one. Part of George Gissing's personal tragedy was the sharp distinction he made between his domestic and his literary life. He made no attempt, really, to reconcile the two. From his father and his early education he had acquired the idea that the intellectual life of a man was hardly, if at all, related to the family of which he was part. As a writer, Gissing never or scarcely ever shared his work. For example only one or two people are known to have read his work before it was published, Bertz being one of them, of course. No one read proof for him. Rarely if ever did he test out the idea for a new book on a member of his family or a friend, or either of his wives. His working life was private to himself. This means that, although in one sense the first period of his life in London extended from his arrival in 1877 to his separation from Helen in 1882, another way of seeing it would be to emphasise the stages by which he established himself as a novelist, indeed the principal novelist who concerned himself with the contemporary scene. The first stage extended from 1880 when he published *Workers in the Dawn* to 1885 when, having finished *Isabel Clarendon* and *A Life's Morning*, he began *Demos*. In these four or five years, and particularly after 1882, his life found its own literary, undomestic direction. Study, experience, temperament led rapidly to the naturalistic novels he was to write in the late eighties: rapidly in the sense that there is such a vast difference between the unfashioned, hesitant, uneven *Workers in the Dawn* and the more assured, though far from perfect *Demos*, five years later.

A lot of ground was covered in this five year period of apprenticeship, something too often begrudged by critics who have judged Gissing haughtily on the basis of his unrevised juvenilia or worst books, giving the impression, complacently, that he mindlessly wrote the same kind of novel thoughout the whole of his life. Nothing is further from the truth. One might as well judge Hardy by reference only to *Desperate Remedies* or Stevenson by *The Pentland Rising*. An essential fact about Gissing is that he thought a lot about what would be genuinely contemporary, what kind of novel could be most appropriate to the contemporary subject, what of relevance would be learnt from past masters whose techniques were no longer relevant: for better or worse he worked out for himself the question of how to write a modern novel, and understandably found this so difficult that he began his career unevenly with a number of very unequal books. Yet this trial and error apprenticeship later allowed him to write a distinctive type of novel that few of his contemporaries were able to match.

Affected not just by his month in goal but also by the way people treated him afterwards, Gissing had obviously spent a lot of time in North America thinking about what he should do with his life. He had returned with his mind made up. For better or worse, Gissing remained resolute in his determination to be a novelist, even in extreme adversity. From this course, whatever difficulties he encountered, he never once deviated. Yes, he admired, indeed revered the classics, but industrial England in the eighteen-seventies did not need an Aeschylus. The novel was the genuinely contemporary form. What else would a *serious* writer write except novels? More and more energy was therefore given to his writing, less and less to everything else. He was not concerned with, had little time for much else. He had few friends. He had little real contact with his family in Wakefield. After 1882, he did not see his wife. He had an existence of his own which was without responsibility. If he had a miserable cold, could scarcely breathe and could not afford coal, was short of food or could not be bothered to go out for it, was lonely or frustrated by the sight of young girls in the London streets, these things simply assured Gissing that he was leading a genuinely bohemian life, and he was therefore happy. At first with Nell and then almost immediately by himself, he thus settled into the routine he was to maintain until his death, after the breakdown of his marriage writing a novel a year: 'Mrs. Grundy's Enemies' in 1882 (unpublished); *The Unclassed* in 1883 (published in 1884); *Isabel Clarendon* in the winter of 1884–85 (published in 1886); and *A Life's Morning* in 1885 (published in 1888). A new novelist had succeeded in establishing himself, at least in his own estimation, and it was this that allowed him to continue. Bohemian did not mean, of course, being carefree, feckless, superficial, irresponsible. It meant (for he had learnt it all from Murger) being deliberately anti-materialistic, anti-bourgeois, not in wild protest, but for intellectual reasons that could easily be explained.

He had established himself at an early age. When Gissing began to write *Demos* in 1885, he was twenty-seven years old, had published two novels, and had two others accepted for publication. Not unnaturally, few people knew very much about what he was doing. How could they? He lived by himself and worked continuously. He kept himself alive for four or five years by tutoring, an occupation which left him with little free time and for other reasons, social ones, tended to hold him to an essentially private, perhaps even secret, role in life. It is not the business of a family tutor to discuss his private life: Gissing liked that. In December 1880, he began to tutor the sons of Frederic Harrison and did so until they went away to school. Early in 1881, he added the daughters of Vernon Lushington, whom he also taught for a number of years. The following year he accepted the two sons of Sir Henry Le Marchant and a nephew of the Duke of Sutherland, whom he taught as a group. There were others, including notably Walter Grahame. In the *Commonplace Book* he 'put down a list of the young aristocrats' he had had as pupils: the son of Lady Albert Gower; the grandson of Sir Stafford Northcote; the sons of the Bishop of Hereford, of Montague Cookson (a barrister) and of George Pepys.[1] All in all he did pretty well from this succession of pupils. By 1882 he was earning £3 or £3·50 a week. Enough to live on. By the end of 1884, his tutoring was bringing him £5·10 a week, which gave him an annual income of between £150 and £200, out of which he still paid £1 a week to Helen. To this would have been added, in 1881 and 1882, the £32 a year he obtained from his quarterly articles in *Le Messager de l'Europe*, so except for the low period of disappointment after the publication of *Workers in the Dawn* in 1880 he was not poor.

Unfortunately, the popular story about George Gissing implies that his whole life, and most of all his attitude to life, were contaminated by a poverty so extreme that he was never able to be 'normal' and well-adjusted, but it is essential to realise that this extreme early poverty lasted only for the first two or three years of his first London period. After that he was never in real difficulty, despite the fact that he grumbled incessantly and lacked the commonsense to put his affairs in order. Frederic Harrison's son, Austin, maintained later that Gissing, though never wealthy, was without financial embarrassments during the years in which they knew each other, a claim that seems to be supported by the facts. Gissing has been given too little credit for the vigour with which he worked for his own independence. After all, there is nothing culpable about not turning to journalism (though he has been chastised for not being a journalist), nothing extraordinary in being prepared to accept tutoring as a means to keep body and soul together while he found his feet as an author. Because of all that happened in Manchester, he liked the anonymous life of the tutor. And why not? The period of tutoring, in his case, is evidence of vast determination: few people in fact manage to earn a living by writing alone. Abnormal patience and abnormal self-restraint are needed. Perhaps Gissing sized the situation up more accurately than his detractors have realised. To gain complete independence as a writer, a heavy price had to be paid.

He was without acute financial embarrassment, but there was little likelihood that others would understand his purposes. This was part of the price. Certainly there was little likelihood that his family would. A main source of information about these years is the correspondence with his brothers and sisters, part of which was published in *Letters of George Gissing to Members of His Family*, whilst the larger part remains unpublished in American libraries. To his family he wrote letters on subjects of common family interest. This must be what happens in most families and it would be unreasonable to expect such letters to be revealing, particularly when one has in mind the respective ages of the correspondents. When Gissing married Helen Harrison in 1879, his brother William was twenty, Algernon nineteen, Margaret sixteen, and Ellen twelve. Though there was a warm bond of feeling between them, by his standards they were naïve, inexperienced, conventional in their attitudes and unaware of the real world. How could they possibly share the life of a man whose classical education was retained and lived out, whose reading in French and German had been so extended in Boston and then in London, whose knowledge of English literature was so thorough, whose intellect took for granted the closest possible connection between all that could be read and all that could be thought? There were already many aspects of his life he could not hope to share with them, quite apart from those matters he wished to suppress or conceal. He could not share his personal or his sexual experiences with younger sisters who were devout church-goers, his domestic problems with a family which still lived securely and honourably within the circle of his father's friends, or his thoughts with people who did not think or (if they did) had no way to test the validity of their conclusions. There is, in short, no likelihood that he would have confided in them: he cannot be seen in terms of, or through the eyes of, his Wakefield family. He was different. They were young, callow, provincial, anti-intellectual, and contributed nothing to Gissing's development as an artist. In any case, people who are by nature secretive confide least of all in their own families.

Six years later, when he began to write *Demos* in 1885, William was dead, Algernon had qualified as a solicitor and had joined a local firm, and Margaret and Ellen, aged twenty-two and eighteen respectively, were still at home having never in any sense broken away from the life that Gissing himself had left when he went away to school fifteen years earlier. There were unbridgeable chasms

between them, except, that is, between George and Algernon in whom
Gissing to a certain extent began to confide after he had finally
separated from Helen. All this means that both *Letters of George
Gissing to Members of His Family* and the unpublished letters to his
brothers and sisters are of limited significance. He told them what
they wanted to hear. He created an image of himself comparable with
what they could be expected to understand. He wrote about books
because they, his brothers and sisters, were still being educated or
were educating themselves and because they thought of him almost
exclusively as a bookish person. He wrote about the issues of the day
because such things were just beginning to concern them. Equally important, as far as Gissing's life is concerned, is the fact that the Wakefield family exerted absolutely no influence upon him.

Apart from the publication of *Workers in the Dawn*, the most
significant event of 1880 was Gissing's meeting with Frederic
Harrison whom he already knew to be a member of 'the advanced
Radical party', a positivist and a man of letters with wide-ranging interests, someone whose articles he had read in the *Fortnightly
Review* and other journals. For the first time, he was brought into
contact with people of intellect equal to his own, while in a more
directly personal way Harrison took him under his wing and ensured
that he had the wherewithal to survive. Harrison became a staunch
friend. He accepted Gissing's past; that is, he accepted the reasons
Gissing gave for his expulsion from Owens College. As a friend, he
accepted their basic incompatibility of temperament. He accepted in
Gissing his 'incurable turn for a solitary life and the study of misery
and the sordid,' while he himself favoured robust optimism and a
much more active, purposeful attitude to life. Intellectually, he
accepted the Gissing who had read Spencer, Comte, Schopenhauer,
the agnostic who was keenly interested in the issues of the day as they
were debated in newspapers and journals, the classicist who was concerned enough about the present to be interested in sociology and
political theory. He frequently had Gissing to lunch after tutoring
sessions, took him on picnics, invited him for weekends at his country
house, asked him to parties, and later invited him to share a family
holiday in Normandy. As he told H. G. Wells shortly after Gissing's
death: 'I was on terms of the most perfect confidence and familiarity
with him and I used sometimes to rally him as being the most hardened
egotist and the most refined sybarite I knew.'[2]

Austin Harrison, though not completely partial to the memory of a
father who 'dispensed his disfavours liberally,' much later gave
various accounts of this friendship. On one occasion he wrote:

> I would positively quake when I heard my father chide Gissing for his
> 'delight,' which by the way was perfectly true, in portraying the nether
> world when life was full of beauty and happiness. Gissing, the pessimist,

would hang his head and look the image of despair, and then his laughing eyes would twinkle, and with his spontaneous and delightful burst of laughter, so characteristic of his attitude towards the people he drew and the life they lived, and he hated this squalor as much as a victimization, he would cry, 'but we must know or we shall never remedy those atrocious (his favourite word) abominations! Someone, I say, must speak out and tell the truth. . . .'[3]

This was part of Gissing which Harrison understood and respected, even though it ran counter to his own 'meliorist' attitudes.

The issues raised by *Workers in the Dawn* were of interest, perhaps urgent interest to Harrison in 1880. He was drawn to it. Even much later, in the letter to Wells quoted above, Harrison was to say: 'What surprises me is that with all this roaring of the young lions about him no-one seems to know his earliest and in many ways his best book – savage and foul though it is.' *Workers in the Dawn* may have been innocent, unfashioned, uncertain in its direction, yet it was descriptively realistic and heavy with the weight of social conscience and social perplexity. Harrison responded to it because it *was* unfashioned, because important social issues were raised but not solved, because there was such a strong attempt to depict the conditions of the thinking, working-class man (the socialist's best hope), and because, despite the heavy, often moralistic tone, there was clearly within the book an active social conscience at work with which Harrison, the positivist, the 'advanced Radical', could identify. Harrison knew he was reading the notes for a powerful social commentary, the raw material for a novel in which life was not idealised. As such he could respond to it. On this basis, the friendship flourished through 1882 and indeed survived the time when Gissing realised that while the older man was set in his attitudes, he himself was not only intellectually still on the move but much more inclined to push his thoughts to conclusions which for Harrison would have been unbearably antisocial. Both men agreed that a condition of relative sanity depended upon the abandonment of outmoded social, political and religious practices. But Harrison thought that wise legislation would or at least could gradually improve life in England, while Gissing thought urban society was irredeemable. Gissing's own intellectual and artistic development meant coming to terms with *Workers in the Dawn*, without doubt one of the most fascinating first novels ever written. This fact has to be emphasized because, during these years, the main events of Gissing's life were literary and intellectual. What he *did*, in the physical sense, can be stated very simply. He taught a succession of pupils whose parents decided when they were free to be taught; he walked the streets of London (the London he called the 'necromancer' of his brain) for hour after hour, day after day, observing with an acuteness not shared by many of his contemporaries, starting, he said, with a map spread out on a cellar floor so that he could identify and search out all the places described by Dickens and his biographer, Forster. He frequented the British Museum and the reading rooms of Oxford Street: 'It astounds me to remember,' he has Ryecroft say, 'that, having breakfasted on dry bread, and carrying in my pocket another piece of dry bread to serve as dinner, I settled myself at a desk in the great Reading-Room with books before me which by no possibility could be a source of profit.'[4] And he worked each day until he was exhausted. For a period he went to political meetings, dabbled in socialism and interested himself in day-by-day affairs.[5] But this interest was short-lived. Nothing happened to him. He allowed nothing to happen to him. In short it was not what he did that mattered, but what he *thought*; he suppressed events for the sake of an intellectual freedom which was independent of them. This meant that in his own life he habitually denied actuality, consciously preferring the world of the literary imagination and never allowing it to be undermined by flesh and blood encounters with other people. It meant, too, that in his writing he could not be anything but completely detached from his characters whose experiences he observed and recorded at the same time specifically dissociating himself from them. So one comes to a paradox at the heart of Gissing's life and work. No one knew more about London and contemporary urban life than Gissing and this knowledge was gained by first-hand experience. At the same time, no one could have been as detached, insulated, from that experience; for Gissing was totally detached and insulated. Detached observation *was* his experience and warmer, more human, more ordinary experiences were suppressed so that it could be developed and become subsumed in fiction. Uneven though the novel undoubtedly was, *Workers in the Dawn* was the key to all this. Mrs. Harrison had remarked perceptively that it had in it material for six novels: it in fact took Gissing the whole of a decade to work the novel out of his system, for not until after *New Grub Street* and *Born in Exile* did he produce work that was not in some sense derived from this vast and ambitious first book.

Workers in the Dawn was first and foremost a study of the growth of the inner spirit, in the tradition exemplified by the Brontës (and particularly by *Villette*, one of Gissing's favourite novels), then brought to maturity by George Eliot, whose works from a technical point of view Gissing absorbed completely before discarding as being too conventionally moral to have relevance in contemporary life as he saw it. The main characters in *Workers in the Dawn*, Helen Norman and Arthur Golding, move through life passively, quietly, but perceptively and intelligently, learning more about themselves, growing to a kind of maturity in the process. Of course young Gissing had done this also, or thought he had. The 'growth of the spirit' novel is a convenient structure for a writer who, still lacking a profound understanding of people, is at such an early stage in his career that he does not even fully appreciate his own lack of a coherent theory of motivation. Why do people do things? They grow up – within themselves. To this story about young people discovering themselves Gissing had added a realistic depiction of Whitechapel in the late eighteen-seventies. 'Come with me, Reader, into Whitecross Street,' he says. Direct description of London preoccupied Gissing throughout the eighties. If people turn a blind eye at the truth, you must make them see! If they cannot understand why the poor behave 'badly', let them be told of the circumstances in which such people live! 'I am constantly astonished,' Gissing wrote in the *Commonplace Book*, 'to think of the small use Dickens made of his vast opportunities in the matter of observation among the lower classes. The explanation of course is, that he did not conceive of a work of fiction as anything but a *romance*. The details which would to me be most precious, he left aside as unsuitable, because unattractive to the multitude of novel readers.'[6] Yet so absorbed was Gissing with these precious details that he had yet to learn to let the detail speak for itself. This took him three or four years, and three or four novels.

A third aspect of *Workers in the Dawn*, which revealed both something of Gissing's own nature and of his early difficulties with the novel form, was the polarising conflict between the two women whom the hero thought he might marry, the one 'refined' and educated, the other 'ordinary,' human, passionate, uneducated. It took Gissing some time to realize that the 'man desired by two women' fantasy was psychologically self-indulgent, untrue, and as a method of structuring a novel inadequate. Incidently, as fantasy, this triangle – as we find it in *Workers in the Dawn* and other early books – is more genuinely and profoundly autobiographical than the alleged guilt and masochism the biographical critics usually emphasise. Like many introverts, Gissing compensated for his loneliness by wanting to be loved, by imagining that he was. He had to grow out of this. An extreme luxury in this fantasy world was to choose between two women who wanted him, maybe rejecting them both. As his skill as a novelist developed he learnt to avoid such naïveté, both by creating more interesting one-to-one situations between people and by devising more complex plots which brought people together in a greater variety of ways.

A fourth aspect of *Workers in the Dawn* which anticipated the way in which Gissing was to develop was the explicit discussion of socialist theory among the working-class men whom Arthur, the hero, met. Gissing at first dithered. He had observed for himself the vast class disparities in the cities, observed hundreds of instances of poverty, suffering and brutality, knew at first hand the extent to which the poor did not even know they were exploited and realised that the divisions between people in England were characteristically English, not universal. Social awareness, though, did not really develop into social conscience. Some of Gissing's characters are given social consciences. He himself tended to remain the detached observer. Part of the problem of Gissing's early work is a lack of passionate involvement which results from his inability to identify completely, innocently, with the type of person he is describing. He wants to describe without the 'romance' to which Dickens succumbed, the shopkeepers, tinkers, rent collectors, prostitutes, publicans, rogues of an east London district and he does so. This is what life is actually like, he says. It is not at all what politicians, moralists and preachers say it is. All the time, though, his sympathies are with the person who separates himself from his environment with the help of books. Gissing attached much more importance to abstracting oneself from an environment, any environment, either physically or mentally, than to influencing or improving it. Neither in practical terms nor doctrinally was he ever a real socialist; indeed, he became more and more frankly élitist. This meant that he had a real problem of point of view when he tried to write novels about the uneducated people even though his work was invariably based upon first-hand knowledge and observation. In *Workers in the Dawn* this shows up in the fragmentary plot: the various parts of the story do not really have much to do with each other. Gissing spent about ten years attempting to resolve the problem of how to write novels about the working class that would be acceptable to the middle class. A difficult task. His only recourse was that haven of bourgeois sensibility, the psychological novel, but a few years passed before he reached it. *Workers in the Dawn* was meanwhile a form of case book of everything that Gissing was thinking about. He had no answers. But after he left his wife the problems remained and he teased them out one by one. Such were the 'events' of his existence.

At the age of twenty-two, Gissing did not have the skill to handle these different themes simultaneously. The best he could do was handle them one at a time. If he were to develop the type of tense, personal situation he had created so savagely between Arthur Golding and Carrie Mitchell, he would find himself writing a mainly psychological novel. If he were to develop or extend the parts of *Workers in the Dawn* in which he attempted to describe London, he would be tending towards naturalism. If he were to develop the doctrinal aspects of the novel, he would have a novel of ideas. When he wrote about *Workers in the Dawn* to his family and friends he emphasised the latter. Was this because he felt that he had to justify it in terms others could understand? Or was he trapped in his own book, unable to see yet that the novel would have been stronger without the moralising and philosophising? Something of both, no doubt, though the statements he made about the novel are unnerving.

One of these statements was the much quoted open letter which he wrote to his brother in June 1880:

> In view of the very kind efforts being made by some of your Wakefield friends to procure a circulation for *Workers in the Dawn*, I think it is better that I should send you a few lines (relative to the book) which I should like you to show to any interested in the matter. The book in the first place is not a novel in the generally-accepted sense of the word, but a very strong (possibly *too* plain spoken) attack upon certain features of our present religious and social life which to *me* appear highly condemnable. First and foremost, I attack the criminal negligence of governments which spend their time over matters of relatively no importance, to the neglect of the terrible social evils which should have been long since sternly grappled with. Herein I am a mouthpiece of the advanced Radical party. As regards to religious matters, I plainly seek to show the nobility of a faith dispensing with all we are accustomed to call religion, having for its only creed a belief in the possibility of intellectual and moral progress. Hence it follows that I attack (somewhat savagely) the modern development of Ritualism, which, of course, is the absolute antithesis of my faith.
>
> In doing all this, I have been obliged to touch upon matters which will be only sufferable to those who read the book in as serious a spirit as mine when I wrote it. It is *not* a book for women and children, but for thinking and struggling *men*. If readers can put faith in the desperate sincerity of the author, they will not be disgusted with the book; otherwise it is far better they should not read it.
>
> I write this in order to relieve you personally from any unpleasantness which may ensue upon the introduction of my book to Wakefield, and you would do me a service if you could show this to such as have manifested the least interest in the matter. I fear it is the fate of many men to incur odium by their opinions, but the odium is only cast by those who cannot realize the sincerity of minds differently constituted from their own.[7]

Poor Gissing knew that because the church-going community of Wakefield would react against the book (it was just the sort of thing someone expelled from university would write!), he had to say something for the sake of his family. Sincerity does not make a good book. Gissing knew that. He simply wanted to avoid the charge of insincerity, sensationalism, shallowness. But there was no escape. The only remedy was to write better books, which Gissing soon did, books less dependent upon ideas and attitudes, and certainly less dependent on the attitudes of the novelist himself.

Meanwhile, he sent the novel to Frederic Harrison, who responded with a letter which is sufficiently important to be quoted in full, because it represents an incisive assessment by a man who was not predisposed to like Gissing's work and because it resulted in a life-long friendship based upon mutual intellectual respect, the kind of friendship of which Gissing was eminently capable.

38 Westbourne Terrace, W.
July 22, 1880.

My Dear Sir,

There can be no doubt as to the power of your book. It will take rank amongst the works of great rank of these years. I have not yet finished it, and I cannot yet make up my mind as to its place as a work of true art. It belongs to a school of which I know nothing, and which I hold at arm's length, at least I think so. I am no critic, and very rarely read a modern romance, and I especially hate the so-called realism of Zola. But your painting of dark life seems to me as good as his, and to have a better social purpose – at least I hope so. I am, as I say, very little experienced in judging fiction, and I made no pretensions to judge at all work so full of power both in imagination and in expression as your story. It has most deeply stirred and impressed me by its creative energy. And I cannot wait till I have read it coolly, and felt it as a whole, before I write to you. It kept me out of bed a large part of last night – I took it up after my work – and that is what very few books have done for many years.

There cannot be the smallest doubt about its power, and power of almost every kind that fiction admits. But as you ask my opinion I will be frank. I do not pretend to offer either advice or criticism, your work is far above anything I could do in that way, if I wished. And I do not wish. But I will tell you what I feel about it – as yet – before finishing it. I am not sure that the social and moral aim is sufficiently sincere, or rather sufficiently strong, to justify the deliberate painting of so much brutality. Perhaps it is. I have not yet read enough to see what your moral and social aim exactly is. I am the last person who ought to pretend to judge such a book, for I loathe books of the *L'Assommoir* class and never open them, nor indeed modern fiction except on rare occasions. Your book therefore goes against all my sympathies in art, so that my admiration for its imaginative power is wrung from me. Whether prostitutes, thieves, and debauchees talk as you make them talk in the night-houses of the Haymarket, I do not know, nor wish to know. It is possible that they are introduced to good purpose. I will try to see it.

But I will not trouble you further with my present half-instructed feeling. That is a personal matter with me, and cannot be of any value. I think I know enough of romances to say this – that you may be sure of your book eventually proving a literary success. There are scenes, I am sure, which can hold their ground with the first thing in modern fiction. The circulating libraries will be very shy of it. I do not think girls ought to read it at all. But men of insight will very soon discover its power. I will myself take care that one or two such read it, and I will urge my own opinion on the editor of more than one literary review. I never presume to 'review' books, as the picking out of scraps, and the saying of smart things about them, is called. And if I did review the book publicly, I might say many things which the author would not like. But you may be quite sure of this – your book cannot be lost sight of. Do not be in a hurry. Books like that are not often written in England, though they sometimes are in France. You will be neglected for a few months, abused for two or three, and in six have a distinct (but not altogether tranquil) reputation. Such is the opinion of an avowed ignoramus in these matters.

If after this letter, which I have not sought to make pleasant, you care to make any further communication to me, I shall on my side be very willing to know more of you. I am one of those Goths, fanatics, or prigs, as we are sometimes called, who think much less of artistic or literary power, than of the objects for which it is used, the principles with which it is associated, and the character of those who possess the gifts of the angry fairy. I have written enough to show you that anything you choose to tell me of yourself, your views and aims, will deeply interest me. I write from the country, and I am going next week to another part of the country. I shall return to London in August, and I shall like to meet you there, if you care to meet me after this frank letter of mine.

I am, yours very truly,
Frederic Harrison.

PS. To show you that I do not write in any unfriendly way I will repeat to you three criticisms or remarks made on the book by my wife, whose judgment in fiction I trust far more than my own.
  1. There is enough stuff in the book to make six novels.
  2. The finer type of London workman has never been so truly drawn.
  3. Where are the 'Workers in the Dawn'?
You had better regard what I have said as premature till I know more of your work and of you.[8]

Naturally Gissing was much affected by this letter. It meant that at least one person, a person whom he already respected, could understand *Workers in the Dawn*. Whether or not he liked it was of secondary importance. Ellen Gissing said that the 'nervous strain he underwent in these years'[9] was too great, that it was then that his health began to deteriorate and that he became embittered by the struggle to keep going as a writer despite his domestic difficulties. This is the view that Korg developed into the 'two lives' theory, one life being that of the writer, the other that of the disillusioned husband, the experiences of the latter influencing the work of the former in an almost compulsive, involuntary fashion. Ellen said that, despite the 'dire need of money', Gissing never appealed to the family for help during these early years.

Yet to cease to be a scholar, or to cease to write fiction, was impossible for him. His domestic difficulties put an end to all friendly intercourse with others, and he was thrown entirely upon himself – the worst thing that could happen to a character already too self-centred owing to the fact that he saw more deeply into life than his fellow men. This kind of egoism might well have become an 'embittered' egoism, for in looking back, though still hardly more than a boy, he felt that the hope of sharing his interests with others was becoming even more remote.[10]

From Ellen's point of view it was respectable to be embittered if your marriage broke down. You were necessarily an outcast. But Gissing seems to have recovered quickly from the difficulties of 1880 and 1881. No one, then or now, positively wants the reputation of having contributed to the breakdown of a marriage. Perhaps Gissing did this, though, when he saw it was contrary to his own interests. At any rate, he lived a normal social life as soon as he and his wife separated, normal in the sense that for a young man who was still only twenty-two he was lucky to find people like Harrison with whom he could share his interests, and normal in the sense that, embittered or not, he bought books, went on expeditions, went to parties, saw plays as funds would allow, which is what most other people do.

Austin Harrison recalled the day Gissing arrived in the house as their tutor, an important and memorable day for the Harrison boys since it marked the beginning of their formal education. Gissing was 'one of the gentlest looking beings we had ever seen.' He immediately began to talk of the Greeks and Romans 'with boisterous enthusiasm,' won the boys over by giving them Latin names and soon became a close friend. At the beginning of the article in the *Nineteenth Century* in which he reminisced about Gissing, Austin gave an interesting portrait of the author as he remembered him.

Thick, brown hair clustered round a brow of noble shape; his head was well-shaped. Though his cheeks lacked colour he looked healthy, strong and vigorous. His facial expression was extra-ordinarily mobile, sensitive and intellectual. I have never seen so sad and pathetic a face. In repose his features contracted into a look of ineffable dreariness, sorrow and affliction, of mute submissiveness and despair. Yet it was a noble face, dignified, delicate, sensuous, thoughtful. And then it would flash and light up, and the eyes would become in radiant transport, and the misanthrope would become a tempestuous schoolboy, and he would thump the table and positively shout with buoyant exuberance. For there was ever laughter in his heart – spontaneous, boisterous, sincere laughter. Gissing, the sad man, had the zest of life, and with it its joy. At times he would laugh so uproariously at lessons that my father, at work in the adjoining room, would come in to see what was amiss. And the Homeric joke would be repeated and we would all laugh the louder and merrier.[11]

Certainly Frederic Harrison did not recommend his son's tutor to his friends because he was incompetent or because he would imbue in them a nasty, pessimistic attitude to life. And certainly Gissing did not succeed as a tutor in this cluster of families because he was gloomy, gauche and a subversive moral influence. As late as 1887, Frederic Harrison felt free to ask Gissing's help with Bernard, his youngest boy, even though he knew Gissing had stopped tutoring in 1885 altogether so that he could devote all his time to his writing. Whatever may have been the philosophical or moral differences between the two men, Gissing and Harrison obviously retained their respect for each other.

By mid-1882, Gissing was out of danger financially. He had eight or nine pupils. When Helen went to the home in Battersea, Gissing began his next novel, 'Mrs. Grundy's Enemies'. Although in March Algernon came to stay with him and they did the town together, Gissing had committed himself to the headlong career of a man whose only genuine existence was in his writing, in the act of moving the pen across the page, in the language and in his own finely tuned appreciation of it. Between February and September 1882, he wrote 'Mrs. Grundy's Enemies', which Bentley accepted on 26 December. While waiting for Bentley's decision he wrote the essay called 'The Hope of Pessimism' which he suppressed because his attack on 'Positivism' and on 'optimistic Agnosticism' would have given offence, particularly to Harrison, and it is possible that during this period (1881–82) he also wrote early drafts of *Born in Exile* and *New Grub Street*. Bentley was to ask Gissing to revise 'Mrs. Grundy's Enemies' and then let a considerable period elapse, two years, before telling the author he would not publish the book he had paid for. Gissing did not know this: he was already at work on *The Unclassed*, which he finished in December 1883. This novel he was also asked to revise, which he did in the early months of 1884, which means that when he started to write *Isabel Clarendon* in September 1884 he had just published *The Unclassed* but did not yet know its fate, and had 'Mrs. Grundy's Enemies' with Bentley, about to be published. This pace was hectic enough, but Gissing accelerated. Because he had to rewrite *Isabel Clarendon* for Chapman & Hall, he did not finish it until September 1885. By that time he had written *A Life's Morning* and in August had begun *Demos*. Since Smith, Elder did not publish *A Life's Morning* until 1888, his position in August 1885 when he began *Demos* was as follows. Bentley had still not told Gissing he had decided against publishing 'Mrs. Grundy's Enemies'. Gissing thought that he had overcome James Payn's objections to the ending (the original ending) of *A Life's Morning*, so that this novel also would be published in the near future. He had worked conscientiously on the revision of both *The Unclassed* and *Isabel Clarendon*: neither books had been a great success, but since Gissing had sold the copyright of both books to Chapman & Hall outright he did not expect a financial return and had yet to learn how completely he had failed to convince the reading public. Three novels published; two about to be published; *Demos* started. At this point he gave up his pupils and devoted himself entirely to his writing, confident that his energy and determination would eventually be rewarded. Restlessly he felt his way towards the naturalistic novel, his experiments with different types of novel proceeding independently of the reception his published novels were accorded. He learned by writing, eliminating possibilities as he wrote. A fearsome business, since he was also reading voraciously.

This, though, is to anticipate. *The Unclassed*, *Isabel Clarendon* and, as far as one can tell, 'Mrs. Grundy's Enemies' were very different from each other. If it is true to say that the apprentice novelist had to work out for himself the novelistic problems implicit in *Workers in the Dawn*, one can certainly see the speed with which he learnt in *The Unclassed*, an excellent novel which by comparison with *Workers in the Dawn* was more controlled, more aggressive (though less didactic) in its attack upon established moral attitudes and more uncompromising in its assertion that natural goodness could and did prevail even when social conventions were flaunted. Like *Workers in the Dawn*, it did not assert that the working-class man had high moral standards or held convictions, derived from his own experience and yet consistent with socialist principles, which made him essentially redeemable in the eyes of the middle class. On the contrary, it tended to suggest that values were relative and that, because of the constant struggle between human beings and their environment, how a person made his way in life, whether he did well or badly in the struggle, was only partly an indication of that person's worth as a man or woman, indeed that talking about the worth of a person was besides the point when so much depended upon circumstance and chance, upon heredity and the opportunities of upbringing. Technically, Gissing is more successful in *The Unclassed* in creating the nucleus of characters essential to the type of novel he was to write during the next decade, the group of uprooted or un-rooted people who must *discover* their relations with each other because they derive no support or guidance whatsoever from social institutions and conventions.

The publisher Richard Bentley rejected *The Unclassed* because he could not tolerate the idea that the emancipated, spirited Ida Starr could be a good person, could wish to be good, despite the fact that she had been a prostitute.

> Though we know in this unfortunate class that there are many with kindly instincts yet the nature of the life tends to deaden and in time destroy the good originally present. It does not appear to me wholesome, to hold up the idea that a life of vice can be lived without loss of purity and womanly nature. I confess that I am of the opinion that the realistic treatment of such a subject works for evil as well as good, and possibly more for the former.[12]

Frederic Harrison also had difficulties with the novel. He 'had not a little sympathy,' he said, 'with many of the champions' of social revolt, but that of 'Waymark is to me mere moral dynamite'.[13] He could not accept the notion that a young man like the character, Waymark, could actually benefit from, might in fact be entirely saved by knowing a girl like Ida Starr, because accepting it would have meant the inversion of established Victorian values, anarchy in fact. As for the Wakefield family, it was extremely startled and Gissing was obliged to instruct it. 'We must not forget that our grounds of actual and literary experience are so different that it is very difficult for you to understand me. Your opportunities have not lead you to writers like Balzac, Turgenev, Dumas, etc. Knowing all these men so intimately, I see my own work is really anything but startling.'[14] Gissing had to sell the lease of the copyright to Chapman & Hall for £30 and was luckily too busy to worry about it overmuch. When Gissing revised the novel in 1895 for the second edition, the obvious similarities between *The Unclassed* and both Hardy's *Tess of the d'Urbervilles* and Meredith's *Lord Ormont and His Aminta* were so striking that people began to realise how bold Gissing had been, more than a decade earlier, in addressing himself so directly to the contemporary theme of relativism in moral questions. In 1884, however, the public, like Gissing, was still learning.

One can guess, nonetheless, that George Meredith, Chapman & Hall's reader, took *The Unclassed* seriously in part because it coincided with the direction of his own thoughts. Meredith was not afraid of novels built on situations that would be offensive to the public, but he thought that the novelist's task was to convey the implications of such a situation inoffensively. He read *The Unclassed* when he was already at work on *Diana of the Crossways*, so that Gissing's assertion of the moral integrity of a prostitute, his insistence that she, by herself, could redeem her own life, and that a genuine but also good relationship was possible between someone like her and a thinking, but fallible man like Waymark, would obviously be of interest to the author who was explaining the psychological complexity of Diana's character, also a woman who committed a socially repugnant act by which the novelist asserted she was not to be judged. Thus Meredith, on behalf of Chapman & Hall, was sympathetic. He asked Gissing to re-structure the book and in part rewrite it. Gissing did so in one week during February 1884, without knowing yet the identity of the man who had given him advice.

Gissing later dissociated himself from *The Unclassed*. The emotions were too raw, the issues too boldly stated. And the novel reminded him of his own experiences during years of hardship, since *The Unclassed* was more directly autobiographical than *Workers in the Dawn*. In 1884, though, he was more than willing to defend it. When he had to answer criticisms from his family, who objected to his intellectual standpoint, to the book's advocacy of immorality and to what they took to be its anti-religious, anti-social thesis, he replied:

> You evidently take Waymark's declaration of faith as my own. Now this is by no means the case. Waymark is *a study of character*, and he alone is responsible for his sentiments. . . . If my own ideas are to be found anywhere, it is in the practical course of events of the story; my characters must speak as they would actually, and I cannot be responsible for what they say. You may tell me I need not have chosen such people; ah, but that is a question of an artist's selection. You see, I have not for a moment advocated *any* theory in the book.[15]

Gissing had right on his side. He claimed the novel was 'intensely human, strong with genial emotion' and it is. 'I repeat, it is not a social essay, but a study of a certain group of human beings. Of course I am responsible for the selection, but for nothing more.' Unfortunately the youthful Gissing did not understand that if you say what people do not wish to hear you will inevitably be accused of preaching, however you say it.

Gissing also tried to appease the Harrisons, whom he had no wish to offend. The day after he had written the letter to his sister referred to above, he wrote to Frederic Harrison.

> It would be much better for myself if I could write so as not to offend people, and yet I cannot do it. I have no circle to encourage me in the course I have chosen, and no-one to follow; it is simply that I feel the irresistible impulse to strive after my ideal of artistic excellence. It is true, as you said, that I have a quarrel with society, and that, I suppose, explains the instinct. But the quarrel is life-long; ever since I can remember I have known this passionate tendency of revolt.[16]

Gissing had moved from Chelsea in March and was living in a one-room flat at 18 Rutland Street, Hampstead Road, and then at 62 Milton Street, thinking no doubt that he could live in one room if he was to be by himself and liking the idea of Hampstead because it was 'the true Bohemian locality'. This did not work. He could not simply revert to the life he had known five years earlier when he had arrived in London. He knew too many people. He had too many pupils. He needed conditions that would allow him to sustain the vast effort he was making. The arrangement only lasted through the summer during the pause between the publication of *The Unclassed* and his beginning the writing of *Isabel Clarendon* in September. During this period of relative unemployment he did a lot of soul-searching with the heavy seriousness of egotists and people who live by themselves. To Mrs. Harrison he wrote in July:

> Of course all this only means that the conditions of my life are preposterous. There is only one consideration, that, if I live through it, I

shall have materials for darker and stronger work than any our time has seen. If I can hold out till I have written some three or four more books, I shall at all events have the satisfaction of knowing that I have left something too individual in tone to be neglected.[17]

Gissing's friendship with the Harrisons survived the publication of *The Unclassed* and he survived the long summer by himself. After all, when an egotist writes about himself gloomily or with self-pity it usually means he is happy. He does not tell people of things which make him genuinely unhappy.

He often walked out to Richmond or Kew. Or sometimes he went by train and rented a skiff. 'I progress in the art of keeping a look-out over my shoulder, and sculling is becoming very easy to me.'[18] During July he spent a great deal of time with the Harrisons, going daily to Sutton and spending an hour and a half in the train each way. And in August he at last had word from Bentley on 'Mrs. Grundy's Enemies'.

Bentley writes to me that there is one way out of our difficulty, – that I should *re-write* vols. 2 & 3 of 'Mrs. Grundy'. This I shall accordingly do. The task is fearful, and especially annoying, as I wanted to get on with a new book. But, apart from the sense of my debt to him, the advantage of having a book published by his house will be very great – they are such ubiquitous advertisers. That he should continue to publish for me is out of the question: we differ too fundamentally. Tomorrow I sit down to the work, and, by dint of Balzacian labour, think to finish it in a month or so, I shall earnestly try to make the thing quite inoffensive, and it will be abominable if he continues to object after that. . . . Someday I shall of course look back with sad amusement at these initial struggles. . . .[19]

Gissing took this in his stride, for he was far too busy and far too confident to worry about the possibility of Bentley's letting him down.

This was the summer, too, when he took Harrison's boys to Bonscale on Ullswater for a holiday in August (because Mrs. Harrison was ill), climbed Helvellyn with the boys and later by himself, rowed on the lake daily, and tramped about on literary pilgrimages through the Wordsworth country. When he gave himself a day off from being with the boys it was to climb Helvellyn from Ullswater, then down to Rydal to see Wordsworth's house, then back through the valley beneath St. Sunday Crags, a twenty-mile walk which he enjoyed thoroughly. The farmhouse at Bonscale which overlooks the lake from a fine position about a quarter of a mile up the hill is simple still and must have been quite primitive then. But Gissing enjoyed the simplicity and the freedom, the terrace from which there was such a wonderful view, the open hillside and fell behind the house. 'I am in amazing health', he told his brother from Cumberland. Indeed he was. Whenever life was not affected by the nervous strain of having to co-exist with other people, Gissing enjoyed himself. Now he had an

ordinary Lakeland holiday, climbing and walking every day, and at
the same time brooding over his work. The setting for the first chapter
of *Thyrza* is, as a matter of fact, the house on Ullswater still to be
seen between road and lake beneath the farm at Bonscale.

On returning to London, he acquired new pupils, the sons of Mr.
and Mrs. Gaussen of Houghton Hall, Lechlade, bought a dinner
jacket because of the number of invitations he was receiving, and in
December 'right gloriously' established himself in a flat just off Baker
Street, where he was to live for the next six years.[20] There, at 7K
Cornwall Residences, he settled down to a characteristic work
routine. 'I am mortally hard worked at present, teaching from 9.30 to
5, with only one hour's interval, and writing from 6 to 12.'[21] He
settled down, in fact, to the controlled, free, private existence he liked
so much. 'When I lived in garrets with uncarpeted floors and un-
pictured walls, I was no less comfortable, in reality, than now. These
external things do not seem to influence my life, which is one of
intense and unmitigated self-occupation.'[22]

Repressed and sensitive people are easily flattered by the attentions
of self-assured women, since it is tempting to mistake attention for
understanding and willingness to listen for genuine sympathy. Gissing was flattered, briefly, by the attention of a Mrs. Gaussen, 'one of
the most delightful women imaginable', and transferred the quality
or tone of the encounter to *Isabel Clarendon* when he rewrote the
novel. Pierre Coustillas has given an account of Gissing's friendship
with the Gaussens in his introduction to the Harvester Press reprint.
He stayed with them on several occasions at Broughton Hall in the
country near Lechlade, flirted mildly with Mrs. Gaussen when she
was in town, played up absurdly to the daughters and accepted one
of the boys as a house guest while he did the inevitable cramming.
'Jean Gaussen comes to live with me for the next six weeks', he told
Algernon in a characteristically quirky letter. 'He will establish himself tomorrow. I am amazed at my being able to do my work, with
the youngster constantly present. At night I sit on one side of the
table & he at the other, & every five minutes I am interrupted for the
quantity of a syllable or the parts of an irregular verb. For a marvel,
I somehow get on.'[23] This tutoring was the firm basis of a friendship
with the mother who just happened to have an amiable, wordly
disposition, saw that Gissing needed someone to mother him, and
from time to time sent him little gifts, like the primroses and snow-
drops mentioned in the letter quoted above. It, the friendship, was not
profound. Nonetheless, Gissing was prepared to defend it to his
family, something which he did not invariably do. His sister, Ellen,
stayed with him for a short while in the summer of 1885, met the
Gaussens, saw the ridiculous side of the relationship, and criticised
her brother for his carelessness in allowing a relationship to develop

while he kept his marriage a secret. When she returned to Yorkshire he wrote, defensively:

> I have not seen Mrs. Gaussen since you left. No one person of course is like another, but her personality is remarkable in a degree you cannot perhaps sufficiently appreciate as yet. When you have been fatigued and disgusted through a few more years of life by commonplace, dreary people, shallow in heart and mind, you will get into the habit of resting in the thought of her.[24]

If Gissing wanted to write a novel that was different in tone and in subject matter from *The Unclassed*, he no doubt received encouragement from his friendship with Mrs. Gaussen. He was susceptible, was temporarily infatuated. But clearly in writing the two pot-boilers, *Isabel Clarendon* and *A Life's Morning*, between October 1884 and September 1885 he was both attempting to extend his range and, within the limits of what he could do, establishing himself as an independent author who could live on his writing. He learned his lesson. The financial return on the two books was slight and he soon realised that he had been dissipating his talent. In the summer of 1885, Meredith told him to return to his own *métier* and that is just what he did, in fact setting to work on *Demos* before he had finished *A Life's Morning*. The period of apprenticeship was over.

5

Naturalism

DURING THE FIRST genuinely creative period of his life, Gissing lived by himself in his three rooms near the corner of Baker Street and Marylebone Road, thinking, studying, writing. Roberts called the flat 'a horrible place of extraordinary gloom' whose back windows 'overlooked the roaring steam engines of the Metropolitan Railway'. Jacob Korg said the building was ugly and simple but 'by no means a slum.' A self-contained flat, whatever its appearance, suited Gissing exactly, for, as he said, having pictures on the walls and carpets on the floor had little effect on his way of life. He was happy if he could get on with his work and the flat allowed him to do that undisturbed. His development to the point in 1885 when he began *Demos* had been exceptionally rapid. Now he kept himself more to himself and accelerated.

Bertz had gone back to Germany. Gissing had separated from Helen whom he was to see for the last time in 1886. Morley Roberts was still in London but in 1887 he again went on an extended expedition which kept him out of England for several years. Except for Walter Grahame, Gissing had stopped taking pupils, though he helped Bernard Harrison once, at his father's request. True, Gissing felt free, because he had the flat, to have members of his family stay with him occasionally, and true also that, in many respects, he lived a simple normal life, going to galleries, seeing plays, accepting the odd invitation to a party, and on Sundays escaping to the country for a walk or a row on the Thames. Yet, between 1885 and Christmas 1891, when he gave up his lease, he lived a mainly solitary life, without ties and responsibilities. For better or worse, this 'egotistical' existence as his family and friends called it allowed him to work at a great pace.

The main event of these years, the matter which took all his energy, was his coming to terms with the naturalistic novel, one of the type of novels which had been implicit in *Workers in the Dawn* and which he knew about from his reading. To appease Harrison, he had told him he had not even read Zola when he wrote *Workers in the Dawn*. Maybe this was true. He had certainly read him by 1885 and understood clearly that the naturalistic novel, in the continental European sense, was contemporary, urban and descriptive: contemporary in that the novelist allowed himself no distance of time between the events related and the fact of narration, albeit that there was the assertion, aggressively put, that contemporary life was as he, the novelist, not as others saw it; urban in that the novelist 'studied' people in their social milieu, as Zola had advocated in *Le Roman Expérimental*, 'montrant par l'expérience de quelle façon se comporte une passion dans un milieu social'; and descriptive in that attention was paid to the surface of life, the part that anyone could see for himself was there if he looked. Romantic idealism was rejected, both as informing metaphysical principle and as a credible source of motive. What could not be seen and studied was omitted. Gissing knew from his own reading what was happening in France and Russia and for these few years at least he went with the stream.

As usual he proceeded with determination, not worrying about the two novels which, though accepted, had yet to be published: *Isabel Clarendon* (1886) and *A Life's Morning* (1889). As usual, too, he did it the hard way, learning by his mistakes, correcting them not in the novel in hand but in the one which followed it, and in effect writing a series of novels, only the last of which was satisfactory.

In the three years between August 1885 and September 1888 Gissing wrote *Demos*, *Thyrza*, 'Clement Dorricott' (unpublished) and *The Nether World*. Little is known about 'Clement Dorricott' but the other three show an increasing mastery of the naturalistic technique. *Demos* had many of the faults of *Workers in the Dawn*, the tone being hesitant, the plot unresolved, the issues blurred. The treatment of working-class socialism degenerated into somewhat facile satire of what happens when uncultured, uneducated men attempt to implement utopian theory, while the plot, designed to bring middle-class and working-class people together, proved inadequate for the purpose. Gissing was writing more strongly; the novel was reactionary enough for it to be successful when published; but problems remained, problems which Gissing tackled when he wrote *Thyrza*.

Here, in *Thyrza*, in almost every respect a better book than *Demos*, he succeeded in being faithful, as an artist, to the area of Lambeth which he had chosen to study. Indeed *Thyrza* is a brilliant depiction of a sub-culture seen in its own terms, not from outside. An independent universe is created, preserved in its detail, and studied for its effect on the behaviour of a wide range of persons, for whom life is essentially Lambeth and nothing more. Whereas in *Demos*, Gissing had concentrated mainly on a single working-class family, he now portrayed a 'society' in which attention moves evenly from one person to another. Even so, Gissing in *Thyrza* failed to devise a plot which allowed people of different social classes to interact, with the consequence that the feeling of resignation to circumstance engendered in Lambeth and accepted by the reader as a function of place, seems somewhat incredible on the larger canvas of the world, where such economic constraints do not exist. *Thyrza* is a much better book than *Demos*, not just its pale shadow as some have suggested, but Gissing had still not succeeded. Nor could he have done when he wrote 'Clement Dorricott', since he suppressed the book voluntarily, even though it had been accepted for publication.

Of Gissing's works only *The Nether World*, written last in the series, is the fully realized naturalistic novel, consistent in its methods and consistent in tone. This is not to say that the book is wholly successful, only that Gissing had worked out for himself, experimentally, the type of novel that could derive legitimately from the confined world of a small, self-contained, unknown area of London where people lived lives according to values and attitudes that to the middle-class novel reader remained a mystery. The three books, *Demos*, *Thyrza* and *The Nether World*, represent not Gissing's developing thought on social issues, but his developing thought on realism. Characteristically, when he had explored the question to the full, he turned away and wrote a different type of novel, *The Emancipated*. A stage in life was over for him.

It is scarcely adequate to say that Gissing devoted these years exclusively to literature. Literary events, that is thoughts, reflections and insights, were the main events of his life. A friend might call and be begrudged half an hour. Domestic worries might loom large in correspondence but only because they took time which was needed elsewhere. Nothing at all happened to Gissing, as far as one can see, which was allowed to deflect him from his main purpose. And at this point in time his main purpose was not to write any kind, but *a certain kind* of novel, and in order to do this he had to resolve a fairly specific set of literary problems. The problem of place: how do you convince a contemporary reader that a place like Lambeth actually exists? And how do you describe it in its own terms without lapsing into attitudes and value judgments? The problem of motive: if a group of people accept their environment, are conditioned by it, and thus accept their social and economic circumstances passively, what would make them do anything that would result in an interesting plot? And the problem of social mobility: if the novelist depicts a stratified society, not as he thinks it ought to be, but as he observes it to be in fact, can the classes intermingle in a credible fashion and can a person, as part of a story, move from one class to another? These, and similar problems, were

perplexing and difficult, especially to one brought up in the early
Victorian novel. In a sense Gissing devoted the best years of his life
to an attempt to find his own solution. In this respect the actual
physical events of his life, his comings and goings, were of relatively
little importance, at least until he had written *The Nether World*.
Then, having concentrated his energy for so long, he first kicked over
the traces completely and travelled abroad for two winters running
and then, as though to compensate for the austere, working life, got
married for the second time. So intense was his period of work at 7K
Cornwall Mansions that it is not surprising the reaction to it was a
violent one.

This being so, the novels written can be seen in some ways as deriv-
ing from the ones which preceded them, in some ways as a group of
their own representing Gissing's pre-occupation with naturalism. If,
further, one extracted from all of Gissing's early novels the strongest
ones, that is the ones which are still the most interesting and readable,
one would have *Workers in the Dawn* (1880), *The Unclassed* (1884),
Demos (1886), *Thyrza* (1887) and *The Nether World* (1889). In such a
grouping, the author's pre-occupation with literary, novelistic
questions would be striking: is an author's interest in the *development*
of character consistent with the *static* description of a place; can he,
the author, describe things as they are seen to be without comment,
with a neutral pen; in particular, is it possible to write about the
appalling social conditions of London life in the eighteen-eighties
without using loaded words like 'appalling'; is it possible for an
author to devise an interesting plot that is not incompatible with the
depiction of ordinary people going about their ordinary, uneventful
lives; can he show the limits of urban existence, that is the physical
limits, the boundaries, the small nexus of streets and alleys that constitute for a community the whole of life and also have characters
cross these boundaries, by escaping or entering from a different
milieu; can class boundaries be crossed by characters in a naturalistic
novel; is determinism implicit in naturalism; is psychological analysis
of character inconsistent with naturalism. And so on. All these
questions are raised by *Workers in the Dawn*; the other four novels
mentioned above show that Gissing continued to think about them.
Whether Gissing thought about a novel in a highly theoretical way or
not is unimportant. Clearly he was preoccupied by problems such as
these, consciously or not, since the novels of this period show a
development of skill, *The Nether World* being a far more coherent
novel than the others, while all of them are independently interesting
in different ways.

These thoughts about the novel were the events of Gissing's life
while he lived by himself and, for a biographer, take precedence over
outward, physical events, some of which were of course important.

The aspiring artist lived his interior life, thought about his craft and worked continuously. The interior life was no doubt affected by exterior happenings: a visit of his sister; a coal-gas explosion in the flat below; the 'misery' of having to give time to domestic matters. Nonetheless, what he thought, read and wrote was more significant than what he did. Any portrait of these years must therefore be primarily in terms of his work.

To see his solitary existence in this way, however, involves an emphasis upon three matters: the extent of his involvement, auto-biographically, in his own work; his reading; and his travels. Each of these is important, but none more so than the question of the autobiographical element in Gissing's work since naturalism and autobiography are incompatible, perhaps not in every sense, but at least on the obvious level where objective description is inconsistent with subjective self-revelation. Most writings on Gissing have either assumed or argued that Gissing's work was autobiographical, that he wrote about his own experiences, that his London novels were coloured by his own misery, and that his work as a whole had a narrow range because he lacked the ability to free himself from his own early formative experiences. Roberts, Swinnerton, Donnelly, Korg and Coustillas have all argued along these lines. But they were seriously mistaken – seriously because it is impossible for a reader to appreciate Gissing's purposes if he is hampered, throughout, by the notion that the novels were little more than autobiographical docu-ments. Whatever autobiographical elements there may have been in these novels of the late eighties, there was much more besides, for Gissing, whether successful or not, was a serious artist.

Evidently, all writers write about themselves. A man cannot write about what he does not know. Thus, in some sense or other, all writ-ings are autobiographical. But in what sense? Most people would feel there to be a significant difference between an author who gives a direct account of his own experiences and one who transforms, transmutes his experiences, imaginatively, within separately con-ceived, independent fictions. At the same time, what *seems* to be a direct account may be completely unrelated to the author's own life *in fact*, while what seems to be an independent fiction may be directly autobiographical. This is a blatant way of putting it; there are, obviously, thousands of subtle variations, a work never being autonomous (as a branch of literary criticism tends to claim) but always, however remotely, the expression of the author's psyche, which can at the very least be identified distinctively by the author's name: Tolstoy, Dickens, Hemingway. Despite all protestations to the contrary, Gissing is thought by many to have been an autobio-graphical writer in the simple sense; that is, that he wrote books that were thinly or badly disguised versions of his own experiences, that in *Workers in the Dawn* he wrote about his first marriage, that in *Isabel Clarendon* he wrote about his relationship with Mrs. Gaussen, that in *Demos* he wrote about his own thoughts on social democracy, that in *Thyrza* he gave his opinion on popular education, and so on. Even if this were true, more difficulties would have been created, from a biographical point of view, than solved, for if some parts of a novel are blatantly autobiographical why are they not all? Are only those parts autobiographical which the reader can identify as having actually happened, something he knows (or thinks he knows) independently? Or are episodes in novels autobiographical even when there is no independent external evidence of events of the same kind having actually occurred in the author's life? In the case of Gissing, the novels have mostly been regarded as *primary* biographical evidence, but this is surely a mistaken approach. If a reader thought, for example, that Ida Starr in *The Unclassed* was a version of Gissing's first wife, Helen, he ought also to think that other things had happened to Gissing, for example that he had once worked as a rent collector. Such a line of thought is speculative and absurd. There is limited usefulness in regarding a novel as autobiographical even when it is. Perhaps one can argue from life to fiction, but certainly not from fiction to life, except in the important sense, implied above, that a man's fictions *are* his life.

Admittedly what the writer himself says on the extent to which his work is directly autobiographical must be taken with a grain of salt. A reader may know that a certain episode is autobiographical, even though the author says the contrary. Nonetheless, what Gissing said should not be entirely ignored. During the first decade of his writing life, he repeatedly emphasized that he was not writing about himself. In 1880: 'It is not *I* who propagate a doctrine, but the characters whose lives I tell. Because I chose to take my subject from a sphere hitherto unused of novelists, shall I therefore be accused of making fiction the vehicle of doctrinal opinions?'[1] In 1883:

> The world is for me a collection of phenomena, which are to be studied and reproduced artistically. In the midst of the most serious complications of life, I find myself suddenly possessed with a great calm, withdrawn as it were from the immediate interests of the moment, and able to regard everything as a picture. I watch and observe myself just as much as others. The impulse to regard every picture as a 'situation' becomes stronger and stronger. In the midst of desperate misfortune I can pause to make a note for future use, and the afflictions of others are to me the materials for observation.[2]

In 1884: 'You see, I have not for a moment advocated *any* theory in the book. Perhaps you have overlooked the few lines at the end of that very first chapter of Volume III? There I speak in my own person, and what I say in reality contraverts all that Casti has just thought, if rightly understood.'[3] In 1888: 'When I am writing I can partly forget myself in the world I create.'[4] In 1890: 'I only represent the prevalent views of our day.'[5] In 1891: 'I do not dogmatize, remember; my ideas are negative, and on the whole I confine myself to giving pictures of life as it looks to my observation of it . . . The world to me is mere phenomenon (which literally means that which *appears*) and I study it as I do a work of art – but without reflecting on its origin.'[6]

These statements are in direct contrast to what is usually said about Gissing. Usually it is claimed that he wrote as he did because he was recording his own misery, his own knowledge of being poor in London, his own perplexity about social conditions and social theory, and his own domestic misfortunes. But these accounts simplify and are much less than the whole truth. He was not poor when he was writing *Demos*, *Thyrza* and *The Nether World*. He was lonely, maybe, since he lived by himself, but not domestically miserable. As a matter of fact, throughout his life he wrote his best work when he was by himself. Whenever he married, his work deteriorated. It is much more useful to see him as someone who was consciously attempting to write a naturalistic novel, a novel which derived from the novelist's attention to the surface detail, which studied the effect of environment upon character, and in which moral and political ideas were proposed only through the characters themselves as the occasion arose.

In any case, he had a sense of his own development. He did not remain the same person throughout his life. 'Heavens!' he exclaimed to Bertz when his friend was reading his early work for an article:

> How it must have brought back old days, to re-read *Workers* and *The Unclassed*! Not for any consideration would I open those dreadful books! All I have ever written seems to be apprentice-work; I fear to examine it. And there is so much of my suffering in it! Yes, yes; you and I have both a share in that literature of struggle and misery. What man but yourself can completely understand the books? It makes me both sad and happy to look back into the fog, and to discern our figures looming there.[7]

He was indeed a different person, finding it more and more difficult, for example, to suppress his feelings about the Puritans in Wakefield, and looking forward to better times, not backwards to the period of early literary struggle when he was attempting to establish himself as a writer.

Part of the difference was his increasing cosmopolitanism. His knowledge of classical and of contemporary European ideas, through literature, was by this time so wide that the moral earnestness of his youth was progressively abandoned. Gissing realized that a significant part of his development had been contrary to the English moral tradition. 'It is my misfortune as a writer of fiction that English writers have so long been taught to look for the moral of such works, and especially in the case of stories that deal with the poor. To say that I am out of sympathy with that view is saying little. My masters are the novelists of France and Russia: in comparison I have given small study to those of England.'[8]

Gissing, probably more than any of his contemporaries, knew well the main trends of European literature at that time, for he continued to read widely in both French and German, as well as English. During the eighteen-eighties, he re-read George Sand and much of Balzac; read Zola for the first time; purchased cheap German editions of Turgenev and read them all; was familiar with Daudet, Flaubert, Tolstoy, Dostœvsky and later de Maupassant; and read Ibsen as his work became available and in the late eighties saw his plays when they were performed for the first time in London. He continued to educate himself and in the process became less insular. He moved away from the preoccupation with the 'slow growth of the mind novel' that he had inherited from the Brontës. He freed himself, in important respects, from the moral influence of George Eliot. He became in fact a European man of letters, as completely conversant with French and German culture as he was with English. He knew there were things being done elsewhere that he could attempt in English. *Demos*, *Thyrza* and *The Nether World* constituted his attempt. As he said to Bertz:

> You, after all these years, are the only man of *European* culture with whom I have been intimate. Of Roberts I see a good deal now, but he is almost exclusively English, and this lack in him is a great hindrance in conversation. So very much of my own culture derives from foreign literature, that I cannot be my real self when unable to refer familiarly to the foreign authors I value . . . How sluggish-minded are the few people whom I know in English! I do not think over highly of my own attainments, but certainly, compared with them, I am a very Casaubon. I keep up steadily my reading in Greek, Latin, German, French; and I do not know a soul – save yourself – who ever reads anything but English – at all events for pleasure. Hence their terrible narrowness.[9]

He also travelled. His main companion was Baedeker. His purpose was to see ancient Europe. To see the places he had read about in Greek and Latin authors was his main aim. He made no attempt to see people, least of all literary people, and seems to have used his expeditions as an opportunity to be completely alone, without ties and responsibilities, without a role to play, or a pretence to maintain. Obviously, to travel at all would tend to liberate him from his own early experiences, would allow him to see life in new perspectives, would mitigate his loneliness, and would confirm his already strong sense of the coherence of literature and life. Meanwhile, he was writing continuously.

In the winter of 1885–86, with *Isabel Clarendon* in the press and *A Life's Morning* still delayed, Gissing finished *Demos*, 'rather a savage satire on working-class aims and capacities'.[10] As usual he grumbled to his family about the labour involved: he proceeded only 'with much toil and endless re-writing'.[11] Nonetheless, proceed he did and, despite the fact that Algernon came to stay with him in December, finished in the early spring. The final batch of corrected proofs was returned on 14 March 1886 to Smith, Elder to whom he had sold the copyright for £100. The book was successful, perhaps for bad reasons. The public interest in working-class conditions, conditions of which the middle class was ignorant, had by this time been aroused. The reader could now cope with descriptions of Emma Vine and Mrs. Mutimer as portraits of people who lived in a world they knew had to be understood. On the other hand, *Demos* did not require them to sympathize with the poor, for it implied a bitter critique of socialist fantasy and demonstrated the difficulty, perhaps impossibility, of marriage across the class barriers. Readers there undoubtedly were who would not have been in the least upset either by the failure of Mutimer to sustain the attempt to build a socialist community on Robert Owen principles, or by the failure of the marriage between Adela, the middle class woman whose social conscience had led her to an interest in social problems and socialist theory, and Mutimer, a working class idealist whose ideals are undermined by wealth. Though the book has many faults, it was recognized as being something other than a mere treatise on the poor. And Gissing's ambiguous, reactionary stance, as author, was mistaken for understanding. Ironically, Gissing's first genuine, albeit limited success had been published anonymously, because *Isabel Clarendon* was to appear the same year. In fact, it was published a few months later, in June 1886, and Gissing was irritated because people thought he had written it after *Demos*. In April he went to Paris for a few weeks. His own lonely emancipation began as soon as he began to build a reputation for himself in his own country.

When he returned to England, he began *Thyrza*, that is, before *Isabel Clarendon*, *A Life's Morning* and *Demos* had been published and therefore before there had been any critical reaction to them. 'I am toiling fearfully over the construction of a new book,' he told his sister, Margaret, 'and fear I shall not begin the actual writing for a week or so yet. I have to go over a hat factory, a lunatic asylum, and other strange places; also to wander much in the slums.'[12] He always used expressions like 'toiling fearfully'. whether things were going well or badly. If he grumbled openly, as on this occasion, it usually meant that he was reasonably contented. On the material level, he had little to worry about. He had just received £100 for *Demos*, not much admittedly, but the most he had ever received, and he had taken back Walter Grahame as a pupil, work which brought him £2·10 a week. Besides, *Thyrza* was a novel which meant a lot to him and he endured the 'depression' that went with constant rewriting. 'I am again day after day in Lambeth; this morning I got home only at 2 o'clock. Ah, but you will see the result, I have a book in my head which no-one else can write, a book which will contain the very spirit of London working-class life.'[13] When the novel was finished he wrote to his sister the next day, 16 January 1887: 'Thyrza herself is one of the most beautiful dreams I ever had or shall have. I value the book really more than anything I have yet done. The last chapter drew many tears.'[14]

The world that Gissing described in this group of novels was on the boundary of the City of London and the City of Westminster. In the case of *Thyrza*, he chose Lambeth, a district of which he had little knowledge until shortly before he began to write the book. He himself had not lived there; nor was the locality associated with any of the experiences of his early life. The result of his 'study' was a fine depiction of a closed urban society, in which most people lived out their lives in an area bounded by a few streets, the 'real' streets of Lambeth Walk, Walnut Tree Walk and Paradise Street, streets which still exist as a route to somewhere else, but which then constituted a self-contained 'urban village' whose inhabitants for the most part remained there for the whole of their lives. Gissing was successful, this time, in his creation of a relatively large group or neighbourhood of characters. There is the thirty-five year old Gilbert Grail who works in a soap and candle factory from 6 a.m. to 7 p.m. each day for forty shillings a week, and whose idealism, trapped and forever thwarted by the pressure of environment, is the 'haunter within – a spirit ever straining after something unattainable'; Luke Ackroyd, Grail's friend from the north of England whose 'rough comeliness' and 'intelligence' are matched by 'a good deal of self-will and probably a strain of sensuality', and for whom 'being in love was, to tell the truth, a matter of vastly more importance than all the political and social and religious questions in the world'; Totty Nancarrow, a nineteen year old Catholic living by herself in Newport Street, who was 'for all the world like a lad put into petticoats' and who was known for her love of 'marmalade and pickles' and her disdain of 'necessity'; Jo Bunce, widower, locksmith, atheist; Bower, a factory foreman whose wife presided over one of the social centres of the area, The Little Shop with the Large Heart; his daughter Mary, who was fanatically religious and even attended the mid-week Special Prayer meetings, and Lydia and Thyrza Trent, twenty-one and seventeen respectively at the beginning of the book, living together in the Grail's house, sleeping in the same bed, working in the same factory and in every way the closest of companions. Gissing allows these characters to co-exist in the novel as he had observed them co-existing in real life. Sometimes one comes into prominence, sometimes another. Focus on one to the exclusion of the others is avoided. The treatment is essentially unheroic, documentary, sympathetic. And successful. Gissing succeeded in making a world where the economic, geographic and social constraints were so strong that social mobility was unknown, and personal aspirations soon developed into fantasies which most people knew they could not afford. If, studiously, Gissing was attempting to write in English the type of naturalistic novel he knew in French, then he certainly came much closer to it in *Thyrza* than he had in *Demos*, at least in those parts of the novel that are set in Lambeth.

To this closed world, Gissing brought an idealist, a man educated at Oxford, called Walter Egremont, whose father was a factory owner in the district and who, troubled by social conscience, has got it into his head that he could help the poor by educating the mechanic class – that is, the people who were one or two pegs up the social ladder from the labourer. There is a harsh contrast between his idealism and the real world of Lambeth. He gives lectures, but he never touches the actual concerns of those who listen to him. He begins to establish a library, but his purpose wavers when he falls in love with Thyrza. Gissing allows both Egremont and Thyrza to fall in love with each other but so contrives the plot that neither has a chance to cross the class-barrier that divides them. The characters all, in the end, are made to settle for the less than satisfactory. The defiant, even iconoclastic social attitudes that informed *The Unclassed* have been replaced by a Schopenhauer-type of resignation. Life is as it is, not as one would like it to be.

Thyrza is an extremely important novel in Gissing's overall development. In it he managed to be less blatantly cynical about idealists, more controlled in his realistic depiction of contemporary urban conditions, more compassionate in his treatment of a large range of characters and more subdued in his intrusions and comments. The book was a success and in fact drew a greater variety of favourable comment than *Demos* had, somewhat to Gissing's surprise. At least it was well enough received for Gissing to be able to continue to write with confidence.

Confidence of a kind he had. For all that, 1887 was unfortunately a bad year. When he finished *Thyrza* in January 1887, he had every reason to be satisfied with himself, since *Isabel Clarendon* and *Demos* had both appeared fairly recently. He was obviously proceeding rapidly. Yet he was also becoming ambitious, or more ambitious than he had previously allowed himself to be.

My next book must be a strong and important one, even though I starve a little in the writing. Everyday I have proofs that people of some weight take an interest in my books. I cannot and will not be reckoned among the petty scribblers of the day, and to avoid it, I must for a time issue only one novel a year, and each book must have a distinct character, a book which no-one else would be likely to have written. I have got a solid basis, and something shall be reared upon it.[15]

This was all very well, but how could it be done? During 1887, living all the time at 7K Cornwall Mansions, Gissing started a literary satire called 'Sandray the Sophist' which he abandoned; wrote a novel called 'Clement Dorricott' which Bentley accepted but which Gissing himself withdrew;[16] and began at least two other novels which he failed to finish, 'Dust and Dew' and 'The Insurgents'. Material from these books may have been used later. It probably was. But during 1887 Gissing's imagination marked time, as though waiting for the moment when something worthy to follow *Demos* had been conceived. 'Yes, I feel that the next book must be of a more solid kind', he said to Mrs. Harrison in answer to her letter about *Thyrza*, 'and I think the plan I have will work out satisfactorily. It must be sterner for one thing; I dread anything like a temptation to make London life pretty. The glorious black depths must not be lost sight of.'[17]

The winter of 1887–8 was extremely turbulent for Gissing. He seemed temporarily to lose his bearings and this may have been partly because he had already begun to feel the effects of his deteriorating health. In the widely scattered correspondence there are references to his colds and coughs and chest problems. If these are brought together, they give a fairly strong indication that Gissing succumbed to the London winter as one of the victims of its foul air. Towards the end of 1887 he took a short holiday on the south coast. Though it did him good, he relapsed once again when he returned to London. After Christmas, he spent the better part of two months in Eastbourne, the conventionally accepted remedy for bronchial conditions, and gloomily recovered some of his energy. From this time on bad health was a major factor in Gissing's life, whatever his protestations to the contrary, and like many of his contemporaries he was affected, in his attitudes and in his ideas about what he was capable of doing, by this physical state long before he could understand this himself. Even so, his health in the spring of 1888 must have worried him for early in June he said that he never put his hand to his mouth when he coughed without then inspecting it for signs of blood. He did not, that winter, go to see a doctor. In fact about five years were to pass before he brought himself to consult an English doctor about his lungs and by that time it was too late for effective remedy.

Gissing himself realized that his confused state of mind had partly psychological causes. He lived by himself and became hopelessly introspective. Or rather, there was nothing to hold his natural habit of introspection in check. 'Morbidness is it?' he said, referring to the hopelessness of his condition. 'I only know that these forecasts are the most essential features of my mental and moral life at present.'[18] The turbulence of spirit, as it combined with quite ordinary depression and bad health, had very much to do with the mustering of energy for a new book. That energy does not come to a writer at a snap of the fingers. Nor indeed does he have much control over the time at which mind and body feel ready for the task. If he wants to write a new book, has planned it, prepared for it, he will feel miserable until he can actually find the strength to write it. This was Gissing's state during the winter of 1887–8. Negatively, he rejected four or five false starts for the imagination knows when it finds itself committed to the wrong course of action, unfelicitously. Positively, he could make no headway. He was beginning to be known but not in ways that were helpful for his writing. Not surprisingly, for example, he turned down an invitation to be an honorary steward at the Newsvendors Provident Institution! He was also leading a more active social life. He went frequently to the theatre and to the Royal Albert Hall, where amongst other things he had his first experience of Wagner. None of this, though, had an immediate bearing on the problem of how he was to write a better book than any he had written before.

Gissing's turbulence of spirit was resolved in a way which demonstrates vividly how even the most clear-headed intellectual is really at the mercy of emotional or physiological forces outside his ken. Unconnected details about the surface of his life give some indication of his existence throughout the winter. He overspent, ran out of money and had to borrow £10 at the end of December to pay his rent. Almost immediately he received £15 from Harrison for coaching and £50 from Smith, Elder for A Life's Morning. Typically, before settling down to correct the proofs, he indulged himself in book purchase: Great Expectations, the plays of Dekker and of Beaumont and Fletcher, 2 volumes of Thackeray. Morley Roberts was his most frequent companion during this period and they fairly often went to Gissing's regular 'eating house' where you could get meat and two vegetables for eight pence. That life was not completely bad is clear from the grumbling of that inveterate grumbler. Yes, he enjoyed those meals yet 'there are few things now I can eat with impunity'. Yes, bottled ale shared with Roberts late at night did cure his insomnia but it also gave him headaches. His semi-bohemian life in the Cornwall Residences was in some respects tolerable but the manager intruded to ask him to clean his windows 'as the appearance was disreputable'. These were the surface details that in small measure expressed Gissing's profound restlessness. After Christmas, as soon as he could get away, he went again to Eastbourne where for part of the time he was joined by Morley Roberts. Even there, he went restlessly from one boarding house to another. He felt desperate.

In Eastbourne, he made an attempt to utilize material about his college days that in all probability he had written many years earlier. Though there is academic dispute over the question, the diary entries for January and February show rather conclusively that Gissing wrote a version of Volume I of *Born in Exile* while in Eastbourne. In that novel, the difference between the first volume which in parts is naïve, in parts verbose and silly, and the second two volumes, which were powerfully written several years later, is easy to see – at least by those who endure the infelicities of the early chapters for the sake of the extremely interesting psychological situation that is developed in the second part of the novel. In the spring of 1888, Gissing did not know how to write a psychological novel. A great deal was to happen to him before he was even ready to try. What seems likely is that, during an extremely confused period in Eastbourne, he mulled over his early notes, began to conceive the character of Godwin Peake (the main character in *Born in Exile*), and in the process moodily reviewed his own position in the world – not so much as a writer, because in a sense he was simply waiting for his book to come to him, but as a man who was deeply troubled, after the struggles of the previous decade, by his inability to make for himself an acceptable existence.

This moody and turbulent phase was brought to an end abruptly when the news of his wife's death was brought by Morley Roberts. As they travelled back to London together, those years before Gissing had moved to 7K Cornwall Mansions seemed far distant. He remembered Helen as a problem, not as a person he had loved. In truth he could scarcely remember her at all, for not only the months and months of their shared unhappiness but also the period of his own restless and unhappy independence stood between the Gissing of February 1888 and the Gissing of 1879 when he had married. He had not seen Helen for about four years. With Roberts he found the boarding house where Helen had died. Of her half share of their furniture only a mattress remained. He found her few clothes, photographs from the time of their married life, her pawn tickets and his letters to her. He could not see in her the person with whom he had chosen to live.

I looked long, long at her face, but could not recognize it. It is more than three years, I think, since I saw her, and she had changed horribly. Came home to a bad, wretched night. In nothing am I to blame; I did my utmost; again and again I had her back to me. Fate was too strong. But as

I stood beside that bed, I felt that my life henceforth had a firmer purpose. Henceforth I never cease to bear testimony against the accursed
social order that brings about things of this kind.[19]

Even though the chief pain of the breakdown of his marriage was
several years in the past, this sudden confrontation with the reality of
Helen's existence was for Gissing a terrifying experience. There was
really no way in which he could cope with it. Whatever he might
think about it he realized was profoundly irrelevant. More terrifying
still, in retrospect, is the fact that Helen's death released him from
the anguish of his own winter. He stayed in London, subscribed to the
Grosvenor Library and began to write *The Nether World*.

Gissing wrote *The Nether World* between 19 March and 22 July,
did a great deal of 'on site' research including an important expedition to the Crystal Palace on 2 April when he brought back 'a lot of
good notes', reported – inevitably – his 'fearful difficulties', which
included incidentally the rewriting of Chapter VI in the second
volume and after the book had been completed the addition of a new
chapter in the third, and then suddenly, after an intense period of
work, felt a free man again. Once more he had managed, after a
struggle, to carry himself forward with courage and determination.
On 23 July he celebrated by purchasing Daudet's *L'Immortel* and a
hat at Heath's, and by treating himself to a solitary dinner at Wilkin-
son's restaurant. He had pulled through.

By far the best novel of the early period, *The Nether World* is
artistically the logical outcome of the attempts at a naturalistic novel
that he made when he wrote *Demos* and *Thyrza*. Gissing abandoned
himself to the world he had chosen to study, gave a detailed account
of the closed, claustrophobic area in Clerkenwell where the whole
action occurs, and allowed no lapses into sentiment and no boundary-
crossing, whether social or geographical.

In *The Nether World* not as much depends upon contrivance of
plot, since not as much happens or matters as in the earlier novels. A
plot is devised which depends upon the mysterious motives of an old
man and a granddaughter who may profit from his will. The mystery
is sustained, just as it might have been, for example, in Dickens. But
in point of fact, there is implicit destructive satire on a plot whose
Romantic consequences are denied. The will is destroyed. The
characters are not affected, after all, by the contrivance which brings
them together. The contrivance only appears to be important, whereas
in *Demos* and *Thyrza* everything depended upon it. In *Demos*,
Richard Mutimer is put to a test, first when he inherits a vast sum of
money and secondly when a will is found and the money is lost to
him. In *Thyrza* contrivance is needed to keep Thyrza away from both
Grail, her working-class fiancé, and Egremont, her middle-class lover,
for reasonable periods of time. Both of these books are 'change of

fortune' novels and, in both, the change of fortune, the favourite device of the Romantic novelist, is treated sardonically. Significant changes of fortune are simply not permitted to occur, either on the personal or the material level. In *The Nether World* Gissing is even more ruthless. Snowdon's will merely appears to influence the lives of the principal characters. In actual fact, the relationships between characters, relationships which shift and change as the book proceeds, do not depend upon exterior contrivance but simply upon people's feelings for each other. All the characters live in the same part of London. Seldom do people come to it from outside. Seldom do people leave. It is a self-contained universe, in which there is no release from the pressures of environment.

This environment is precisely drawn: it is the area of City Road, St. Luke's Hospital, the Metropolitan Meat Market, St. John's Lane. Once again, Gissing had set out to 'study' an area of London with which he had previously been unfamiliar. This area is at one point described through the eyes of one of the characters, Clara Hewett: from her room she looked towards the 'black majesty' of St. Paul's; the 'surly bulk' of Newgate; 'the markets of Smithfield, Bartholomew's Hospital, the tract of modern deformity, cleft by a gulf of railway, which spreads between Clerkenwell Road and Charterhouse Street', the urban world in which people, individuals, seemed to lose themselves and their identities, never escaping from the mill for long enough to make a personal assertion of any kind. 'Down in Farringdon Street the carts, waggons, vans, cabs, omnibuses, crossed and intermingled in a steaming splash-bath of mud; human beings reduced to their due paltriness, seemed to toil in exasperation along the strips of pavement, bound on errands, which were a mockery, driven automaton-like by forces they neither understood nor could resist.' This was the bird's eye view of one of the characters, Clara Hewett. At street level, it was a world of activity, jostling people, noise. 'Three work girls had just entered and were buying cakes, which they began to eat at the counter. They were loud in gossip and laughter, and their voices rang like brass against brass.'[20] The book is full of details of this kind: the working man's club behind the pub, for example, with the gas jets in the upstairs rooms, the smoke, the banjo, the 'nigger' entertainment, and by contrast whole families, like that of John Hewett, living in single, unfurnished, unheated basement rooms. Gissing responded, as observer, to the myriad life of Clerkenwell, and portrayed it in detail. Able to a much greater extent to respond to it in its own terms, he was less prone to moralize. Certainly the moral bombast of *Workers in the Dawn* was largely eliminated.

Because the locality in *The Nether World* is described in its own terms, because it is not contrasted with any other place, whether better or worse, and because Gissing relied less on the set-piece and more on the continuous description of streets and houses and incidents as they occurred, as they were seen by the characters in the course of the action, the element of satire that characterized *Demos* is here minimal, ordinary things being seen more simply for what they are. There is a mass of detail: the hat factory at which girls are paid piece-work starvation wages, the filter factory, the burial club from which a member absconds with all the funds, the flower factory, the alcoholism and the vinegar drinking, the counterfeit money trade, the pubs and the music halls and the working men's clubs and the debauchees of public holidays. For once Gissing did not take away with one hand what he gave with the other. He did not undermine his own description with satire or aloof, moralistic comment. The fact of death is feared: John Hewett's feelings about the burial club are at the centre of existence. Rents, however low, had to be paid: the street oratory is now about something immediate and real, by contrast with the idealistic socialism of the earlier novels. Illness for the poor was a multiple tragedy: Gissing showed it, without himself standing between the implication of poverty and his reader. To a much greater extent than before he allowed the facts to speak for themselves. He thus wrote one of his most convincing accounts of an area in London.

One of the high points of this account is Chapter XII, 'Io Saturnalia', in which the rival gangs from Clerkenwell go to Crystal Palace to celebrate August bank holiday. On the same day, in the morning, John Hewett's son Robert had married, not Clem Peckover whose desire for him was only matched by a more general ferocity of character, but Penelope (Pennyloaf) Candy, whose fate – after this celebration – was to continue her work as shirtmaker and share a room with her husband in Shooter's Hill. Hardly anywhere in Gissing's early work are there more colourful passages, or passages written with a greater flair, than these in which he showed the rival gangs travelling to and arriving at Crystal Palace. 'Everything was new except her boots – it had been decided that these only needed soleing. Her broad-brimmed hat of yellow straw was graced with the reddest feather purchasable in the City Road; she had a dolman of most fashionable cut, blue, lustrous; blue likewise was her dress, hung about with bows and streamers. And the gleaming ring on the scrubby small finger.'[21] How uninhibited had Gissing become, relatively, to be speaking of colour at all! On the same train travelled Jack Bartley, leader of the rival gang, with two pounds ten to spend, so it was rumoured, and suitably resplendent: he 'wore a high hat – Bob had never owned one in his life – and about his neck was a tie of crimson; yellow was his waistcoat, even such a waistcoat as you may see in Pall Mall, and his walking stick had a nigger's head for handle.'

When they arrived at Crystal Palace, the vast throngs settled down to a day of British sport:

> Did you choose to shy sticks in the contest for cocoanuts, behold your object was a wooden model of the treacherous Afghan or the base African. If you took up the mallet to smite upon a spring and make proof of how far you could send a ball flying upwards, your blow descended upon the head of some other recent foeman. Try your fist at the indicator of muscularity, and with zeal you smote full in the stomach of a guy made to represent a Russian.

So the day passed in sport, idleness, drinking, until the sun set and the gas lamps within the Crystal Palace were lighted. By then the

> dancing has commenced; the players of violins, concertinas, and penny-whistles do a brisk trade among the groups eager for a rough-and-tumble valse; so do the pick pockets. Vigorous and varied is the jollity that occupies the external galleries, filling now in expectation of the fire-works; indescribable the mangled tumult that roars heavenwards. Girls linked by the half-dozen arm-in-arm leap along with shrieks like gro-tesque maenads; a rougher horseplay finds favour among the youths, occasionally leading to fisticuffs. Thick voices bellow in fragmentary chorus; from every side comes the yell, the cat-call, the ear-rending whistle; and as the bass, the never-ceasing accompaniment, sounds myriad-footed tramp, tramp along the wooden flooring. A fight, a scene of bestial drunkenness, a tender whispering between two lovers, proceed concurrently in a space of five square yards. – About them glimmers the dawn of starlight.

The long day ended with a fireworks display; love-making and drink-ing on the train home; an ambush and a street fight; and the sleep of utter exhaustion.

Gissing did not resist the temptation to call Bank Holiday Monday a 'panacea,' to suggest 'an entire change of economic conditions' or to indulge freely, much too freely, in the emotive words that marred some of his earlier work. He is still obsessed by 'vulgarity' of dress, 'animal' behaviour, and 'deformed' appearances. On the other hand, however uneasy a modern reader may be about Gissing's point of view, the novel as a whole and chapters like this one in particular, have an immediacy and power consistent with Gissing's greater skill and the novel's more clearly defined structure.

The novel is about two families, the Snowdons and Hewetts, and their friends. The very slow forward movement of the story is caused partly by the Hewetts' poverty, which is so extreme that just to con-tinue is next to impossible, partly by Clara Hewett's desire to escape from her family and from her whole 'background,' partly by the appearance of Jane Snowdon's grandfather and his wealth, which he

secretly intends Jane will later use for 'good works,' and partly by
Sidney Kirkwood, who is the Grail or Mutimer of the story and who
loves Clara, almost becomes engaged to Jane Snowdon and eventually, after her accident, takes up with Clara again.

In a sense, *The Nether World* is Gissing's acknowledgement that a
fairly-drawn, realistic depiction of urban life in all its detail is incompatible, at least for him, with a genuinely dramatic treatment of a
psychological situation involving thinking people who are self-aware
and self-critical. Since in *The Nether World* Gissing's interest in
locality is fully extended – it is his most successful book in this respect and the closest, for instance, to Zola – it follows that the scope
for psychological analysis is sharply reduced. As many critics have
pointed out, this is because Gissing is not really making a novel out of
working-class attitudes. He is ascribing to some people in Clerkenwell a sensibility that most of their neighbours lack. To do this
successfully, that is without straining the reader's belief in the action,
he is forced in this novel to reduce his basic equation about people to
minimum terms. In the process of simplification, the inherent vul-
nerability of his attitude to character – at this time – becomes quite
obvious.

All the characters in the book occupy a secular, non-political,
confined working world. All are part of a 'system' over which they
have no control. Most of them live at subsistence level. Though the
ramifications of the story prevent gross over-simplification, in retrospect one can see that Gissing's attitude to his characters was an
ethical one and that the dividing line between groups was very precisely drawn. In Gissing's world, in the environment of *The Nether
World*, to be a human being meant self-control, restraint, resignation,
honesty. Sidney Kirkwood represented this ideal. His idea of himself was based upon a cool assessment of what it was reasonable to
expect from life (very little), and a determination not to lose self-
respect by doing anything rash. To be out of control, passionate,
bitter against fate, assertive but assertive without self-knowledge, was
to be less than human. Not to know what was at stake, not to know
the importance of restraint, is to be merely animal. In this novel, Bob
Hewett, Jack Barclay, Clem Peckover, Mrs. Peckover, Joseph
Snowdon and Scanthone are amoral. Ethical considerations are for
them not real. Gissing's overall attitude to people is here being expressed in minimum terms in the sense that it is not good conduct
but emancipation that is at stake. Control, restraint and honesty are
freedom from the corruption and meaninglessness of the world in
which one finds oneself. Jane Snowdon and Sidney Kirkwood
represent this twilight, unassuming, unpassionate self-control as is
seen, for example, when they so easily come to an understanding
about Kirkwood's engagement to Clara Hewett. Jane's friendliness to

Kirkwood despite her bitter disappointment, her decency, her willingness to repress her own feelings and her preference for open talk give the understanding they reach its characteristically Gissing flavour.

The episode gives the novel its tone. It is representative of the way Gissing handled things at this point in his career but at the same time it is a good example of the point at which Gissing stopped short. Jane Snowdon's self-sacrifice has multiple critical significance. First, the sacrifice means that a conflict between Jane and Clara is avoided. It is this avoidance of perfectly legitimate clashes of temperament and psychological interest that leaves Gissing open to criticism. Why should Jane not press her own case? Why *should* she be nice to Kirkwood? And why should Gissing so arrange things that Kirkwood does not have to decide between two women, both of whom not only love him but are known to love him? One cannot say that Gissing ought to have dealt with something he avoided, but the avoidance certainly contributes to the type of fiction that Gissing created. Secondly, Jane's self-sacrifice is consistent with Victorian concepts about women: her self-abasement is heroic. So Gissing gets it both ways: everybody behaves properly (unlike the Clem Peckovers and Bob Hewetts of the world!)

The Nether World is undoubtedly one of the more successful of Gissing's early novels and this was in part because he hit upon a formula which allowed him to describe an environment without having to be too explicit in questions of motivation. In a naturalistic novel motivation, except of the day by day kind, is played down. The novelist can reduce the reader's interest in motive if he represents his characters as being governed by the conditions which prevail in their environment. As soon as environment is not the main aspect of the novel an author wishes to write, he must return to the question of motivation. What is the extent of a character's freedom of action? What makes him act as he does? What determines the way he will respond to other people's actions? Do people in 1888 behave in a significantly different way from their grandparents? If so, in what way? And how?

When Gissing completed *The Nether World* he had reached the point in his career at which these questions positively demanded an answer. He never returned to the writing of novels about 'working class' areas of London, because he knew that in *The Nether World* he had already written the novel of restricted personal freedom. That degree of restriction ceased to interest him. Eventually his work developed in two main directions. Firstly, he became much more interested in the question of how to write a psychological novel, that is one in which the motives and aspirations of complex characters intermesh and conflict. *New Grub Street* and *Born in Exile* were his first serious attempts. Secondly, when he wrote novels set in London he explored the motives of that restless, mobile, modern population of semi-educated, ambitious yet frustrated people who lived on the periphery and were were in a sense classless. This allowed him to write novels like *In the Year of Jubilee* in which the fate of the characters, though not rosy, is nonetheless not represented as being predetermined by environment. This, however, anticipates Gissing's later years. For the time being, he was simply glad to have finished what he knew to be a good book. He was so relaxed about it that in August he took his mother and his two sisters, Nelly and Madge, to the seaside at Seascale and then, in September, went on to see his brother, Algernon, at Broadway. Having done his duty, he set off for Italy on the expedition he had for so many years been promising himself. He left London by train on 26 September, spent an unsatisfactory night at the Hôtel Atlantique in rue J. J. Rousseau, moved the next day to the Hôtel Londres in rue Linné where he could make his own meals with the spirit lamp he had taken with him, and soon settled down to the enjoyable task of getting to know Paris. He felt marvellously free, so much so, incidentally, that he had left London without knowing for certain that Smith, Elder would accept *The Nether World*.

Gissing travelled with a newly made friend called Plitt, a companionship of convenience in that the two men had little in common, wanted to see different things, and almost immediately disagreed about the domestic details of the way they should or could live while they travelled. Gissing wanted to live as economically as possible but, in a fine case of the pot calling the kettle black, thought Plitt was mean. The difference between them was that, whereas Plitt was brutally economical, Gissing only wished to do without those things he felt, subjectively or snobbishly, did not matter. He told Bertz about Plitt in a sour little note: 'His experience of living will be very valuable to secure cheapness of living. I am sorry to say that there is nothing but the most superficial sympathy between us.'[22] Though Gissing regretted that Plitt was not 'intellectual' and though they were soon in disagreement, nothing could have prevented Gissing from enjoying himself. While in Paris he learned from his sister that Smith, Elder had offered £150 for *The Nether World*, the largest sum he had ever received. He browsed happily along the *quais*, spent hours in the Louvre, attended public lectures and explored the city, Baedeker in hand. Never again did he return to the desperately confined urban world he had just described so tellingly. He had escaped and in the process of escape the Gissing version of the Victorian double standard re-asserted itself. He had tried his best to write sympathetically about fellow human beings trapped within an inhuman environment but he could not in his heart completely sympathize with them, because whatever the promptings of social conscience, of social concern, he remained convinced – as he did throughout his life – not just that it was better to be educated than uneducated, but that educated people were better than those who were not.

> I experience at present a profound dislike for everything that concerns the life of the people. Paris has even become distasteful to me because I am living in this quarter, in a house thronged with work people, and where, to get away, I must always pass through the dirty and swarming streets. All my interest in such things I have left behind in London.[23]

Out of context this diary entry reads harshly. A charitable view would be that after the intense labour of *The Nether World* a reaction was inevitable. While at work he could enjoy the luxury of self-deprivation. Work and a type of non-conformist asceticism were associated in his mind. When he was not at work, self-deprivation lost its appeal. He then wished to live quietly and simply as an educated Victorian gentleman. This desire could be satisfied in his private world, given his advance of £150, but only if he was left to his own devices. In this sort of mood he left Paris bound for Italy on 26 October.

As usual he had been secretive about his intentions, only telling his mother that he was going for a short time to Paris, whereas he had at the outset a definite plan to go to Naples by steamer from Marseilles and then return by a fairly leisurely progress through the major Italian cities. As usual the impetus was literary. In *The Private Papers of Henry Ryecroft* Gissing has Ryecroft recount the spirit in which he went to Italy.

> In his *Italienische Reise*, Goethe tells that at one moment of his life the desire for Italy became to him a scarce endurable suffering; at length he could not bear to hear or to read of things in Italian, even the sight of a Latin book so tortured him that he turned away from it; and the day arrived when, in spite of every obstacle, he yielded to the sickness of longing, and in secret stole away southward. When I first read that passage, it represented exactly the state of my own mind; to think of Italy was to feel myself goaded by a longing which, at times, made me literally ill; I, too, had put aside my Latin books, simply because I could not endure the torment of imagination they caused me. And I had so little hope (nay, for years no shadow of reasonable hope) that I should ever be able to appease my desire. I taught myself to read Italian; that was something. I worked (half-heartedly) at a colloquial phrase book. But my sickness only grew towards despair.[24]

The first part of this paragraph is in fact a paraphrase of Goethe's entry for 12 October 1786 as Gissing himself noted in his *Commonplace Book*. Gissing was not interested in contemporary Italian life. Nor was he very much interested in Roman life except in as far as it

gave rise to Latin literature. On several occasions he commented on
the discrepancy between the literary sophistication of the classics and
the relative barbarism of the times in which they were produced. He
did not think of art as in any way reflecting life. On the contrary,
Life and Art were in necessary opposition. Consequently the dead
languages had a special appeal for him, since they had evidently survived the physical conditions in which they had at first flourished.
Gissing was not totally unaffected by contemporary Italian life when
he actually arrived there (least of all when his observations allowed
comparison with aspects of English life he did not like!) but his
motive for going was predominantly literary and for the most part he
only visited places with literary associations.

He reached Naples in early November and began to write enthusiastic letters to Bertz, letters simply about everything that happened to him. 'I generally go out for my breakfast: a good *caffè latte*,
two rolls and a piece of butter, cost 35c. My midday meal consists of
bread, fruit and wine, eaten wherever I happen to be. I buy grapes
for 10c a pound (*one penny* a pound!) and figs at the same rate, figs
just off the tree. My wine – of very good quality – costs 60c a bottle!'[25]
After a period of intense concentration, which had lasted through his
years at 7K Cornwall Mansions and had seen his separation from his
wife, her illness and death, as well as his sustained absorption in the
social conditions of London, suddenly he was free to enjoy himself,
to follow his own interests, to respond to art and to the beauty of
what he saw, even the view from the window of his room in Naples
from which he could just see 'one end of Capri.' As a simple tourist
he discovered Italy and because he was convinced the experience
would be a significant one, so it became.[26] His two companions were
Baedeker and the classics.

> For guide books it would scarcely be possible to improve on Baedeker.
> I bought in Paris his three volumes, north, middle and south Italy, and
> they are my constant companions. Oh, I must tell you. Just beyond
> Posillipo is the little island of Nisida. Whilst I was looking at it, I con-
> sulted Baedeker, and he reminded me that it was hither Brutus came
> after the murder of Caesar, and here that he was visited by Cicero; hence
> he set out for Greece, for Philippi. That was a thought! The coast and
> the islands have not changed. As I see Capri, Ischia, Nisida, so did Vergil
> and Horace and Cicero see them. One cannot speak of such things.

With Baedeker, he energetically visited places he had known through
his reading for many years: Lake Avernus, identified for him by 'an
old boatman' ('There I gathered some flowers, and one of them I send
you.'); Vesuvius, by tram and horseback; the museums – on Sundays,
when they were free; Salerno, Amalfi, Paestum, Pompeii, Castellanse
and Sorrento, and 'finally for a couple of days to Capri!' Whatever

Plitt's influence may have been, there was some significance in his
going first to Naples, since for the rest of his life he was to feel comfortable in southern Italy which he associated so directly with Latin
literature and Roman history.

From Naples, he travelled to Florence, Rome and Venice, and then
home. He revelled in the experiences which allowed him to relate his
knowledge of classical literature to the present. 'Perhaps the supreme
moment of my life was that when I woke one night in Rome, & lay
with a sense of profound & peaceful *possession* of what for so many
years I had desired. Before going to bed I had read Horace. Never
have I been so free of temporal cares (in soul, that is to say) & so
clearly face to face with the ideal of intellectual life.'27

On his way he corrected the proofs of *The Nether World* and in his
letters to Bertz commented on tourists, on Italian manners, on the
lack of 'English rowdyism' and 'giggling shop girls', on the lack of
an oppressive sense of class distinction, and on the 'domesticity' of
the people when they met in public. 'Again I notice the democratic
character of Italian society', he remarked when he reached Venice.
'Here promenade, side by side, the gentleman and the gondolier, the
lady and the girl who makes wax-matches. There is no feeling in the
poor people that they are out of place. And it is more remarkable in
the case of women, seeing that here the work girls have a distinct
costume.'28 Both in Florence and Venice he visited – or, as he said,
worked at – the museums and galleries, before setting out for England
on 27 February 1889. He went by way of Milan, Strasbourg, Brus-
sels, Antwerp and Harwich, arrived in London on 1 March, by that
time already deeply engrossed in his plans for his next novel, in which
he had told Bertz he intended to use his 'Italian experiences for the
background.'

He used them, in fact, for much more than background. Throughout his writing life, up to this point, he had been preoccupied with
characters whose artistic sensibility set them apart from their fellow
men. Arthur Golding in *Workers in the Dawn* was the first of these.
Now, in *The Emancipated*, which he wrote in 1889 between 3 June
and 13 August, he created as it were a mature version of Arthur
Golding, an artist called Mallard whose self-assurance as a man came
from his deeply ingrained appreciation and knowledge of art, particularly Italian art, and whose brand of respectable, agnostic
bohemianism derived from or consisted in the feeling that one could
be both sensitive and a man of the world, responsive to art, even
'decadent' art, and yet be a man of integrity. Certainly the setting of
this novel, which is partly in Naples, reflects Gissing's recent travels,
but much more important is the change represented by Mallard. In
the previous novels there had been characters who wanted to be
emancipated. Now Mallard and eventually Miriam Baske *are*

emancipated, and the fact – coming as it does from Gissing's Italian experience – is a very significant one in Gissing's career. He never reverted to a view of the world in which people are totally dominated and conditioned by environment.

6

The Second Marriage Disaster

IN 1889 Gissing reached the point of personal crisis. For as long as he had remained relatively unsuccessful, there had at least been a type of coherence to his life. Young writers traditionally lived in garrets, kept alive on whatever happened to be in the stew pot and accepted, of necessity, other people's opinions about them. What did it matter? They had to be unconventional, different, even bohemian if they wanted to write. The modest successes of the late eighties changed this, because Gissing came to have less reason for suppressing his very natural desires and ambitions. He wanted to live in reasonable comfort without financial strain. He wanted the companionship of a woman with whom he could live peacefully. He wanted to be accepted for what he was, one of the few writers in England who was managing to live by his pen alone. By the time he had completed *The Emancipated*, it was natural for him to feel that some of these desires might be satisfied. Natural, yes; but credible? Was he himself capable of changing from what was essentially the student life he had found it convenient to retain or was this so deeply a habit for him that he had long since lost the ability to adopt a different style of life?

Gissing knew that he could only give a negative answer to that last question. Having struggled so desperately for his independence, having worked so hard, having from his own point of view retained the integrity of a novelist determined to write intelligently conceived books at a time when the market for fictional trash was expanding, he did not find within himself any reason to alter. Other people would have to learn to accept him. He, in his fashion, accepted them after all. Both his natural pride, now weathered and tested by experience, and his idiosyncratic life-style, which depended hardly at all upon the possessions and routines by which others shaped their lives, stood, immensely, between himself and anyone who might think of living with him. He knew this. Knowing it, however, did not reduce his desire for the happiness of companionship and he began to imagine himself desperately in love with almost every eligible woman whom he met.

In this way it happened that, as he completed *The Emancipated* during the first part of 1889, as well as during the months that followed, the manifest improvements in his public life did little to assuage his more profound desires, his longings. On the surface he became more sociable. He received invitations and accepted them. The confidence that came with modest success allowed him to relax and enjoy himself, not least when he was with Morley Roberts. This was probably the time when the two men were closest to each other. When Gissing was leading this bachelor or student existence he was always at his best, witty, vivacious, full of stories and talk, just like many of the characters in *New Grub Street* and *Born in Exile*, the novels which were to follow this period. He and Roberts got to know the painter Alfred Hartley and the writer W. H. Hudson and the four men, quaintly dubbing themselves the 'Quadrilaterals,' spent many an evening together.

Gissing at the same time attached a lot of importance to his relationship with the Smith family of Smith, Elder. He had four novels with them, was accepted socially by the family and spent several evenings at their house. One of these evenings he described to his sister in a letter written towards the end of July. He enjoyed both the informed talk between authors and publishers about other authors, alive and dead, and he enjoyed the uninformed talk, too, because other people's ignorance about the only thing that mattered in life, literature, bolstered his own confidence.

It was a wonderful evening. The Smiths' house has a large balcony, & a lot of us (we were some twenty altogether) sat out there, smoking, drinking coffee, hatless, shawl-less; a glorious moon in the sky right before us. I felt thoroughly well & content & hopeful for the future, & answered people's questions merrily about *Thyrza*. Then old Smith came & sat down by me, & said: 'Come now & tell me all you can about the Brontës.' So he began his stories. It was a wonderful thing to think that this man had entertained Charlotte in his house some forty years ago, just as he was now entertaining me. (He is about sixty-four, hale to look upon, a luxurious liver, just had a fit of gout, a great traveller.) Of course he was a young man in those days, & he hints that he is the original of 'Dr. John' in *Villette*. It is not unlikely. He says that he actually did accompany Charlotte to see Rachel act, as in the story. Charlotte had a strange weakness; she was very vain of her narrow waist & small foot, & she laced herself so tight as to injure herself. – One day she attended a lecture of Thackeray's, &, when she went up to Thackeray to speak to him after it was over, he suddenly exclaimed aloud to some standing near: 'Oh, let me introduce you to Jane Eyre!' A day or two later, Charlotte was in the Smith's drawing-room, & Thackeray came in. She rose & gave him a prime scolding. 'Suppose you came down into Yorkshire, do you think I should present you to people as Mr. Pendennis?'

Well, all this is glorious. A happy thing that I have not come too late to talk with these people; if I live thirty years more, the memory will be interesting.[1]

Meanwhile, Gissing read as widely as ever, with the same unbridled curiosity as during his youth but now with an intelligence tempered by experience. Of course he continued to read the Latin, Greek, English and French classics, but of the particular titles he noted in his diary during the second part of 1889 there are a number that indicate fairly and squarely the direction in which his thoughts were carrying him. Besides books like J. P. Jacobsen's *Niels Lyhne* and Frederick Bremer's *Hertha*, he also read Taine's *English Literature*, Bourget's *Études et Portraits* as well as the *Essais psychologiques*, A. H. Buck's *Treatise on Hygiene*, W. B. Carpenter's *Principles of Mental Physiology* and the books he just mentions as Ribot's *Hérédité*. In a manner that was wholly characteristic of him, he realized he needed to know more about why people acted as they did, more about motivation, more about the interaction of people in urban conditions. That he was aware of his position is clear from a letter he wrote to Edith Sichel, a new friend, in June.

It is my misfortune as a writer of fiction that English readers have so long been taught to look for the moral of such works & especially in the case of stories that deal with the poor. To say that I am out of sympathy with that view is saying little. My masters are the novelists of France and Russia: in comparison I have given small study to those of England.[2]

This highly interesting letter was actually in response to Miss Sichel's comments on *The Nether World*, but it has a wider significance. If in a novel there is not a moral for which the average English reader can search, the implication is that when the characters in the novel become involved in a complex situation the issues between them are not moral. Were the conflict moral, the conclusion would have to be moral as well. Gissing had realized that the alternative had to be psychological, for indeed he had trained himself to observe how people actually behaved, as opposed to how they were supposed to behave. But to perceive the irrelevance of moral precept and moralistic description was only part of the problem: it was much more difficult to arrive with one stride at a psychologically credible idea of human motive. He therefore took himself off to the Grosvenor Library and the British Museum; the results of his 1889 researches were destined to appear for the first time in *New Grub Street* and *Born in Exile*.

On 20 August, the day he delivered *The Emancipated* to Bentley, he set out with his sister, Madge, for a holiday in the Channel Islands and Brittany, as usual with a suitcase full of books. He badly needed a holiday and enjoyed this one, despite his irritation at Margaret's unintellectual conversation. Of two sisters who epitomized a certain type of straightlaced, narrow-minded, provincial Victorian woman, Madge was even more naïve and conventional than Ellen, which predictably Gissing found a considerable strain. Nonetheless, they had an enjoyable time on Guernsey and then, instead of going over to Brittany, which they decided would be too expensive, went to Sark. Gissing had always been responsive, as indeed he remained, to places of extreme natural beauty. He enjoyed clambering about, exploring, botanizing, getting to know a new place. It was a pleasant interlude and distracted him from deep-seated personal problems and thoughts of the future. He was also giving himself the sea air he believed his lungs needed.

The precarious balance between the successful writer and the man whose personal life was still severely dislocated was for six months threatened by his friendship with Edith Sichel, an emancipated woman of the kind Gissing portrayed two years later in *Born in Exile*. Unmarried, widely read, interested in the social questions of the day, independently wealthy, she wrote to Gissing about his books because she liked and was interested in them. That was on 10 August. After his holiday in the Channel Islands he accepted an invitation to go down to see her in the country at Chiddingford in Surrey, duly reporting in his diary that he had 'had a very pleasant day, with much gossip'. As the friendship quietly developed, it became clear to Gissing that this was something with which he could not yet cope. He saw that her motives were civilized, direct, friendly, that it was natural for an emancipated woman to enjoy meeting someone whose books showed he understood contemporary life and that there was nothing wrong with her taking the initiative in their relationship. But he found it difficult to reciprocate. He had never been put to the test in this simple way before. A vestigial awe of conventionally polite young women prevented him from accepting her as a human being with the same feelings, desires, thoughts as himself, even though his intellect told him that equal friendships between men and women just had to be possible. He unconsciously resisted her and invented little difficulties, wishing to have her friendship and yet fearing it. That he thought about, analysed, cared about and eventually understood this predicament (that is the predicament of a man who wishes to be 'modern' or 'liberated' in relationships with women and who meets a woman who already is), becomes completely clear in *Born in Exile*, especially in Gissing's portrayal of Marcella Moxey whose offer of a loan of money, out of friendship, Godwin Peak feels mysteriously compelled to refuse.

In the autumn, Gissing wanted, needed the friendship and companionship of a woman who was his intellectual equal but when he met Edith Sichel the experience was more troublesome than joyous.

At 4.30 went by appointment to see Miss Sichel, at 7 Barkston Mansions, Earls Court. A luxuriously furnished flat. Waited in the dark for a minute or two till she entered: then we talked of London & its aspects. Lights & tea brought in. Much talk of my books, till at length a younger Miss Sichel with a girl friend appeared, returning from the Popular Concert. Miss Sichel interested me; for some reason her face pleased me more than when I first saw her down in Surrey. I half think she is beautiful. Left at 6.30. Spent the evening in a troubled state of mind, occasionally glancing at Darwin's *Origin of Species* – a queer jumble of thoughts.[3]

The extent of Gissing's excitement is evident even from the length of this diary entry, which is so different from the one or two terse sentences he usually wrote, but as for the jumble of thoughts he was too inexpereinced in the ways of the world, too unsure of himself, too inept socially to resolve all the questions raised by the simple fact of someone else wanting to know him. In October he had sold *The Emancipated* to Bentley for £150, with an agreement that more money would accrue if the books sold well; (£50 after the first 850 copies sold, and a second £50 for the next 1,000). With enough money in his pocket for the winter, he set out in November on the second of his cultural expeditions. He had been to France and Italy. Now he must go to Greece.

As a typical, albeit well-educated Victorian tourist, Gissing's way of seeing and thinking about another country was pre-determined by his notion that the only importance it could have was cultural. The actualities of place were more of an irritation to him than a pleasure. Modern frames of reference which might have been congenial to him intellectually did not yet exist. He had always wanted to go to Greece because of its importance in the cultural universe that he himself had always inhabited. Now he satisfied his ambition. If he had been a social anthropologist or had been interested in comparative politics, he would have been able to engage himself in what he saw. If he had a sense of myth, he would have been able to retain his sense of the importance of the Greek past, without mixing that up with his sensations of the present. As it was, his historical attitudes were naïve and he tended to accept accounts of ancient events uncritically. It was consequently inevitable that if, when he went to Athens, he did not in some vague way at least feel the continuity of cultural life, as he had (vaguely) in Italy, he would be disappointed, seeing monuments with the eyes of an intelligent tourist and reacting against the modern Greek because so obviously he was not an ancient Greek. He was indeed disappointed.

You know that the scene of Aeschylus's *Eumenides* lies at the foot of the Areiopagos, by the well sacred to the Eumenides themselves. This well still exists; it is in the furthest recess of some huge, wild rocks that are heaped about the foot of the hill. One goes in search of it with enthusiasm; but what does one find? The whole locality is simply a vast *lieux d'aisance* for the public. The air is poisoned, and you cannot step without treading in human ordure . . . Such a place to be subject to such defilement!4

It was most unfair. He wanted to respond to Greece. He desired a significant experience. But though he enjoyed so much, he was in the end put off by the contemporary realities of the country.

Gissing's voyage to Greece from Marseilles took six days including one spent in Genoa which he spent rambling round the city with two French-speaking Greeks and in the evening going to the opera – 'an astounding entertainment'. So great was his longing to see at last the place he knew so well from his reading that he endured the staunch work done by 'Boreas' on the last day. His anticipation was intense and characteristic. 'We drew near, and there before me was Sphakberia, with the harbour at Pylos! Great heavens – to behold such places! I rejoice that I know my Thukydides [*sic*] pretty well.'5 He put up at the Hôtel de la Couronne and though greatly discomfited by the sun, the dust and by the fact that 'not a blade of green growth is anywhere to be seen' immediately set out on foot to see as much as he could, regretting like so many tourists before and since that so much of archaeological interest was in a fragmentary state but particularly enjoying himself when he could imagine seeing things in the same way as the ancient Greeks. 'How it helps one to understand the Greek writers!' he told Bertz towards the beginning of his stay. 'For instance, whenever I am on the Akropolis [*sic*], I have but to look westward, and there I see the white road winding away to Eleusis, the Sacred Way of the Mysteries. At a very little distance lies a hill, among the olives of the Kephisos, which is no other than Kolonos.' This letter and equivalent entries in the diary completely give the tone of Gissing's stay in Athens, which in effect was part of a self-imposed cultural regimen. 'So this is my last letter from Athens', he wrote on 14 December. 'My education slowly progresses; in a few years I hope to be a decently cultivated man.'6

As usual, Gissing had a solitary, lonely time. Apart from what he called a 'little intercourse' with a young Greek named Parigory, he seems to have spent the month entirely by himself. He dismissed Greeks in general as 'uninteresting' and ignorant of their own antiquities. As usual, too, he expressed his loneliness in a singularly graceless fashion: 'No one could imagine what I have lost by making those journeys without a sympathetic companion.' (Why, after all, *should* anyone imagine it?) Furthermore, he was ill. He several times gave his cough as the reason for his not going out of Athens and spent a lot of time in the hotel reading Aristophanes and Plato. He could read Greek but not speak it. It was with something like relief that he left Greece for Naples late in December 1889. Certainly he had satisfied an ambition, but it is probably also true to say that his cultural earnestness had brought him to yet another cul-de-sac. All his life he had distinguished sharply between Art and Life. He had not thought that the two could be reconciled. Now, in Athens, he realized that Art could not be a complete substitute for living, that in life some things were better than others, and that the personal achievement of culture, his achievement, did not lead to ultimate, personal satisfaction. Being a 'decently cultivated man' is of no avail if you are friendless, sexually deprived, and in the intellectual sense perpetually being driven into an arid set of nihilistic attitudes. It is likely, therefore, that Gissing's altered attitude to his own life, an altered attitude that led to his second marriage, as well as his shift as a novel writer away from social commentary based upon conscience to social commentary based upon satirical or ironic critique, derived from his Greek experience which taught him that one could not simply combine Baedeker and Thucydides and make personal happiness.

As always he enjoyed his stay in Naples, particularly because of the civilised, worldly company at the dinner table in his boarding-house but, sick at heart and physically ill, he was also glad when he could set sail for England by way of Gibraltar. His enthusiasm for the exotic had burnt itself out.

When Gissing returned to England at the end of his trip to Greece, he was thirty-two years old. Loneliness began to overwhelm him. He had published eight novels yet was relatively unknown. He had read widely in European literature and was well educated in the classics; there was next to no one who appreciated this, so he thought. He had travelled in Italy and Greece, felt at home in both countries (though much more so in Italy than in Greece), knew himself to be a man of the world, of sorts, yet had no one with whom he could share his experiences. He knew his determination was beginning to have results, that he had established himself with his pen exactly as he had intended, that he had managed by and large to write the books he had wanted to write and see them published, yet as usual he had less than a hundred pounds in the bank and scarcely a course of action open to him except to settle down to his next novel immediately in order to keep body and soul together. The house at 7K Cornwall Mansions was a gloomy place to be by yourself after the light and warmth of Greece.

The return to England made him more than ever conscious that a whole phase of his life was over. Helen had been dead for two years. Except when he had to identify her, he had not seen her for four or five years: the last time seems to have been 1886. The years before the death of his wife, and before his two major expeditions to the continent, and before the writing of his naturalistic novels, must in the spring of 1890 have seemed very distant indeed. He was a different person. To make amends, as it were, he took his sisters to Paris but the experience only confirmed his own sense of loneliness. Exhausted after his travels, he spent the summer with his family in Aybrigg, in a kind of capitulation, but it was a desultory summer, a spiritless one in which he made many starts on books without finding the strength or interest to sustain anything to a conclusion. In this mood, he began to reflect on his own situation, coming in the end to quite alarming conclusions.

When Gissing returned to London in August 1890 and settled down once again in his flat to write, he was bored and restless. He could not every year go to Italy or Greece: he had 'done' Greece and had satisfied his notion that all educated people *ought* to have been there. Though he was only thirty-two, the travelling had exhausted him. Besides, the prospect of years of solitary travel reinforced his despondency. On the other hand, the four months he had spent with his sisters had been sufficient reminder that he did not, within himself, aspire to the bourgeois bliss of a well-ordered household if that meant that he, too, had to be ordered and orderly. Gissing was disorderly, egotistic, selfish. He concluded that he wanted companionship but that he did not want the management that his mother had imposed upon the Gissing household during his youth; that he wanted the sexual companionship he had known with Helen but that he did not want the pretence that women like his sisters were intellectually interesting to live with; and that he wanted the creature comforts that he saw some wives brought to a man's life, but that he did not want to live with a woman who would interfere with his writing or his literary life in general.

That was one aspect of the matter. There was a contrary aspect. Though he had a craving for companionship, had many close friends and often wrote about the pleasures of friendship, particularly friendship between men, he did not believe that friendship should impinge upon a man's own life. At least he never behaved as though he had any inkling of shared experience. The men in his books *exchange* ideas: they do not share ideas. They meet in bachelor rooms at night to talk about literature: they do not share their daytime experiences. They do not work together. They do not go on expeditions together. They are rarely even shown eating together. Gissing's own enjoyments were real enough, yet he seems never to have understood that his sensibility was not unique and indeed that his pleasures might have increased had they been shared. Similarly, though he was sexually lonely, he was not capable of accepting in a simple way that others, especially women, would have known the same loneliness. The intermesh of companionship, sexual love, family affection and shared ideas was beyond him because he had never experienced them. Consequently, in the early part of his life he felt, absurdly, that men could meet as equals but not men and women. The conclusion of *The Emancipated* is an expression of Gissing's aloof and patronizing attitude: the woman, if she is to have any hope at all, must learn the man's values, aspire to them, and work humbly in order to be a fit companion for him. Yet there is no doubt that, beneath the condescending attitudes, was a genuine confusion of the spirit. Within himself, he understood that his views of society were at odds with what he actually felt about himself. Theoretically, a modern intellectual man, who despised middle-class life and who observed that his pleasures were anti-democratic, élitist, private and almost exclusively literary, ought to have been able to do without women, since women were nearly always uneducated, unintelligent and lacking in sensibility. Gissing, however, found that this could not be. He desired a wife.

His preoccupation with these matters shows in the work he did during 1890–91. In the autumn of 1890 he wrote *New Grub Street*; during the winter he revised *Thyrza* for the second edition; in the spring he completed *Born in Exile*. He was taking up work that for the most part he had begun before writing *The Emancipated*. Both *New Grub Street* and *Born in Exile* derive from earlier, unfinished drafts. Neither novel is a finished book, though both represent a move away from social realism towards a type of psychological novel. *Born in Exile* Gissing was rewriting and revising even after it had been accepted for publication; *New Grub Street* he later revised when Gabrielle Fleury proposed a translation. Both books grew from the agitation Gissing felt as he yet again assessed his own life, the solitary life of the returned traveller.

This agitation was distinctly that of a stock Victorian figure; the agnostic who has veered towards nihilism, not towards 'good works.' No one more than he represents more painfully the dilemma of the nihilist, of men like Astrov in Chekhov's *Uncle Vanya* who long for love but intellectually have decided meaningful relationships are impossible. Gissing knew very well that he was a dispossessed European intellectual. He thought negatively, had rejected Victorian values and institutions, had long ago abandoned the idea that the normal biological processes of life had meaning, and in short was self-consciously anti-bourgeois and 'decadent.' He knew too that he was exceptional in the rigour with which he rejected whatever he could no longer believe in. Yet he was intellectually and sexually lonely. In fact he felt the deprivation all the more for his not believing in those daily domestic habits that make life tolerable whether one believes in life or not. How will an emancipated man find brute intellectual and sexual contentment in an age when women are not emancipated? Characteristically he applied his mind to the question.

He became obsessed by the subject, worried at it for seven or eight years, and in the process wrote some of his better books, each novel in the series giving, as it were, a different set of solutions to the same problems. *The Emancipated* had been satirical: Gissing imbues the couple who ought to have been emancipated with solid, middle-class virtues and lets them settle down. In *New Grub Street*, he explores the idea of marriage by calculation as opposed to the old-fashioned marriage for love which led to the breakdown and destruction of Edwin Reardon. In revising *Thyrza* he re-examined, one could say, his reasons for not allowing happiness to his main characters. The class barriers that separated Walter Egremont and Thyrza Trent remain rigid, the final relationship between Egremont and Annabel Newthorpe being one of limited expectation, limited possibility, based essentially upon an acceptance of the fact that not much can be expected of life. Then, in *Born in Exile*, *The Odd Women* and *In the Year of Jubilee*, he continued to ponder the problem of the age: the institution of marriage under pressure from social change. He himself, however, could not wait until the problems of the age were solved. Why should there not be solutions for him as well as for his characters? Was he to live a solitary, sexless life to the end of his days – he who understood the issues so very well? He thought not and consequently rushed headlong into a matrimonial disaster that made his first marriage seem positively arcadian. In *Born in Exile* there is a nihilist character called Malkin who, for intellectual reasons, despaired of making a marriage to his taste, since well-bred girls would be stupid while lower-class girls would be gross and ignorant (he thought), and therefore decided to choose, secretly, a fourteen-year-old girl who could be educated to his specifications and be rendered, by the age of seventeen or eighteen, marriageable. This Gissing himself was to attempt.

While the novels show that Gissing was preoccupied with ideas about marriage, it is clear from other sources that he himself was in a turmoil. He was aggrieved. Why should he not know the pleasures and comforts that other, ordinary people took for granted? In Wakefield, during the summer of 1890, he had met Connie Ash, with whom he imagined himself to be in love. 'Met Mr. and Mrs. Ash, Connie, younger sister Gertie, a pretty, dark girl, and boy Norman. Had much music. Gertie plays the mandoline. Connie sang a good deal, and beautifully. I am in love with her, and there's an end of it. – Wrote to Nelly about her.' Such was Gissing's diary entry for 11 August. He wanted to be in love with someone. Perhaps he *was* in love with her. However that may be, he visited her again in her parents' home on 14 August, then never mentioned her again. He had been rejected and, from what happened later, one can guess that the reasons were in part financial. No doubt he had been egged on by his sisters, later resenting the fact: he would not expose himself in the same way again. A. C. Young once suggested that Henry Shergold, a character in Gissing's story 'A Lodger in Maze Pond', in effect spoke for Gissing himself when he said: 'Perhaps it is my long years of squalid existence. Perhaps I have come to regard myself as doomed to life on a lower level. I find it an impossible thing to imagine myself offering marriage – making love – to a girl such as those I meet in the big houses.'[7] In Wakefield, at least, where Gissing's past was known, this would indeed have been difficult. He could not demonstrate that he had succeeded at his chosen career and knew that his books would be misunderstood or misinterpreted. In Wakefield, he was a man who had been expelled from University, had been in prison, had failed to help his family, had lived in London and had written unattractive novels. The obstacles to friendship with a girl like Connie Ash were considerable.

The following day, 15 August 1890, he wrote to Bertz from Wakefield: 'Since last I wrote to you, I have been ill in body and mind, all but on the point of madness . . . This solitude is killing me. I can't endure it any longer. In London I must resume my old search for some decent work-girl who will come and live with me. I am too poor to marry an equal, and cannot live alone.'[8] In the same letter, he mentioned that he wanted to be back in London as quickly as possible so that he could get his work done before the lease of his flat expired at the end of the year. On 21 August he did in fact return to London. On 23 August, he noted in his diary that he had begun a new novel, 'a jumble of the various ones I have been engaged in all summer', but work did not free him from loneliness, for in the same diary entry he said: 'Am on the verge of despair, and suffering more than ever in my whole life.' On 6 September he told Bertz that he had been in London for seventeen days without speaking to a single person, commented on the fact that Bertz had just married (in England 'he would not be admitted to general society') and toyed with the idea of living 'for brief periods in a succession of boarding houses', since they had not been much used in English fiction.

In the same letter to Bertz appeared what, in retrospect, has to be regarded as a crucial paragraph:

I live alone, as usual, and dare not, as yet, make any effort to change this state of things; my financial position is too shaky. I shall see what can be done when the book is finished. But you are quite right in what you say: a continuation of my present miseries would be fatal. Marriage, in the best sense, is impossible; educated English girls *will* not face poverty in marriage, and to them anything under £400 a year is serious poverty. They remain unmarried in hundreds of thousands, rather than accept poor men. I know that my danger, if I become connected with a tolerable girl of low position is very great: I am weak in these matters. But then, reflect: there is no *real* hope of my every marrying anyone of a better kind, no *real* hope whatever! I say it with the gravest conviction.[9]

By this time, Gissing was reduced to a condition of such complete loneliness and despair that any companionship would have been welcome. He was genuinely ill, though he did not fully accept the fact and indeed did not understand it. There was little he could do to improve his lot. He had to keep writing in order to stay alive, yet he could no longer endure the agony of going on and on by himself. He craved the love that he believed impossible. In this state of mind he met the girl who was to become his second wife, Edith Underwood, probably on 23 September. The effect on his work was immediate. On 15 September he had recorded 'a complete breakdown'; on 1 October he begins again: 'It will be *New Grub Street*.'

Gissing did not write to Bertz again until 25 October, though Bertz had written to him. What Gissing said about himself in this letter has to be taken seriously. It can be taken seriously because it relates directly enough to known facts. 'I cannot answer properly, for I am physically ill', he said. Indeed he was. He never looked after himself. He had a perpetual cold. He had always stinted with fuel in the winter and did so now. And his lungs were already seriously affected. He told Bertz, too, that 'he was gravely troubled in mind'. As well he might be. He found himself attaching importance to knowing a girl he had met casually in Oxford Street, someone whom he knew could never provide intellectual companionship of any kind.

This girl came to his flat and they were soon seeing a lot of each other. On 5 October they went by boat to Putney Bridge and walked over to Richmond where they had supper. The next day Gissing told his sister that he might 'possibly' get married at the end of the year. He was desperate. That week he saw Edith twice, took her to Kew and at the weekend visited her home at 25 St. Paul's Crescent, Camden Square, for the first time. He went there several times during the month of October, meeting no one until 5 November when he met her father, no doubt as a result of bad organization or bad luck on Edith's part. At any rate the father made it plain that Gissing's presence in the house was not welcome and he in fact did not go there again until Christmas Day, when he had dinner with her. 'Afterwards, her sister Flossie came into the room, and we had some games at cards.' Gissing, by this time, was aggressive, importunate, unrelenting, at one moment clear-headed in his perception that he could not continue without companionship of some kind, at the next completely confused and incapable of thinking clearly about what kind of life he and Edith might make for each other. Edith found herself under immense pressure, for Gissing was not to be denied. On 9 January he even recorded what must have been a somewhat absurd interview with Edith's father: 'In the evening to Edith's: saw her father, and told him that I wish Edith to come to me at Exeter in a month's time. He "would think it over", but E. says she has made up her mind.'

The excitement of this encounter allowed Gissing to complete *New Grub Street*, just as his meeting Helen years earlier had allowed him to complete *Workers in the Dawn*. When he told Bertz about this new friendship, he seemed to acknowledge that it was a case of brute need. As early as October, the possibility of her living with him had already been mooted. 'I have made the acquaintance of a work-girl who will perhaps come to live with me when I leave this place, at Christmas. But everything is dark and almost hopeless.' This seems to mean that he realized that living with Edith Underwood would not solve anything: he had been born in exile and had to live with the impossibility of reconciling the social and intellectual sides of his existence. 'I must consider nothing but physical needs,' he said.

He considered his physical needs and wrote rapidly. Some months later he was to tell Bertz that his relations with Edith had been platonic. But that was in the letter in which he told Bertz he was thinking of marrying her. It's much more likely that the relationship before marriage was frankly sexual on both sides and that only after marriage did Gissing revert to his conventional, puritan ideas about sex. At all events, he wrote the rest of *New Grub Street* rapidly and by the end of the year had sold it to Smith, Elder for £150. Whatever Gissing may at times have said to the contrary, he preferred a relationship which did not make demands on him.

The way in which he eventually rejected Edith Sichel makes this clear. He did not really want a friendship which involved that mutual honesty in which, in theory, he sincerely believed. He did not want to talk about his past; he did not want to disturb his present. Undoubtedly Gissing himself understood this, for in *Born in Exile* he permits Godwin Peak to realize that the pretence of respectability, which he had hypocritically assumed in order to be accepted socially, was unnecessary for both the women who loved him: they saw as clearly as he did that a thinking, emancipated life and conformity to Victorial social and moral norms were incompatible. Gissing knew in his heart that an outwardly 'refined' woman might accept, even desire, the bohemianism he practised. He knew in 1890, wha the literally had not known in 1885 or 1880, that women were as much influenced by modern ideas as men, and that the appearance of conformity often concealed an actual intellectual freedom. (Thus there is a huge difference between Miriam Baske in *The Emancipated* and Marcella Moxey in *Born in Exile*.) Since Gissing knew that emancipation was a reality, his fear of friendship with women like Edith Sichel must have had other causes. 'Let me tell myself the truth', he later had Ryecroft say; 'do I really believe that at any time of my life I have been the kind of man who merits affection? I think not. I have always been too much self-absorbed; too critical of all about me; too unreasonably proud. Such men as I live and die alone, however much in appearance accompanied.'[10] But the pride was an expression of, or at least related to, sexual inhibitions, reinforced by his experiences at Manchester, which denied sexual equality between people of the same class but which did not prevent unequal relationships. Gissing wrote to Edith Sichel just before Christmas to say that he did not know what would happen to him, that he could not see her for a while, that he was 'all headachey confusion,' and that he was temporarily leaving London. He did not tell her that he had already decided to live with Edith Underwood, that he had given up the lease of his flat, and was about to begin his search for a place in Exeter, and that his personal problems had at least been resolved enough for him to have completed *New Grub Street*. At least towards Edith Sichel he had not behaved as Edwin Reardon would have done!

Then again, Gissing never really liberated himself from his family in Wakefield. Gabrielle Fleury was later to complain of this fact. It was easier to think of living with someone who would not be in a position to pass judgment on Wakefield. 'I strongly doubt', he entered in the *Commonplace Book*, 'whether husband and wife ever become as much to each other as relatives by blood.'[11] That Gissing did not have anything more than a shallow relationship with the Wakefield family was of little consequence: it was a shallow relationship that he wanted. His brother and sisters did not invade his interior existence. Not only did they not understand it, he knew they did not. Therein lay his personal security, his essential privacy. An intelligent wife would have been a different matter indeed.

Edith Underwood was fourteen years old when Gissing first met her. How old Gissing thought she was is another matter. Since he had, in all likelihood, deliberately set out to marry a young girl who could be trained to act as a companion, *hausfrau* and mistress, he would have known that Edith was young. Yet she, not knowing what would come of their meeting, would undoubtedly have concealed her real age. You have no need to be completely honest with a man just to go with him on the Thames as far as Kew Gardens. Nor do you dwell upon the question of age if the man evidently likes and accepts you as you are. From the point of view of their getting on together, his being thirty-two was just as much an obstacle as her being fourteen, one might say. Edith seems to have been fourteen, but the evidence is conflicting. On her marriage certificate she is given as 'Spinster, aged 23, of 25 St. Paul's Crescent, Pancras, daughter of James Underwood, sculptor'. If this information were correct, she would have been born in 1868. Her death certificate states that she died on 27 February 1917 at the age of forty-five. If this certificate were accurate, she would have been born in 1872 and would have been nineteen when she

married. Neither certificate can be regarded as reliable. The reasons
for giving a false age when she married are obvious. As for her death
certificate, she died in Fisherton House, Salisbury, an asylum 'for
private insane patients'. No one there would have been able to check
the details of her life. Indeed she was entered as 'wife of . . . Gissing
occupation unknown'. There is no birth certificate which corresponds
even approximately to either the marriage or death certificate; that is,
there is no entry for an Edith Underwood between 1867 and 1873.
There is, however, an entry for Edith Sophia Underwood, born 24
August 1876 at 2 Cologne Street, of John Underwood and Mary
Underwood, formerly Raby.

Even when it is admitted that Edith, Gissing's wife, cannot be
associated conclusively with this birth certificate and that many
births went unregistered, the evidence for her having been young is
strong. He had the idea that he could train a wife and for this purpose
gave up the lease of his flat and disappeared into the country, to
Exeter. He did not tell his family that he intended to marry until he
had already moved. When he did marry, he kept Edith away from his
friends: the Harrisons, for example, were not permitted to meet her.
Meanwhile, his letters were extraordinary. In a letter to his sister, a
month before his wedding day, he said: 'As you write so kindly, I
think I will really ask you to send just a line to Edith. Her address is
Miss Edith Underwood, 25 St. Paul's Crescent, Camden Square,
London NW. You may be sure I should not ask this if I were not
convinced that she is quite worthy of some attention . . . I quite
believe that with a year's time there will be no great fault to find with
her demeanour.'[12] A week later, in a further letter to Nelly, he wrote:
'Well, once more a new epoch is beginning with me and under
reasonably favourable auspices. We shall see. My life passes in
experimenting like that of so many people in our time.'[13] 'Experiment' is a somewhat eerie word as used by Gissing: he may well have
thought there was justice in the arrangement they had made. He had a
companion who brought an end to sexual deprivation and the
extremes of loneliness. She, too, had a companion, a husband, and
thereby a chance to better herself. Whatever the extent of their
understanding. however, the consequences were ruinous.

Gissing did not have in mind that there would be compromise. She
would have to adapt to him. He would not be expected to adapt to
her. Edith, like any young wife, naturally had a great deal to learn.
George, established novelist and experienced traveller, had few
deficiencies of character and certainly no reason for change. From
his point of view an ideal household consisted of a den in the attic for
him, a kitchen under ground for her, and between the upper and the
lower a small house in which they could from time to time live a
respectable married life in a way that was unnatural to both of them.

George was as inept as Edith at the business of living with another person, a fact which was obvious enough to her but not to him. He assured his family that his experiment would work. When Nelly received an 'extraordinary' letter from Edith, he told her firmly: 'I have so often told you that the uneducated have seldom any natural delicacy. But perhaps a little may be cultivated in the process of time. Thank goodness: there is much docility and some slight capacity for household work – a very exceptional thing let me tell you.'[14] When he at last told his brother, Algernon, that he had married, he said in a letter dated 6 November 1891: 'Edith, as you know, is uneducated but I am more than satisfied with her domestic management. She has many very good qualities and most distinctly improves. I feel our Kate [Mrs. Algernon Gissing] would not feel it impossible to see a little of her now and then.'[15] Gissing was well past the age at which his family in Wakefield thought that he ought to have been married, stressed his wife's ability to manage in the house because that is what they wanted to hear, and could not yet imagine that she might not want to adapt to him in a way that was acceptable to his brother and his sisters. Characteristically, the egoist, in planning the experiment, had failed to anticipate the girl's actual personality which was as proud and determined as his own. With such a beginning conflict was inevitable.

What is utterly extraordinary is the fact that Gissing wrote *New Grub Street* during this period between his first meeting with Edith Underwood in August or September 1890 and his leaving London for Exeter immediately after Christmas. It is extraordinary because Gissing appears not to have associated his treatment of marriage in the novel with his own attitude to the possibility of living with Edith, whether married or not. 'Is this, then, what you think of marriage?' one can imagine an orthodox fiancée exclaiming when she read the manuscript. Gissing would have replied, of course, in the negative. 'No: these are two possibilities, the one Romantic, the other practical and modern, both of which I reject.' He had in fact rejected them. He did not want a bourgeois romance; nor was he prepared to marry for money, like Jasper Milvain. 'Well then,' the fiancée might have said, 'are there possibilities for us, do you think, that your book denies, for example, to Amy Reardon?' And in an honest mood Gissing would have said: 'Yes: *possibilities*. We may grow to like living with each other.' However, he was not honest. As far as Edith Underwood was concerned, it is far more likely that Gissing behaved before their marriage in the possessive, jealous manner that in *The Odd Women* he attributed to Widdowson, who became infatuated with a shop girl. And he probably felt no need for consistency between his own behaviour and his treatment of marriage in *New Grub Street*.

Nonetheless, *New Grub Street* in its unrevised form is undoubtedly an interesting commentary on Gissing's state of mind in the latter part of 1890, that is, once it is understood that the book is about marriage and not about nineteenth-century publishing. *New Grub Street* is such an important novel in the Gissing canon that the point is perhaps worth emphasis. Some literary critics have wrongly identified Gissing, the author, with Edwin Reardon, the character, claiming that in depicting a novelist whose inspiration had failed and who was, then, at the mercy of alien market forces to which he could not respond, Gissing was in some way writing about himself. Not so. Edwin Reardon is represented as a Romantic idealist who cannot find it within himself to complete his third novel whether for the contemporary market or not. Gissing, on the other hand, when he wrote *New Grub Street* was a successful novelist who had just written and published six novels in as many years. Gissing obviously did not see himself as an idealist; nor is there any similarity between the marriage of the Reardons in *New Grub Street* and Gissing's own first marriage, except in the very general sense that all writers feel some conflict between the demands of work and the demands of family life. Furthermore, *New Grub Street* gives very little contemporary information about the publishing world. It has two novelists, a journalist, a few editors and what we would now call a research assistant, but it has no publishers, agents, publisher's readers, printers, booksellers or even, for that matter, practising, normal writers. If the book shows anything at all, it is Gissing's ignorance of the publishing world, a fact that is not really very surprising in that, throughout his life, he was exploited by his publishers. *New Grub Street* is about a group of people who happen to be on the fringe of London literary life, but it is their personal, not their literary, life that is the principal concern.

If a reader of *New Grub Street* does not start off with the preconception that Gissing is to be identified with Edwin Reardon, and that therefore the reader is in some way being asked to sympathize with Reardon, even though as a man he is a dreadful failure, he will see that the novel is in fact about two types of marriage, or at least about two men, Jasper Milvain and Edwin Reardon, who have different attitudes to marriage just as they have different attitudes to life. Jasper Milvain is modern, pragmatic, practical and realistic. Reardon's marriage was based upon the dream that he would be a successful writer and when the dream is shattered the couple, having no common ground on which they can discuss their predicament, quickly become alienated, Amy by Reardon's inability to do anything of a practical kind, Reardon by his wife's stubborness in refusing the love on which their dream of life together had been based. Jasper Milvain's attitude, on the other hand, was that he would not be a great writer, but that he might be successful; that to be successful he needed money and that it made sense to marry for money, especially if that established a basis for understanding between husband and wife; and further that to marry for love, when everything about marriage was arbitrary and accidental, was the height of foolishness. Gissing handled this contrast with, for him, a new boldness. He allowed the idealist, Reardon, to languish and eventually die. He allowed the realist, Milvain, to flourish and eventually marry Reardon's wife, Amy. Reardon is oppressed with a sense of guilt and hopelessness: he had lost everything he had believed in. Milvain, on the other hand, commits a modern act of bad faith by abandoning the girl who loved him and to whom he was secretly engaged in order to marry Amy Reardon, who has the inherited money that Marion had been expected to have. Gissing himself did not say that Reardon's life was tragic or that Milvain's was despicable. He leaves the contrast between the two sets of values to make its own point. Nevertheless, no one could reach the conclusion, on the basis of *New Grub Street*, that the author wanted to assert the values traditionally associated with Victorian marriage, for only the cynical and the worldly are allowed to prosper.

It is as though the novel represented for him the more or less dreadful matrimonial possibilities he observed existed in New Grub Street. Were there better alternatives? Promiscuity had no attraction for him: he wanted the emotional security of possession. A mistress would have been expensive. One can understand the process by which he came to the cynical conclusion that only a 'docile' young girl could be trained to see him as he saw himself. Edith was in fact selected for her docility and Gissing seems to have had no notion that she might develop opinions of her own. Thus the inevitable conflict was postponed.

Edith did not at first know the man she had married, remaining as 'pliant' as when Gissing had first met her. Gissing moved by himself to Exeter, with his belongings, at the end of 1890, apparently only telling Wakefield that he intended to do so in a letter to his sister, Nelly, dated 26 December 1890. In the first week of January, Smith, Elder offered £150 for *New Grub Street*, so Gissing was able to marry. The wedding date was set for 17 January, but Edith procrastinated. She had previously kept Gissing away from her family by saying that her father would not allow them to see each other in his house, a strategy which prevented an unnecessary or premature discussion of her age or background, but which surprised Gissing, according to a note in the diary, since he had been led to believe the father did not mind Edith's visiting Gissing's flat. Mr. Underwood probably never knew about the visits any more than he knew his daughter was on the brink of matrimony. If so, it would not be surprising that Edith refused to get married immediately. Eventually, Gissing told Edith by letter that they would either marry on 25 February, exactly three years after the death of his first wife, or not at all. On that date, then, they were married in the St. Pancras Register Office and afterwards travelled directly to Gissing's new home at 24 Prospect Park, Exeter.

Gissing, with a book in the press, was happy again. He had with him, he told Bertz, bundles of notes which were 'material for all the rest of my life'. The 'miseries and difficulties' of 1890 were behind him. He had moved his furniture to Exeter and was 'happily . . . able at length to write' in his 'own orderly room'. The house at 24 Prospect Park, where he rented a set of rooms for six shillings a week, was, he told his sister, 'in the highest part of Exeter, not a quarter of an hour's walk from the heat of the city, yet within sight of absolute rurality.' The coast was only ten miles away. Before long, after some hesitation because of the cost, he joined the Devon and Exeter Institution, with the reading room and library that together were essential to him. He could now keep in touch with all that was going on in the world of literature, without the inconvenience of having to cope with people in London whom he knew.

Here, however, as Gissing the author settled in a new part of the country, the tragedy of his existence is most evident. What he had then, in January 1891, were the essential ingredients of his personal happiness: a book in the press and another one in progress; the English countryside where he could 'botanize' as his father had done; a library where he could read the journals and magazines; and privacy – privacy which enabled him to work hard without interruption and which at the same time allowed him to indulge in that particular brand of self-pity that, throughout his life, showed his soul was temporarily at peace with the world. He developed a great affection for Exeter and the surrounding countryside; 'the early coming of spring in this happy Devon gladdens my heart', Ryecroft said. Sitting above the green valley of the Exe and 'the pine-clad ridge of Haldon' for the first time was 'one of the moments of my life when I have tasted exquisite joy'. Throughout his first year in Devon, he walked almost every day.

> Now inland, now seaward, I follow the windings of the Exe. One day I wandered in rich, warm valleys, by orchards bursting into bloom, from farmhouse to farmhouse, each more beautiful than the other, and from hamlet to hamlet bowered amid dark evergreens; the next, I was on pine-clad heights, gazing over moorland brown with last year's heather, feeling upon my face a wind from the white-flecked Channel. So intense was my delight in the beautiful world about me that I forgot even myself; I enjoyed without retrospect or forecast; I, the egoist in grain, forgot to scrutinize my own emotions . . .[16]

He responded eagerly to the beauty of Devon as he had earlier responded to the Lake District. He explored the villages around Exeter and took Edith for a short holiday to Budleigh Salterton. He celebrated the countryside in several warm passages in *Born in Exile* and later books. And when he became ill in 1897, it was to Budleigh Salterton that he returned for his convalescence, just as later, when he was actually writing *Ryecroft* in France it was Devon that provided his strongest memory of England. Yet, despite such a great joy in his new surroundings, the note of tragedy was dominant. He was ill. He was poor. And he had perpetrated another disastrous marriage.

It is possible that Gissing would have been a happier man if he had not been able to complain so openly to his family in Wakefield. 'I have an uneasy feeling', he had told his sister three weeks before he married, 'that you are all shaking your heads and viewing me rather gloomily. It gets more and more difficult for me to believe that people regard me indulgently.'[17] In so many ways he needed not an indulgent family, nor indeed a wife, but a tough-minded friend who would put his affairs in order, tolerate or endure his fits of depression and yet share a house, perhaps with the help of the kind of housekeeper Gissing later allowed Ryecroft. Certainly he would have been a happier person in the twentieth century, for his attitudes, many of them, would have been superfluous. As it was, he worked hard at *Born in Exile* and indulged himself – almost as a condition of working hard – in characteristic introspective fits.

> Of course I have no society here. My ambition now is to make my name known, while personally I remain unseen and unheard of. In a time when any man of any shadow of distinction does his best to keep always in the sight of the public, one may reasonably find solace in the thought of winning reputation whilst remainining in quiet corners. We shall have to see whether I can keep my mind active without the help of congenial minds. I have the feeling of being deserted by all who ought to be my companions: but then these miseries are useful in giving a peculiar originality to my work.[18]

This from a man who had coolly left London without telling his closest friends where he was going – a man who at the same time, January 1891, was urging the young girl he had met four months earlier to come to Exeter to live with him and who was already at work on *Born in Exile*, a book in which educated people of no means consistently fail to marry happily.

Gissing himself did not think there was any point in attempting to reconcile intellectual and domestic life. Intellectually, he was a nihilist and as such was apolitical. When, a few months later, his sister wrote to him about the 'meaning' of *New Grub Street*, which had just appeared, his reply showed that, whatever advances he may have made as a practising novelist during the previous decade, he had not altered his basic attitude to life. 'At best it seems to me, only not intolerable. As for human aspirations, I know not their meaning, and can conceive no credible explanation – even as I am unable to understand what is called the instinct of animals. The problem does not trouble me either. I have reached the stage at which one is content to be ignorant.'[19] This rather icy, inhuman part of Gissing's nature was, of course, not known to Edith since he did not believe that what he thought had anything to do with her. They went on walks through the Devonshire lanes as they had walked together along the Thames. They spent their evenings together as they had done in Gissing's flat. Their companionship was not intellectual; it was directly sexual. Edith did not know him, really. Nor did he know her. She, too, though for different reasons, thought there was a difference between 'life' and 'work' and wanted, sometimes, to have a husband who was not working. From Gissing's point of view this was a bizarre imposition.

From his own point of view, one comes to the conclusion that Gissing (however perverse the whole business may appear in retrospect), had created the conditions necessary for the writing of two of his most important works. He said he *had* to write them. Textual and bibliographical evidence strongly suggests that both *New Grub Street* and *Born in Exile* were written from earlier drafts. Both contain fossilized, autobiographical fragments which could be associated more readily with his early immature work – fossils such as Godwin Peak's snobbish reasons for leaving college and, in *New Grub Street*, the Yule family which is so reminiscent of Gissing's own family in Wakefield. Together the two novels represent a turning point in his career, away from social realism towards a type of psychological novel, albeit a limited type. They also represent his coming to terms with issues that concerned *him*, personally, in contrast to the neutral, anonymous attitude he had adopted in the eighties. Neither is a perfectly fashioned book. On the contrary, he revised *New Grub Street* for the French translation and said that he would have done so for an English edition as well, if he had owned the copyright. Equally, he recognized the unevenness of *Born in Exile* but said, in effect, that it was something he had to get out of his system. Yet, despite the imperfections, the two books are most important. They mark Gissing's escape from continental naturalism. They mark a real advance in expertise, especially in the case of *Born in Exile*. To achieve this breakthrough, it would seem that Gissing needed the new conditions made for himself. He needed the change from London. He needed the resurgence of health that the countryside for a short time gave him. And he needed the personal and sexual excitement of a close, though brief, relationship with Edith. But when Edith became pregnant and *Born in Exile* was accepted for publication, the episode was as good as over.

7

Collapse

WHATEVER BOND EXISTED between Gissing and the young girl who had
been persuaded to marry him was soon tested by the extreme loneliness of their life in Exeter. Gissing had moved his possessions, clothes,
books, furniture from Cornwall Residences intact, quickly re-
assembled them in a way which suited him, and continued to live
much as he had always done, reading, walking and writing continuously. *Born in Exile* was written during the first months of his
stay at 24 Prospect Park, so he must have been pretty steadily at his
desk. Edith, on the other hand, had little to take with her, found little
provision for when she arrived, and was soon lonely. She had got to
know Gissing in his leisure hours: the man who enjoyed walks in
Richmond Park, long expeditions on the Thames and comfortable
evenings chatting by the fireside when the day's work was done. This
man now possessed her, had done her a favour, had domestic
expectations not previously revealed and, worst of all, wanted to
educate her. According to Ambrose Bierce in *The Enlarged Devil's
Dictionary*, marriage was 'The state or condition of a community
consisting of a master, a mistress and two slaves, making in all, two.'
Such was Edith's position. Like Helen before her, she not only had to
combine the roles of wife, mistress and servant, but had literally
nothing to do during the seven or eight hours a day when Gissing was
writing. After two or three months she found the loneliness in-
supportable.

Theoretically, things should have worked out well for the Gissings.
New Grub Street, published in 1891, was well received. *Denzil
Quarrier* was published on 5 February 1892 and *Born in Exile* on
24 April. For the first he received an advance on royalties of £105 and
for the second £135, amounts which in the old days would have
allowed him to manage easily enough, even though he was disappointed by his agent's negotiations over *Born in Exile*. Yet Gissing

was unprepared for the practical responsibility of a household, for the need to plan in advance, and for the circumstance in which his old strategies of self-deprivation would not work or could not reasonably be applied. Very rapidly he found himself overwhelmed by domestic miseries that compounded themselves into a major personal misery of such proportions that in the end he turned his back on it all and went away to Italy. To say that another man would have been able to cope is to say nothing. Gissing had no practical aptitude whatsoever. He had scant experience of living with another person. He did not want to become practical and he saw no need for him to learn how to live. The marriage quickly foundered in a way that left Gissing with the feeling that there was nothing he could have done to save it. And in all probability he was right.

Both George and Edith found their rooms in Prospect Park cramped, confining, claustrophobic. Sharing the facilities of the house with the 'people downstairs' was a far from perfect way of starting their married life together. By the end of April, Edith knew that she was pregnant and saw a doctor. It was her bad luck to have a trying time during pregnancy and this was not helped at all by her husband, who wrote in his diary when she had morning sickness: 'Edith ill with dyspepsia or whatever it may be. – Constant sickness and misery', not meaning of course misery for her, but for him.

They needed to find a more permanent home before the arrival of their child, but first, when Gissing finished *Born in Exile* and sent it off to Smith, Elder in July, they had a brief holiday in Clevedon in Somerset. Gissing throughout his life believed in holidays, knew how to choose the type of idyllic rural retreat he could enjoy, and on this occasion must have realized, once he was free from work, that they both needed the change. So they spent an enjoyable few weeks at Mrs. Elston's of Stonington Villas, Old Church Road, at a cost of sixteen shillings and sixpence a week, before Gissing went back to Exeter to find them a house, staying meanwhile in rooms over a shop in Princes Street. They had left Prospect Park with 'profound misgivings' (Gissing had noted in a letter to Bertz that 'there had been no possibility of associating with the people downstairs, who are extremely selfish and vulgar beyond belief')[1] so he was extremely relieved to find for £19 10s. per annum a house which 'suited marvellously' at 1 St. Leonard's Terrace off Wonford Road – relieved not just because he had found a home for his wife and the child that was expected before Christmas but also because, with *Born in Exile* unsold, he knew he had to write a new book as rapidly as possible. Despite the fact that Gissing considered Exeter 'intellectually very dull', the library and the reading room made staying there possible since – as he put it – 'one cannot do without a glance at the day's literature' and he was 'so perpetually in need of works of *reference* on the most unlikely subjects'. The new house gave the family new hope and Gissing was excited and proud of his achievement.

> Heaven be thanked. I am at last established in a house of my own. And a very satisfactory house indeed. The neighbourhood is beautiful; not easily matched, I should think, in English suburbs. We are a mass of garden, flowers and leafage in every direction; a view from every window of the house is one of unspoilt grace. Inside, every convenience. To-morrow I sit down to work once more. My study is small but very quiet.[2]

As usual Gissing managed in the new house by dint of extreme frugality; for example, they managed with the minimum of coal, and paid the penalty with a succession of colds and 'flus. Nonetheless, Gissing had succeeded in achieving exactly what he had set out to achieve. His income still came only from his writing. He had married. And he was living independently in his own house.

All the more surprising, then, is the ferocity of his reaction against his wife when he discovered that their having a house, far from bringing them together, actually accelerated the process of alienation in that he at least and perhaps both of them, affected to be living to 'standards' that were foreign to both. Gissing had married Edith in order to get around or avoid the middle-class expectations of the kind of educated women he would more naturally have married, only to find that it was he who had those expectations or at least that having a wife and child had certain unavoidable consequences which led him, not Edith, to the bourgeois remedies of house and servants and a conventional domestic routine. Gissing did not think that he had any responsibility to be fair towards her: he had no sense that there might be a consistent relationship between what he thought and believed and the way in which he behaved towards people whom he knew, or that anyone else might expect or look for such consistency. The habit of concealing what he did from some people and what he thought from others was deeply ingrained.

He had half faced the question of perverse or secretive introversion in *Born in Exile*, a book in which Godwin Peak persists in concealing his motives from his friends and from both the women who love him until it was too late for him to establish honest and straightforward relationships with them. Peak realized that they might have loved him still, or loved him more, had he not concealed his thoughts and motives but the instinct to conceal, where privacy is confused with pride, was in his case the essential egoism of a man whose self would have been endangered if not supported by a strong sense of alienation and the feeling of indignation that went with it. It was easier to believe that he was not and could not be understood than face the challenge of being understood by someone who loved him, since the frank acknowledgment of strengths and weaknesses in his character would have taken away from his élitist attitude the belief that he was in some way special and set apart from mankind. Actually, Gissing allows Peak a degree of self-knowledge and this fact alone makes *Born in Exile* one of his most interesting books. Nonetheless, he in the end kills him off in a literal exile abroad, just as he disposes of Edwin Reardon in *New Grub Street*, thus obviating the need to ask what would happen next. What would happen, in other words, if people, a man and a woman, achieved a measure of understanding and self-knowledge, saw through each other, and yet continued to live together? To this point in his career, Gissing had avoided the full force of this question, though there are hints of a humane, though limited solution in the marriages of Egremont and Annabel in *Thyrza*, Mallard and Miriam Baske in *The Emancipated* and Amy Reardon and Jasper Milvain in *New Grub Street*. Gissing's question had always been: *can* an intelligent, educated, classless, penniless *man* reconcile himself with life? Not *how*. Or not nearly to the same extent. Consequently, though he had thought deeply about marriage, he had come to no conclusions that were relevant to the way he lived himself. Indeed, he had not himself been through experience of the kind that Walter Egremont, Miriam Baske and Amy Reardon had. So he was not prepared for Edith any more than she was prepared for him. She was not prepared for the violence with which he would react against her after he had persuaded her to marry. Nor was he.

The birth of their first son, Walter, on 10 December meant that from then on there was no disguising the differences between them. George of necessity and by preference had to work continuously. Edith had to look after the baby. Until then, they had managed well enough. In fact, though Gissing later said in his usual way that he had achieved nothing that autumn, his career took a new turn when he met A. H. Bullen of the new publishing house, Lawrence & Bullen. It was in the early nineties that the stranglehold of the circulating libraries was finally broken. A new novel no longer cost a guinea and a half for its three volumes, but six shillings or even half-a-crown. To some extent the railway book shop replaced the circulating library as the means of distribution for publishers, which meant that there was renewed demand both for magazines and for one-volume novels that had been manufactured inexpensively. Gissing was to respond to both aspects of this demand during the eighteen-nineties and was encouraged to do so by A. H. Bullen, who wrote to him in September to ask for a single-volume novel. Gissing immediately told Bertz about it. 'The new publisher, Lawrence & Bullen, who publish Roberts' new books have written to ask me for a novel in one volume. They offer me one shilling on every six shilling volume sold, and, what is better, will pay £100 on account, when they publish. Accordingly, I have got to work, and am writing a book called "The Radical Candidate".'[3]

Gissing was naturally enough impressed and encouraged by this turn of events. A. H. Bullen was making a vigorous attempt to capture authors and in November visited Exeter to see Gissing. They had dinner together in the Clarendon Hotel in Cathedral Close. Gissing took a liking to the publisher, who had found a way to put him at his ease. It was a new sensation to be sought out by someone interested in his books. He liked Bullen as a classicist who was also well-read in English literature. And he knew as well as any other person, from his own experience, that a reform of the business relationships between publisher and author was long overdue. When the contract along the lines described in Gissing's letter to Bertz was signed later in November, it was the first time Gissing had received an advance against royalties. *Denzil Quarrier*, the new name for 'The Radical Candidate' (Bullen thought the word 'Radical' might alarm the womenfolk), did not do at all well but the business arrangements made for it were nonetheless a great improvement over anything Gissing had previously experienced, in that Bullen succeeded in selling the American, Colonial and Continental rights, told Gissing he had done so, and was willing in principle to give Gissing his share of whatever income accrued. In the event, Bullen gave Gissing only part of the £40 or so that derived from these sources, the rest presumably being set against the advance (so even Bullen did not bring himself to be fully professional in his business practices), but from Gissing's point of view life was suddenly very much better, not merely financially – and he certainly needed that hundred guinea advance when Walter was born – but also psychologically in that he felt he was at last understood. As the leaves turned and they awaited the birth of Walter, Gissing toiled away in his study at the top of the house, the result being *Denzil Quarrier*, written with Gissing's normal speed between 7 October and 12 November and dispatched immediately to A. H. Bullen. Though Bullen did not like it, he kept to the agreement and the novel was published on 5 February 1892.

Lawrence & Bullen published six of Gissing's books: *Denzil Quarrier*, *The Odd Women*, *In the Year of Jubilee*, *Eve's Ransom*, *The Whirlpool* and *Human Odds and Ends*. Equally important, as it seems at least in retrospect, was the incentive the firm provided for a revision of Gissing's early work. They wanted to republish Gissing's early, three-volume novels in single-volume editions provided there were no copyright obstacles. Since Smith, Elder were doing well with the five novels they had published, Gissing had to turn his attention to the others, *Workers in the Dawn*, *The Unclassed*, *Isabel Clarendon* and *The Emancipated*. Despite the fact that he disliked rewriting his early work because it reminded him both of his own youthful gaucherie and of his days with Helen, he revised or tried to revise the first three of these in the house in St. Leonard's Terrace. *The Unclassed* was published by Lawrence & Bullen in one volume, this second edition thus providing the definitive text of what in its revised form is an excellent novel. The revision of *Isabel Clarendon* was begun and rapidly abandoned. Gissing must quickly have realized that it was too weak a novel to be rescued.[4] As for *Workers in the Dawn*, because it had been written in two parts, the second part which concerned Harriet being much more strongly written than the first, it was only the first part that really needed revision. Gissing did the work but the novel in its revised form was never republished, either by Lawrence & Bullen or by anybody else.[5] The relationship was soon to come to an end. Lawrence & Bullen over-extended themselves and went out of business, whilst Gissing went more frequently abroad in the later nineties, and needed an agent – one who had a free hand to negotiate for terms with a variety of publishers. Though Gissing's friendly business relations with A. H. Bullen were short-lived for these reasons, they were extremely important. During the eighteen months in St. Leonard's Terrace, Gissing reviewed his career to that point. Lawrence & Bullen provided the incentive. The labour of revision was the occasion. In many respects he needed to take stock and *The Odd Women*, his next book, showed that he had done so successfully.

Gissing's professional successes reduced his chances of being reconciled with Edith. She could not share his thoughts about his career as a writer. Nor was she invited to do so. When Gissing had felt depressed about his future, when they first met in London, he had needed her company. Now he was more on top of things he did not need her. In any case, on 10 December Walter was born and there followed six months or so of domestic confusion, made worse by Edith's not being able to feed Walter herself so that he had to be put out to a nurse in a farm a few miles away, and by the Gissings' complete inability to get on with the nurse and maid George Gissing at first felt were essential to survival. From this time, on Gissing complained continuously about Edith's behaviour, her stupidity, her ill-health and her inability to manage the servants, without ever fully acknowledging to himself that he had deliberately married an uneducated person, that she genuinely was weak and out of sorts after Walter's birth, if not seriously ill, and that their having servants to satisfy his feeling about how they ought to live in fact separated Edith from a part of their existence in which she might have felt at home. Gissing saw nothing strange in forbidding his wife from going into the kitchen. Nor did he understand then, though he may have understood later, that his edicts about the management of the house, far from having to do with his needs as an author, reflected as much upon his character as upon Edith's, making him a stereotype of that bad type of Victorian husband who essentially regarded his wife as a chattel. Gissing's later books show that he thought about this. During the winter of 1891–2, Edith derived little comfort from his thoughts. Probably she was unaware of the direction of Gissing's work. If she was aware of it, she would scarcely have been gratified by the anarchic, anti-matrimonial implications of *Born in Exile*, which appeared in April, and *The Odd Women* which he completed in October 1892.

Though they took a week's holiday in Penzance in the spring of 1892, as soon as Gissing had finished correcting the proofs of *Born in Exile*, the publication of the novel in April made no difference to the way in which they lived and Gissing noted in his diary that Edith was 'constantly groaning with neuralgia, and discontent at our loneliness'. He allowed his sister Madge, the youngest and least critical of the Wakefield Gissings, to visit them in May and described the visit, briefly, to his brother. 'We have had some good walks, and Madge has become much sunburnt. Yesterday we spent at Budleigh Salterton, and returned with a great quantity of yellow iris, growing thickly in the marshy meadows about there.'[6] This was in June, Gissing had never told people why he went to Exeter and since Madge found them both discontented, though for different reasons, they talked naturally enough about a later return to London 'when the infant is out of arms'. Gissing's diary entries, however, tell a different story. On 19 June he noted: 'Madge's visit fairly successful, but of course no hope of genuine understanding between her and Edith.' On 25 June, when Madge had left, he wrote: 'visit, as regards E, profoundly disagreeable, and rendering prospects of future intercourse with Wakefield very doubtful'. The truth was that, in the face of criticism from Wakefield, he did not have it in him to be loyal to Edith any more than he had been loyal to Helen. It was not his fault if they could not live up to the Wakefield standards. Nor indeed was it his fault if he used their failure to live up to the Wakefield standards as a secret pretext for his not living up to them himself. In the practical affairs of life, the radical Gissing was customarily sacrificed to the bourgeois.

Whenever they had difficulty with servants, Gissing resented the time he had to give to Walter. When the nurse and the maid walked out on them he blamed Edith, never dreaming that there was anything extraordinary about the household that would make a person disinclined to work there. He managed to write *The Odd Women* during the summer of 1892, the final spell of writing taking him from 18 August to 4 October. On that day he noted in the diary: 'finished the last chapter. I shall call the book *The Odd Women*. I have written it very quickly, but the writing has been as severe a struggle as ever I knew. Not a day without uproar and wrangling down in the kitchen; not an hour when I was really at peace in mind. A bitter struggle.' After a brief holiday in Weymouth, Gissing and Edith parted company for a while so that he could visit his family, she hers. Each of them was ready for a change.

Gissing went to stay with his brother in Worcestershire and enjoyed himself. From there to Birmingham where he stayed for three
or four weeks gathering material for 'The Iron Gods', a book about
the industrial Midlands which he had been contemplating for some
time and which he all but finished, but never published. The travelling, the company and the new project took him out of himself and
back in Exeter he told Bertz about it with enthusiasm. 'I have been
away from home for five or six weeks, partly living with my brother
in Worcestershire, and partly getting materials for a new book in the
so-called Black Country – the region to the west and north of
Birmingham, a veritable inferno, flaring at night with the chimneys
of iron-works, and blasted by coal and iron-mining.' He said in the
same letter that he would not write about the working-class of the
district but would use the location 'as a picturesque background to a
story of middle-class life, insisting on the degree to which people
have become machines, in harmony with the *machinery* amid which
they spend their lives'.[7] The life of the writer proceeded as well as any
writer could reasonably expect, During the winter months, he continued to plan his new book. He corrected the proofs of *The Odd
Women* and at Bullen's request rewrote the first chapter. He also
'corrected' a copy of the first edition of *The Emancipated* for the cheap
edition that was eventually brought out by Lawrence & Bullen in
the autumn of 1893. Gissing was now thirty-five and deeply committed to the direction he had chosen for himself as a writer. It is difficult
to see that he could have done more than he actually did.

That, however, was not enough. He became increasingly bitter. He
had been angry when a letter from Edith had obliged him to return to
Exeter from Birmingham because Edith's sister did not wish Edith
and the baby to stay with her any longer. 'No dealing with these low-
class Londoners', Gissing had noted in the diary. With the turn of the
year, however, Gissing gave this bitterness full rein. On 31 December
1892, he wrote in the diary: 'the year of 1892, on the whole profitless,
marked by domestic misery and discomfort. The one piece of work,
The Odd Women, scribbled in 6 weeks as the autumn drew to the end,
& I have no high opinion of it. Have read next to nothing; classical
studies utterly neglected. With my new plan of having a study away
from the wretched home, may hope to achieve more in year to come.'
He was referring here to the fact that for six shillings a week and the
cost of fires he had rented a sitting room at 7 Eaton Place on the
Heavitree Road so that he could work. Happiness, though, would
not have been an achievement, certainly not the happiness of friendship and affection. For Gissing intellectual and domestic happiness
were mutually opposed; the former could scarcely give rise to the
latter and domestic happiness was a superfluity if one's intellectual
life was vigorous and absorbing. It would have needed a much more

mature and comprehending and loving woman than Edith to draw
Gissing away from the uncompromisingly puritanical attitudes and
the intellectual snobbery that constituted the outward expression of
his repressed self. After two years of marriage, a marriage on which
he himself had insisted, he wrote in his diary:

> on way home, at night, an anguish of suffering in the thought that I can
> never hope to have an intellectual companion at home. Condemned for-
> ever to associate with inferiors – & so crassly unintelligent. Never a word
> exchanged or anything but the paltry everyday life of the household.
> Never a word to me, from anyone, of understanding and sympathy – or
> of encouragement. Few men, I am sure, have led so bitter a life.

In this state of mind, he began to anticipate his return to London.
Edith had become sharp-tongued, vixenish, angry. They found no
comfort in each other and Gissing, overwhelmed by circumstance,
did not and perhaps could not pause to appease her or to consider
the extent to which he had brought about a situation in which neither
of them had any recourse. Such at least is the impression to be gained
from the correspondence which has survived. One has to bear in mind
that it was Gissing's Wakefield family that re-made his image. Much
correspondence was suppressed or lost. The correspondence reproduced in *Letters of George Gissing to Members of His Family* did
not constitute the whole. Nor does the unpublished correspondence
in the Beinecke Library at Yale. There would obviously have been an
exchange of letters, for example, when Gissing's mother visited
Exeter in May 1893, perhaps of course of a trivial kind that would
have made preservation absurd. The image of Gissing that the family
preserved was of a man who had been wronged. They had no more
reason to be sympathetic towards Edith than towards Helen. Yet had
they been sympathetic they would have had every reason to be surprised and disturbed by the extraordinary domestic situation that
prevailed in Exeter: a struggling author who rented a room in another
part of the town so that he could write; a lonely mother, who was still
a girl, incapable of satisfying her husband and abandoned already to
the anger of frustration and personal hostility. If Gissing ever told his
Wakefield family that they were wrong in thinking he had married
unwisely, the letters have not survived. If he ever frankly accepted the
responsibility for the situation he had created, the letters must have
been suppressed or lost. More and more, the double standard that was
the basis of his decision to remarry reasserted itself. When Walter
Grahame visited him in March 1892, for example, he treated him to a
lunch of 'a couple of fowls, apple tart (from the pastry cook's) with
cream & a bottle of Burgundy', and when his mother came down the
next month, for Easter, he took them all off for a holiday in rented
rooms in Paignton. In other words he did not really accept the
domestic situation he himself had created. In May, Edith and Walter

went with his mother for another brief holiday in Burnham, Somerset, while he tried to finish 'The Iron Gods', the Birmingham novel he had been working at throughout the winter. As Edith talked with other people about her predicament, Gissing felt increasingly isolated in his. His bitterness was given nourishment, there was no longer any point in living secretly in Exeter and, when he moved his family back to London in June 1893, he was determined to lead his own life, married or not.

In retrospect, it is perfectly obvious that his difficulties were financial as well as domestic. In 1892 he had an income of about £275. This was a healthy sum by comparison with earlier years, but it came from the accident of his publishing two novels in the first few months of the year (*Denzil Quarrier* and *Born in Exile*) and in any case disappeared rapidly because of the larger house, the nurse for Walter and the maid. It had to last until Gissing received the advance on royalties for *The Odd Women* in April 1893. Gissing's income did not pick up until 1894, when short story writing combined towards the end of the year with advances on *In the Year of Jubilee* and *Eve's Ransom* to give him just short of £450. By then the marriage was a broken one. The hundred guineas advanced for *The Odd Women* had to last until the publication of *In the Year of Jubilee* about a year and a half later, supplemented only by a small, though growing, income from short stories, so the fact that his income fell to about £190 in 1893 tells only half the story. The Gissings had to survive a terribly bleak period and only barely succeeded in doing so. When he returned to London in June, he rented the top two floors of a house at 71 Burton Road, Brixton, and an attic in Kennington, at 36 Cranmer Road, so that he could write. Determined though he was, the arrangement could not last: by January 1894 the family was living on less than a pound a week. Gissing emphasized Walter's health as a reason for taking rooms on the south coast but, given a knowledge of his income, it seems much more likely that the house in Brixton was sublet while the family took rooms at off-season rates in Hastings, St. Leonards and Eastbourne. At all events, they went first to 23 East Ascent, St. Leonards and then, a few weeks later, to 6 Crewe Road, where they rented rooms for twenty-five shillings a week, returning to London on 4 April after being away for almost exactly two months. Quite apart from the child's ailments and the serious illness of the father, this was a time as unsettled for Gissing as any he had known. Clement Shorter had commissioned Gissing to write a novel for serialization in the *Illustrated London News* but in the spring of 1894 Gissing was finishing *In the Year of Jubilee*. Not until the summer would Gissing give his mind to the commissioned work. He moved the family back to the same rooms they had previously occupied in Clevedon, wrote *Eve's Ransom* in a burst of energy between the 4th and 29th of June, met his deadline and was promptly paid £150. The day had been saved.

The winter of 1893–94 was a traumatic experience from which the family never really recovered. Too much had been laid bare. Too much suffering had been involved on both sides. Gissing over-reacted violently. In September 1894, with the money from *Eve's Ransom* and the expectation of the advance for *In the Year of Jubilee*, he took a house at Epsom (Eversley, Worple Road, for £40 per annum) where they were to live for the next three years as it turned out and where Alfred, Gissing's second son, was to be born. Having succeeded in making physical provision for his family, Gissing evidently felt that he was free to live as he wished; having been lonely, he would be sociable; having dissociated himself from the literary world, he would now participate; having endured solitary confinement with a woman he had never liked, and indeed had come to hate, he would now waste as little of his time as possible with her. The end of 1894 and the greater part of 1895 were thus marked by a frenzy of activity. Early in 1895 there appeared a second edition of *In the Year of Jubilee*, a few months after the first; the American edition of the same book which was published by Appleton; and, simultaneously, the serial version of *Eve's Ransom* in the *Illustrated London News*. In London, Gissing had cemented his relationship with Clement Shorter, who was editor of three periodicals, the *English Illustrated Magazine*, the *Illustrated London News* and the *Sketch*, and wrote a number of short stories for him in the early part of the year. At the same time, he had introduced himself to W. M. Colles of the Author's Syndicate, joined the Society of Authors, and allowed Colles to act as agent for the placing of his short stories. Through Colles, for example, Gissing arranged for a series of short sketches called 'Nobodies at Home' to appear in the magazine *Today*, which was edited by Jerome K. Jerome. These stories, and others, he wrote in May and June. Over and above this, Gissing found time in 1895 to write two short novels. In the spring he wrote *Sleeping Fires*, which was commissioned by Fisher Unwin for his Autonym Library, and in the late summer *The Paying Guest* for Cassell's Pocket Library, also a commissioned work. He was now quite blatantly writing for money and in this he succeeded for his income in 1894 was about £450 and in 1895 comfortably over £500. On the other hand, it was this somewhat frantic bustle of activity that, ironically enough, established him in the public eye. He was now accepted as a major author. People began to search out his earlier work. For the first time his work was used as a standard by which other work might be judged.

Away from his home Gissing was sociable, urbane, talkative. He began to accept invitations, having previously refused them. In June, 1895, he joined a party at Aldeburgh: 'our party consisted of Grant

Allen, Shorter, L. F. Austin, a literary solicitor named Whale, and Sir Benjamin Ward-Richardson, the great authority on hygiene.'[8] This was at the house of Edward Clodd and, after staying there, he went on to Yarmouth to find a place for the annual family holiday. In July he went to the Omar Khayyam Dinner and met George Meredith again, Thomas Hardy, Max Pemberton, L. J. Austin, Edmund Gosse and many others. These two events, and ones like them during the next twelve months, brought Gissing into fairly regular contact with literary people for the first time in his life, allowed him to feel more confident about his own position and very much improved his chances of being widely published and read. He struck up warm friendships with people like Edward Clodd and Edmund Gosse. Since he never talked about his home life with his literary friends, in fact never mentioned it at all, he came to be known as a vivacious, knowledgeable person and a companion not less prized by his fellow authors for the difficulty he had had in establishing himself as a serious author. One wonders what would have happened to him if he had been thrown into this type of company ten years earlier, when the question of what kind of novel he would write was an open one.

Although Gissing's literary life prospered, he was very soon in great personal difficulty once again. His health was deteriorating rapidly, his relationship with Edith was at breaking point and his financial prosperity was short lived. As with most egocentric people, Gissing's statements about his own health lacked objectivity: when his spirits were up and things were going well with him, he declared himself to be unusually fit; when a fit of depression hit him, he bordered on the hypochondriac. Nonetheless, he was already seriously ill when he married Edith. During his years in the Cornwall Residences he had complained of long successions of coughs and colds. He ate badly and sometimes not at all. He did without fires. He took no care of himself whatsoever. There was no one who could force him to acknowledge that chronic fatigue was the result of sustained over-work and he in fact, with a typically Victorian sense of virtue, enjoyed the torment of managing when most normal people would have given up. In 1890, he had had to break his journey home from Greece, to consult a doctor in Italy. 'When I ought to have been sailing from Naples', he told Bertz, 'I was lying ill in bed, with congestion of one lung'.[9] That was the year in which he had spent the summer convalescing in Wakefield, 'ill in body and mind'. With Gissing as ill as that it was not surprising that the marriage had not got off to a good start. And like many Victorians, he continued to behave absurdly. In one letter from Exeter, for example, he described the water freezing under his feet when he came down in the morning for his bath.

By the end of 1894, his lung condition had been diagnosed as emphysema and a vast number of ineffective remedies had been prescribed. He became increasingly worried by his fatigue, by the almost immediate bad effect of hot weather, and by the difficulty he had in breathing. He dreamt he had cancer. Then in 1895 and 1896 he was forced to acknowledge the unrelenting presence of illness within him and went frequently to the seaside in the belief that the change of air would help his lungs. He spent the greater part of March 1895 at the seaside, ill with bronchitis; part of June; the greater part of August. It would hardly be too much to say that the last ten years of his life constituted one long, slow death. From time to time during that period he pretended he felt better, but his own defensive actions show that he was aware of the seriousness of his condition. Not easy for Edith was this marriage to a near invalid who was, nevertheless, so proud of having coped by himself throughout his life that he delayed until too late the search for diagnosis and treatment. 1895 was tempestuous. She managed the house. She nursed him. He went away for periods only to return. Alfred, his second son, was conceived in what, in self-justification, Gissing called a moment of weakness. They fought. Bad temper and bitterness on both sides prevailed.

Gissing had already vented his feelings on the woman question, notably in *The Odd Women*. He had a theoretical belief in the equality of the sexes but, throughout his life, had taken male dominance for granted and believed that only a slow process of education and brain development could affect the desire to change it. Women simply had not evolved. In 1893, for instance, he had written a letter to Bertz, just before leaving Exeter, which was highly charged with his own feelings about his marriage.

My demand for female 'equality' simply means that I am concerned there will be no social peace until women are intellectually trained very much as men are. More than half the misery of life is due to the ignorance and childishness of women. The average woman pretty closely resembles, in all intellectual considerations, the average male *idiot* – I speak medically. That state of things is traceable to the lack of education, in all senses of the word. Among our English emancipated women there is a majority of admirable persons; they have lost no single good quality of their sex, and they have gained enormously on the intellectual (and even on the moral) side by the process of enlightenment, that is to say, of brain development. I am driven frantic by the crass imbecility of the typical woman. That type must disappear, or at all events become altogether subordinate. And I believe that the only way of effecting this is to go through a period of what many people will call sexual anarchy. Nothing good will perish: we can treat the forces of nature, which tend to conservatism.[10]

The forces of nature did not conserve very much for Edith Gissing. Whatever her faults, she discovered she had married a man who had never loved her and who would always put himself first, though he said the contrary. She felt the callousness; whether she understood that it had the type of pseudo-intellectual basis that is represented by this letter to Bertz is difficult to determine. Gissing, at all events, had opted out of his own marriage in a way which was consistent with what he said about 'sexual anarchy'. 'Of one thing I have very seriously thought,' he wrote to Morley Roberts on 5 March 1895, 'and that is – whether it would be possible to give up housekeeping altogether & settle as a boarder with some family on the Continent.'[11]

There was a curious sense in which Gissing's knowledge that he had behaved stupidly by marrying Edith in the first place absolved him from any further responsibility in the matter. Very rarely did he accept responsibility for his actions or bother to think about them in a normal context, because he did not see himself in a normal context and, from a philosophical point of view, nurtured the fantasy that people were not ultimately responsible for what they did. A few years after this (the three years he spent with Edith in Epsom), he was to find himself faced with the problem of telling Gabrielle Fleury about his earlier life. He succeeded in concealing the fact that he had been married to Helen Harrison. He could not conceal Edith and what he said is an interesting commentary on his second marriage, even though tarnished by memory and self-justification. In August 1898, for example, he wrote as follows to Gabrielle Fleury before he had joined her in France:

> Today I shall speak only of my wretched marriage. It was the result of utter misery and hopelessness. Eight years ago, I was poor and solitary and tormented by my emotions. It seemed to me that I should never succeed in literature – which meant that I could never hope to win the love of a woman who was my intellectual equal. In recklessness (of course *criminal* recklessness) I offered marriage to the first girl I happened to meet – and the result was what might have been expected. Few men have paid more bitterly for such foolish weakness.[12]

Certainly Gissing wrote this in self-justification, but one doubts whether he felt criminal any more than he had felt himself to be a criminal when arrested and put in prison for theft. He often withdrew from something he wanted or might have wanted: he never lost something that he possessed and prized. Few people in Gissing's life affected him deeply by disagreeing with him or by withdrawing their affection. He depended on people, but in a special way – by keeping them at arm's length. Edith was a silly, ignorant, bad-tempered girl. What had that, really, to do with him?

1896 was a particularly bad year, even though Gissing sustained the modest social life he had begun when he returned to London from

Exeter. At various dinners and lunches he met people like Austin
Dobson, Andrew Lang and Israel Zangwill. Late in the year he met
H. G. Wells at an Omar Khayyam dinner. He was in demand with
magazine editors and his stature as a writer was accepted as self-
evident by a growing number of fellow-writers. Personally and
domestically, however, there was a steady deterioration throughout
the year. On 26 January his second son, Alfred, was born. Immediately there was the same increase of domestic tension as when Walter
was born in Exeter. Gissing's writing life simply could not be reconciled with the domestic duties: to look after Walter and complete
'Benedict's Household,' the novel Gissing was working on in the
spring of 1896, was beyond his powers. Walter was therefore sent for
a spell to Wakefield in April and, even then, Gissing could not settle
properly to work. Temporarily united, the family had a long holiday
in July and August at Yarmouth, after which Gissing abandoned
'Benedict's Household' and, between 25 August and 18 December,
wrote *The Whirlpool*. Adversity seemed to stimulate him and the book,
when it appeared the following year, was immediately recognized as
one of his strongest novels. Though the book represented a tremendous achievement, a tremendous feat of imagination and will, the
year was a disastrous one financially. In his account book he called
1896 the 'year of terror' because his income had amounted to only
£101.13s.4d. The effect in any case had been too much for him. He
felt under stress because of his eyes, went to Aitchison's, the opticians,
and ordered a pair of spectacles. 'My eyes are greatly astigmatic', he
noted in his diary. He was also, at the end of the year, forced to see a
doctor again and was told he had a 'weak point' in the right lung.[13]
'But I am to paint with iodine and take syrup of hypophosphates.'
All this would have placed the best regulated of households under
strain and Gissing's was not well regulated. Completely unable to
cope, he himself was near breaking point.

This point was reached early in 1897. On 10 February Gissing left
Epsom seriously ill and deeply frustrated by perpetual fights with
Edith. He went first to Morley Roberts and then, almost immediately, to Henry Hick, the old school friend who was then in practice in
New Romney. Hick in turn referred Gissing to a lung specialist called
Philip Pye-Smith, who told him he needed a change of air and a complete rest. As a result, Gissing rented a room for himself in Budleigh
Salterton in Devon where he spent the next three months. The enforced rest was necessary for survival and Gissing knew it. He needed,
too, to escape by whatever means from the tensions of family life –
an escape which was necessary, as it were, for his psychological survival. They were grim times for him. Although he was by himself in a
place he liked and remembered well from the Exeter years, he wrote
little, but instead did part of the preliminary reading for the historical

novel that a few years later became *Veranilda*. His sister, Madge, went down with Walter to see him in May and brother and sister came to an understanding about the care of Walter, although they kept their understanding to themselves until later in the year. He also had a visit from H. G. Wells and Mrs. Wells. Wells urged Gissing to go abroad for a while and here too an understanding must have been reached, because a year later the friends did in fact meet in Rome. To pretend that Gissing was capable of shouldering the responsibility of family life was pointless. From the spring of 1897 no one bothered to make the pretence. As for Gissing himself, when he returned to Epsom at the end of May, he had obviously decided that he had no option but to fend for himself.

Ill-health, over-work, domestic strife, financial difficulty, confusion of mind, were by that time so desperately intermingled that it is impossible to say that this or that single cause brought about the breakdown of Gissing's second marriage. Certainly the financial difficulties of 1896 were a prime cause: he had written some fifteen books without the benefit of any royalty accumulation that would have allowed him to work at a less hectic pace. Certainly his ill-health was crucial. He had become too ill to cope with his family problems in a rational way and his wife was simply an enemy who could not do anything for him at all. On her side, nothing alleviated the miserable situation in which they were always wrangling about the management of the house and the behaviour of the boys. A miserable, only too recognizable situation had been created in which man and wife could offer each other no comfort at all. They needed to be apart at a time when to separate without acrimony was virtually impossible.

Morley Roberts, though confused about the dates, gave an account in *The Private Life of Henry Maitland* of Gissing's leaving home in February 1897.

> After shaking hands he asked me, almost breathlessly, to allow him to wash his face, so I took him into the bathroom. He removed his coat, and producing his elastic band from his waistcoat pocket, put it about his hair like a fillet, and began to wash in cold water. As he was drying himself he broke out suddenly: 'I can't stand it any more. I have left her forever.'[14]

What Gissing could not stand was Edith's bad temper, which by that time had become the only means of self-assertion at her disposal. Gissing, maybe of necessity, had entirely stopped thinking of Edith as a person. There was no longer, perhaps had never been, any possibility of accommodation, whether practical or psychological, between them. They related to each other only in their quarrels about the children and Gissing is remarkable as a copious diarist and letter-writer for never once seeing or attempting to see things from Edith's point of view. The tone is always egotistical, self-righteous, self-pitying, unsubtle. In the diary, for example, he recorded what he called two recent stories concerning what *he* (not of course they) had had to endure.

(1) In coming to live in the house, which I have furnished with special view to E.'s wishes and vanities, I made it my one request that she would keep out of the kitchen, and not quarrel with the servant. After the servant's arrival (and she is very hard-working) I hear tumult from the kitchen. There stands E. cleaning a pair of boots, and railing at the servant in her wonted way. – I had to put a stop to that by an outbreak of fury; nothing else would have availed; and this will only be effectual for a week.

(2) To-day, the little boy has not been very well, owing to wet weather. At eight o'clock to-night, as E. did not come down to supper, I went quietly to the bedroom door, to listen, as I often do, whether the boy was asleep. To my amazement I heard E. call out 'Stop your noise, you little beast!' This to the poor little chap, because he could not get to sleep. And why not? Because the flaring light of a lamp was in the room. I have begged – begged – again and again that she will *never* take a lamp into the bedroom, but she is too lazy to light a candle, and then uses such language as I have written.

But for my poor little boy, I would not, and could not, live with her for another day. I have no words for the misery I daily endure from her selfish and coarse nature.[15]

Two things accentuated the tragedy of this period of Gissing's life. The first was the determination with which he had attempted to understand the 'woman question'. The second was his affection for Walter.

Gissing did not have a solution to the problem of how people should live together in sexual pairings for the whole of their lives. There is no solution and perhaps there is no need for one. He did realize, however, that the matter was open to discussion, that marriage was not sacred, that incompatibility was as frequent as compatibility, that new social or economic conditions created new attitudes to marriage, and biological or sexual needs determined the attitude of men and women to each other to a greater extent than was ever openly acknowledged. He knew too that only the most stalwart, or the most limited, individuals could bear to live without companionship. And he knew that sexual deprivation was one of the more bitter and unacceptable forms of personal loneliness. All his better books after *The Emancipated* addressed themselves to the question of how men and women might live together – or live apart – and the plots of *Born in Exile*, *New Grub Street*, *The Odd Women*, *In the Year of Jubilee*, *The Whirlpool* and *The Crown of Life* simply represent different experimental arrangements for putting the matter to the test. No writer went into the question more thoroughly that Gissing. Indeed his penetrating analyses of such a variety of situations represent, when taken together, one of his chief claims to fame. That so many of these marital or 'interpersonal' relationships were left unresolved in the novels is of no consequence, of course, since no resolution is possible other than the brute fact that a particular man and woman do or do not discover a way to live with each other. Gissing was often brilliant in his depiction of this particularity. He knew that men and women were often alienated from each other, that the alienation often derived from a very basic type of psychological incompatibility, and that this incompatibility was often rooted in a puritanism or set of inhibitions that was determined by heredity or environment in ways that lay outside an individual's control, and he knew also that in the eighteen-nineties men and women did in fact come to arrangements with each other, for the sake of coping with existence, arrangements that, made public, would offend the orthodox but which, if not made public, represented a new tolerance, a new honesty, a new type of moral pragmatism that saved them from hypocrisy and from the unwilling conformity with convention. The novels mentioned above are peopled with characters who in one way or another understood all this. They are not identical to each other. They are not mere puppet figures mouthing sets of ideas. On the contrary, Gissing's approach in these novels was as experimental and inventive as it had been in his earlier books. Having investigated one type of situation, he turned to another, and so on. That none of this applied to his own relationship with Edith is not at all surprising. Why should there be a connection, after all? But it was certainly tragic that an author whose view of 'modern' characters was in his books dispassionate and so remarkably humane should fail miserably to cope with the domestic situation in which he found himself.

His attitude to Walter was equally enigmatic. Undoubtedly they had happy times together. When the boy was only two years old, Gissing bought an old, two-wheeled, wooden milk-cart so that they could go on long expeditions together and in the diary he recorded the effort of doing this on the Downs when they stayed on the south coast. It frequently fell to Gissing to look after Walter when he was ill. During 1893 he was 'perpetually' ill with coughs and colds, no doubt caught from his father and not improved, to say the least, by the cheerless, fireless, cold house. In November it was 'bronchial catarrh', which forced Gissing to extremes: 'Had to light bedroom fire, use a bronchitis kettle and sew the little body into cotton wool.' When he first left Walter with his aunts in Wakefield in the spring of 1896, he said 'he missed the little lad grievously,' which was no doubt true, since for George Gissing Walter had become the be-all and end-all of the marriage. On the other hand, the affection was not matched by understanding, least of all when the child was caught in the

crossfire of argument between the parents. Just as Gissing had a tendency to revert to being a stock Victorian husband so, in times of stress,
he lapsed into being the Victorian father – that is, the stereotype Victorian father whose lack of understanding of members of his own
family as human beings was unparalleled. Once in Wakefield, for
example, he described a typical family scene:

> Madge bathing him, and of course he refused to come out. He fought and
> shrieked – a worse outbreak than I ever knew. I had to seize him and
> carry him to bed. When I reproached him with having hurt his aunt, he
> (sobbing in penitence) could only think of the fact that he had scratched
> *me*. 'Oh, never mind me'. – 'But I think more of *you* than of aunt', wept
> the poor little chap. A doleful business altogether, and showing that it
> would be criminal to take him back to the old life in our home which is
> no home. He must stay here, evidently, and be tamed.[16]

Spine-chilling diary entries of this kind lead simply to the conclusion
that in family matters Gissing was completely at sea, for he would
have been just as bemused to have this quotation used against him as
he would have been amazed to find anyone sympathizing with Edith.
Gissing had to his mind used the word 'tamed' in the same omniscient
but benevolent spirit as on another occasion, when in his diary, he
described Walter as 'ill-tempered, untruthful, precociously insolent,
surprisingly selfish', because of a scene in which Walter had played
off the mother and father against each other. Gissing was not in
doubt about his love for Walter and would have been surprised, such
was his own egotism, had anyone suggested that the evidence, or some
of it, implied the contrary.

One of the final rows between George and Edith Gissing concerned
an absurdly trivial argument over whether Gissing was deliberately
hiding something Edith and Walter were looking for. When Edith
accused him of lying, Gissing appealed to his son, who burst into tears.

> At the sight of his tears, E. shouted: 'There, that's the second or third
> time you've made him cry with your ill temper'. I was very angry, and
> told her I would not be accused of lying before my own son. Thereupon
> she screamed, with a violent gesture: '*Hold your beastly noise, or you'll
> have this plate at your head!*' – Hating the odious necessity of what I did,
> I turned to the boy, and said gently, 'Walter, repeat to me the words
> your mother has just used'. He did so, poor little chap, with tears, and I
> wrote the sentence at once in my pocket-book. My reason, of course,
> was that E. invariably denies all her words and actions a day after they
> have been spoken or performed, and I was determined to allow her no
> possibility of that in the present monstrous instance. – Still raging, she
> then addressed herself to Walter, and commiserated him on having such a
> father, a father unlike all others – who never bought him a toy (verbatim
> thus), and who was never in a decent humour – with much else of the
> usual kind. There it is. Decisive, I should think, for ever. Weather much
> better to-day.[17]

In these terms Gissing recorded the incident in his diary. That was on 25 August, and since he had already decided to leave Edith there was little she could do to stop him, so heavily were the dice loaded against her.

After their holiday in Castle Bolton in Yorkshire, the family travelled back to London at the end of August, at which time there were only a few weeks of the rental agreement at Epsom to run. Quite obviously Gissing had already planned to go abroad when the rental period ended. To earn the necessary money he had worked hard throughout June and July on his new novel, *The Town Traveller*, for which he obtained advances of £300 for the English and £100 for the American editions. Not only had he done the research for *Veranilda*, or a good part of it, but he had also secured a contract from John Holland Rose, an old Owens College friend, to write a book on Charles Dickens for the Victorian Era Series published by Blackie & Son. In other words, he had enough work before him to make the venture a tolerably safe one. He must, in addition, have made enquiries about where to spend the winter because in opting for Siena he selected a town on a hill with good air and a long-established sanatorium for the treatment of diseases of the lung. When he only had himself to consider, Gissing could be practical enough. Only on 6 September, however, did he reveal his intentions to his wife, having already sent Walter back to Yorkshire to live with his sisters. There followed a week of bitter argument, recrimination and anger, until 17 September when Gissing left London bound for Siena determined not to live with Edith ever again.

Two women, Clara Collett and Eliza Orme, had begun to play an important part in Gissing's life. He had first heard about Clara Collett when his sister read an account of a lecture on Gissing's work reported in the magazine *The Queen*. Evidently she was a remarkable woman whose independence of mind and character allowed her to identify with many of the women characters in Gissing's novels, particularly those in *Born in Exile*. Having obtained a degree in political economy from London University in 1885, claiming to be the first woman to do so, from that point on she devoted her life to public service and to her writings on social questions. Like Beatrice Webb, she began her professional career as a researcher for Booth's *Life and Labour of the London Poor*, and then worked in various departments finally reaching the Ministry of Labour (1917–20) and the Trades Board (1921–32). When Gissing knew her she was chief investigator for women's industries in the Labour Department of the Board of Trade and had published her first book, *Statistics of the Employment of Women and Girls* (1894). Ruth Adams described her from a photograph as 'a plump, short woman, with a glance of good sense and reasonableness.'[18] That was some time after Gissing's death, however. When she first wrote to him in Exeter she was thirty-three, had already been President of the Association of Assistant Mistresses in Public Secondary Schools and co-founder of the Economics Association (later the Royal Economic Society) and was just beginning the most active part of her career. Despite several letters, a packet of papers and books, and a portrait, Gissing at first declined to arrange a meeting but, once back in London, he changed his mind and visited her at 34 Hill Street, Richmond, on 18 July 1893. In this way began a friendship that lasted until Gissing's death.

The strong bond of understanding between Gissing and Clara Collett grew from their shared interest in contemporary social problems. Miss Collett must have identified with the recently published *The Odd Women*, since she would otherwise have been unable to approach Gissing as directly as she did. In that novel, Rhoda Nunn and Barfoot arrive at an essentially un-Romantic, pragmatic view of each other even though sexually and by temperament attracted into a situation that conventionally would have resulted in marriage. One of the strengths of *The Odd Women*, one of its many strengths, was Gissing's ability to hold the masculine and the feminine attitudes in balance equally. Clara Collett obviously liked the book. She must also have admired *Born in Exile*, in which Gissing vividly depicted two or three intellectual and 'emancipated' women, since he gave her the copyright of the book. People have wondered why an intimate friendship did not develop between Gissing and Clara Collett of the kind Gissing evidently rejected when he destroyed his relationship with Edith Sichel. This ignores two facts. The first is that Clara Collett admired Gissing because, from his novels, she saw he understood that a woman might not wish to have her life defined exclusively in terms of domestic, sexual or matrimonial relations with a man. How could an intelligent woman in 1893 get to know a married man unless she were clear-headed on this point? The second fact was Gissing's evident ill-health. Gissing's haggard expression, spent appearance, perpetual cough, and the difficulty he had even to breathe were hardly encouragements. Clara Collett saw immediately that he was desperately ill and tried to help him.

She tried to help the family. Before the end of July, she had been to Brixton and together they had been on several occasions to the theatre. On one of these occasions, when Clara Collett had taken Edith out, Gissing received a letter from her offering to take charge of Walter should the need ever arise. Later events showed that this offer was based upon a full knowledge of Gissing's life, for when Gissing died, Clara Collett was one of the few people who knew about both Helen and Edith, just as she was one of the few people who knew about his expulsion from Owens College. At the time, Gissing's reputation as a novelist was very high indeed. He was recognized as one of the major serious writers and was compared only with Hardy and Meredith. Clara Collett thus saw an important and, to her, compatible novelist in dire straits. Her help was not needed immediately because Walter was sent to Wakefield, but she was named with Algernon as executrix of the will Gissing had drawn up in 1897 and, after his death, played an active part in protecting his interests and did her best for his son.

Gissing met Eliza Orme at a dinner party given by Lawrence and Bullen in 1894. To Gabrielle Fleury, Gissing later described Miss Orme as a very strong-minded woman, aged 'about 53', who had been a good friend to him when he left Edith. Eliza Orme assessed the fearful predicament of the Gissing family as coolly as Clara Collett and as generously attempted to help them. When she learned of Gissing's decision to leave the country, she immediately – on 14 September 1897 – offered to let Edith and Alfred live with her rather than go into lodgings. This was impractical. She did not realize that the two hundred pounds she asked for was beyond Gissing's means. In any case, Edith did not wish to live with her. This meant that when Gissing left England he had no idea of how his bitterly unsatisfactory relationship with Edith could ever be resolved, but he at least had a sensible and generous friend who would guard Alfred's interests if she could. And this proved to be necessary.

Edith and George Gissing never again lived with each other. Between their marriage in 1891 and this separation six and a half years later Gissing had written much of his most important work. *Born in Exile*, *The Odd Women*, *In the Year of Jubilee* and *The Whirlpool* stand out as the major accomplishments of an extremely productive period. Their two sons had been born and ought to have brought them happiness. Instead, in their different ways, they destroyed the marriage – a marriage which had been grotesquely unequal at the outset and which was never given a chance to prosper. Gissing died six years later, abroad. Edith died nineteen years later, in an asylum. They had only the bitterest memories of each other.

8

The Crown of Life

GISSING DIED IN 1903, six years after separating from Edith. Undoubtedly he knew he was dying, knew his condition had been imperfectly diagnosed, knew throughout the whole period that there was very little on which he could depend. Nonetheless, he worked with characteristic determination. In 1897, although worn out by the long illness of the previous winter and by the breakdown of his marriage, he quickly wrote the commissioned work on Dickens and perhaps the first draft or, if not, extensive notes for the book that was eventually called *By the Ionian Sea*. Living by himself in Dorking, he wrote *The Crown of Life* during the winter of 1898–99. In the same year he began the Dickens' Prefaces, finishing them in 1899, a year in which he also wrote an unpublished novel 'Among the Prophets' as well as *Our Friend the Charlatan*. Though he was now forced to take medical advice, it was without much conviction, for he knew how ill he was, understood the extent of his own enfeeblement and resisted dependence as much as he could, preferring private remedies that alleviated the symptoms. At the end of 1898, for example, he told Morley Roberts that he had resorted to a concoction consisting of 'cocain, lead, zinc oxide, yoke of egg with milk!'[1] So he persevered, managing indeed to write three more books before he died: *The Private Papers of Henry Ryecroft*, *Will Warburton* and *Veranilda*. Whatever one may think about the extraordinary personal events of the last few years of Gissing's life, there seems little doubt that he devoted himself *primarily* to his writing.

Gissing's final years were extraordinary in many respects, but chiefly in the way in which he compulsively repeated the pattern of the earlier events associated with his two marriages. On earlier occasions he had abandoned the personal and professional contacts of a fairly settled existence. For one reason or another he had made a complete break of this kind when he went to the States, when he left

Boston, when he first went to London, when he moved to Exeter, when he settled in Brixton. He was rootless, restless, dislocated. In 1897 he had left his family and gone to Italy and in a sense, psychologically, was repeating himself, even though the immediate causes were his ill-health and his alienated wife. When he returned to England in the spring of 1898, he was miserable, ill, lonely, just as he had been during the months before he met Edith after his return from Greece. He needed to write a good book just as he had almost a decade earlier. Exactly at this time Gabrielle Fleury came into his life, liberated his imagination exactly as Helen and Edith had done, allowed him and provided him with the incentive to work, and gave his life a new interest which temporarily distracted him from himself. By himself in England, he rapidly wrote *The Crown of Life*. Then in the spring of 1899 he went to France to live with Gabrielle Fleury, who was to be his companion – he said 'wife' – for the rest of his life.

Once again an initial ecstasy was followed by an intense period of work in which the practical but fascinating difficulties of life loomed large. Once again he had rejected life, then craved for it; rejected one wife, needed another; rejected one kind of domesticity, then committed himself, almost immediately, to another kind. The dupe of his own ambitions, he not only planned to put his intellectual and literary plans first, but in fact did so, only to find himself haunted by the desire for friendship, a woman companion, the pleasures of hearth and home. Within this pattern of events, Gabrielle Fleury was an unwitting but loving and understanding accomplice, for she had the same needs.

When Gissing wrote to Bertz to tell him he was going to Siena, he said that his motives were several. 'First of all, though my health seems greatly improved, I still have a little cough, and I want, if possible, to get rid of this altogether. Secondly, I am weary, for the time, of England, and long unutterably for the glorious warmth and colour of the south. Thirdly, it is clear to me that my historical novel will benefit greatly by studies made on the spot.'[2] A pretty cool explanation, one thinks at first, from someone in the process of leaving his wife and children. For better or worse, Gissing really did believe egotistically that *his* life was separate from that of his family, that it was *his* not his family life he could share with his friends, and indeed that there would be no point in doing otherwise, because no connection existed between his main concern, writing, and these other domestic matters which in his mind – so he pretended to himself – were of subsidiary importance. He seems to have been unaware of the ironies implicit in his own position or of the possibility that a neutral observer might have questioned his motives. What he had decided to do was bound to be reasonable. More than that: it was necessary and close to having been forced upon him by circumstance. Thus, in this same letter of 13 September 1897, he gave his friend a straightforward account of what he intended to do.

> My plan is this. As I have promised to finish the little book on Dickens by the end of November, I go first of all to Siena – a tranquil place, which will not excite me, and where I can work steadily day after day. This task will, I hope, be finished in time to leave me a month or six weeks of fine weather, and this I shall use in a journey of serious purpose. From Siena I go by rail to Rome, and from Rome I shall travel by carriage along the Via Appia, through Terracina,and turn off at length to Monte Cassino, where I hope to lodge for a day or two in the monastery of my old friend St. Benedict. Thence, to Naples, where I have to call upon Marion Crawford, the novelist, (he lives at Sorento,) who, I hope, will give me letters of introduction to useful people in Calabria. Thus furnished, I take ship at Naples (the Messina steamer) for *Paola*, on the Calabrian coast, where these steamers call. (This is the town of S. Francesco di Paolo, you know.) Thence I can travel by diligence, across the mountains, to Cosenza, where Alaric died. Here I touch the railway again, and with its help I mean to explore all (or nearly all) Magna Graecia, which may possibly yield me material for a book of travel-sketches. The Editor of the *Daily Chronicle* has asked me to send him anything I think likely to suit the paper. I shall buy photographs, and make rough drawings, for the illustration of my proposed book.[3]

A long paragraph from this letter is quoted in its entirety because it confirms once again the way of living that had been Gissing's throughout his life. He did more or less exactly what he said in this letter that he would do. To his various friends he fed various versions of his plans. To some he said nothing. Later he would rationalize his actions and in particular blame his awful domestic life for his decision to go to Italy. Yet he was clearly doing exactly what *he* wanted to do. He was not cut out for a more stable existence than the one he had adopted, so deeply ingrained was his rootless, *fin-de-siècle*, wandering attitude to life. This fact was rarely acknowledged to those people to whom he wrote letters. Nonetheless, fact it was. As such, it determined the kind of friendship of which he was capable and influences the view that must be taken of his friendship with Gabrielle Fleury.

To Siena he went as he had planned, settling first at Via delle Belle Arti 18, and later at Via Franciosa 8, within five minutes' walk of the cathedral. There is an interesting juxtaposition in the recently published letters of Gissing to Henry Hick as edited by Pierre Coustillas. In his letter to Hick from Epsom dated 14 September 1897 he said: 'I am utterly worn out with my confusion of business – can hardly hold the pen tonight.' Not many days later, in the next surviving letter which he wrote in Siena on 27 September, his tone was very different: 'Comfortably settled in private lodgings, and already at work.' In the same letter he described his quarters in the Via Belle Arti with a relish that in England would have been uncharacteristic of him. His room had four ten-foot high windows 'with sun shutters outside, and board shutters within' and a 'glorious view of the Cathedral' just up the hill, 'gleaming marble agst deep blue sky'. In short, he had found a secret, quiet place in which he could work, the domestic side of life being entirely taken care of by the Italian family with whom he lodged for just £4 a month for full room and board.

The twentieth-century visitor to Siena can see easily enough why Gissing found the city a congenial work retreat. The deeply-shaded, narrow alleys that twist and turn down the hill toward the old city walls are typical of the kind of place Gissing customarily searched out for himself on the Continent, and indeed elsewhere. Always he chose a place that was inexpensive, hidden away, and free from distracting noise. (Italian voices, organ grinders, street sounds were not distractions: English voices and tourist sounds were.) Thus he could tell Bertz that there was much 'shouting and howling' day and night and a 'great row' from the carts trundling between the houses without being disturbed, really, by the noise of a life that did not in the slightest way impinge upon him. The second of his Siena houses in particular, to which he moved only because someone died in the first was very like, for practical purposes, the family house in Wakefield, though so very dissimilar in appearance: he could retreat within it, secretively, in an extreme of privacy. Because in Siena he was known to be a stranger, an outsider, and was treated as such, he could live naturally; that is, in a way that was natural for him, in that he did not have to be anxious or concerned at all about other people. In a happy, relaxed state of mind he quickly wrote the book that had been commissioned by Holland Rose and which was eventually published by Blackie as *Charles Dickens: A Critical Study*. The manuscript was posted to his agent, Colles, on 8 November 1897; by 9 December he had returned the corrected typescript and by 2 January had despatched the corrected proofs of the English edition to Dodd, Mead in the States for the American edition that was to appear more or less simultaneously. This book, written from memory, was a critical *tour de force*. Admittedly, he had been thinking about it for half a year or so. Still, to write an assessment of the whole of Dickens' work in so short a space of time was a considerable achievement. His health held. Though he had chosen Siena not only because of its hilltop location which he anticipated would be good for his lungs but also, perversely, because of the fact that he did not like the place and could therefore expect to work, he seems to have had a relaxed, productive time there. And why should he not have had? The past had once again been obliterated and, as he told Bertz, he felt 'a great desire to get away to the glorious south'.[4]

Gissing realized that his attempts to recapture the atmosphere of

the Roman Empire would be incomplete until he had visited Calabria. Armed as always with his guide book, and with crystal-clear recollections of Latin authors and also of Gibbon (and maybe carrying
with him many of the relevant volumes, for he was once interro-
gated in Southern Italy for carrying so many), he once again reso-
lutely set out, determined to see as the Romans had seen, and at the
same time record his sensations and experiences for the sake of the
later book. Despite the protestations of his Neapolitan friends that
he ought not to waste his time in Calabria, he was once again driven
by a harsh, private desire of the kind that he had never hesitated
throughout his life to satisfy.

In *By the Ionian Sea*, the book in which this journey was recorded
in a simple, direct way, Gissing described his mood as the steamer
moved away from Naples.

> From my seat near the stern of the vessel I could discern no human
> form; it was as though I voyaged quite alone in the silence of this magic
> sea . . . The stillness of a dead world laid its spell on all that lived. To-day
> seemed an unreality, an idle impertinence; the real was that long-buried
> past which gave its meaning to all about me, touching the night with
> infinite pathos. Best of all, one's own being became lost to consciousness;
> the mind knew only the phantasmal forms it shaped, and was at peace in
> vision.[5]

In this state of mind he travelled, despite great discomfort and inconvenience, to Paolo, Cosenza, Taranto, Cotrone, Catanzaro,
Squillace and Reggio, searching out en route the ikons, ruins and
monuments that would allow him to conjure up Aleric and Cassio-
dorus and meditate on the changes that had occurred during the
previous thirteen or fourteen centuries.

For whatever the cause, whether the intense spell of work which had
allowed him to complete the Dickens book, or the frequent drenchings
he received while travelling, or the totally inadequate diet he allowed
himself, he became seriously ill in Cotrone – seriously enough, that is,
for him to be carried back to his hotel unconscious, for him to submit
to the care of the local doctor, one Dr. Sculco, and for him to be
delayed indefinitely (and this worried him intensely!) while his letters
were waiting for him in another town. He had a high fever, accentuated, as the doctor confirmed, by serious congestion of the lung.

> The night which followed was perhaps the most horrible I ever passed.
> Crushed with a sense of uttermost fatigue, I could get no rest. From time
> to time a sort of doze crept upon me, and I said to myself, 'Now I shall
> sleep;' but on the very edge of slumber, at the moment when I was falling
> into oblivion, a hand seemed to pluck me back into consciousness. In the
> same instant there gleamed before my eyes a little circle of fire, which
> blazed and expanded into immensity, until its many-coloured glare beat
> upon my brain and thrilled me with torture. No sooner was the intoler-

able light extinguished than I burst into a cold sweat; an icy river poured about me; I shook, and my teeth chattered, and so for some minutes I lay in anguish, until the heat of fever re-asserted itself, and I began once more to toss and roll.[6]

Whatever Gissing may have felt about this he concealed, at least in *By the Ionian Sea*. Instead he indulged himself and his reader with chat about the 'medieval' doctor's prescription of meat and Marsala, the commotion in the inn, and (apparently without an awareness of the psychological implications) the dream in which on the second night his suffering was 'alleviated'. He felt 'as one involved in a moral disaster' that he might never live to see 'the Lacinian promontory', and La Colonna. Half-delirious, he dreamt of being there and *saw* the place, in multiplicity and detail'. One dream he recorded in detail. When Hannibal was about to return to Carthage, he made Cotron his headquarters and slaughtered those Italian mercenaries who refused to accompany him to Africa. 'This event I beheld. I saw the strand by Croton; the promontory with its temple; not as I know the scene today, but as it must have looked to those eyes more than two thousand years ago. The soldiers of Hannibal doing massacre, the perishing mercenaries, supported my closest gaze, and left no curiosity unsatisfied.'[7]

Gissing did not recover, but he recovered enough to continue, enduring the vast squalor and inconvenience of small wayside inns for the sake of a deeply treasured set of sensations, before returning to Naples and then to Rome. He wrote in the final paragraph of *By the Ionian Sea*:

So hard a thing to catch and to retain, the mood corresponding perfectly to an intellectual bias, hard, at all events, for he who cannot shape his life as he will, and whom circumstance ever menaces with dreary harassment. Alone and quiet, I heard the washing of the waves; I saw the evening fall on cloud-wreathed Etna, the twinkling lights come forth upon Scylla and Charybdis; and, as I looked my last towards the Ionian Sea, I wished it were mine to wander endlessly amid the silence of the ancient world, today and all its sounds forgotten.

As he travelled back during the early part of 1898 he began to recover his other self. In Rome, he stayed first at Via del Boschetto, 41A, another hideout, and then at the Hôtel Alibert; from Rome he commented gloomily on modern life. Roused by the Dreyfus case, he told Bertz that the French nation was 'making a very base and disgusting figure before the world'.[8] Of the Italian nation he said in the same letter that it was being 'crushed by poverty, swamped in the ignobleness of modern life with none of its compensating luxuries'. In February, on the 12th or 13th, he moved to the Hôtel Alibert so that he could get food without going out for it and so that he could be with H. G. Wells and his wife, who arrived early in March. He showed them the sights, was at ease with them, acted as interpreter and of course talked literature – in a way, no doubt, which helped Wells form his own ideas of the kind of book he wanted to write. But at heart Gissing was restless. He wanted to be back in England. He wanted to be at work again. He had done all he had intended and now the misery of his illness was exasercbated by the fact of his being abroad where he believed he could not expect better medical attention than he had received in Cotrone. Bertz prescribed creosotal (creosote carbonate in an oil base) and Gissing gallantly said it helped his cough. In truth, though, he was at the end of his tether. Eventually, after about a month in Rome with Wells, he left on 14 April, spent four days first in Berlin then in Potsdam with Bertz – his only comments on this disappointing visit related to his 'evil German bed' which had no sheet or blanket but only a huge feather pillow to cover one. Germany otherwise was dismissed in a single, terse and characteristic diary entry: 'the sheer *commonness* of it all, after Italy' – and, sick at heart, he returned to England on 20 April, when he went as usual to spend a few weeks in Wakefield.

By dint of elaborate arrangements for the forwarding of mail, arrangements which were essential to a writer who needed to keep in touch with his publishers, Gissing had been able to correspond with Eliza Orme and he therefore knew as he travelled back to England both that it was impossible for him ever again to have direct dealings with Edith and that provision, of a sort, had been made for Alfred. If only he could stay out of their way, he felt he could manage.

From Gissing's point of view the situation he left behind him was insoluble, because naturally enough Edith would not agree to any arrangement that involved giving up Alfred. She must have had an extremely miserable few years, moving from one place to another, looking after Alfred single-handedly and never having an adequate explanation of what had happened to her husband. Eliza Orme bore the brunt of her violent bad temper. 'Long letter from Miss Orme, telling of brutal attack and fury' was a typical diary entry during the winter of 1897–8. After about six months of trying to cope, Miss Orme recommended a legal solution and this was arranged in March 1898 by Gissing's solicitor, Brewster, Gissing to pay her twenty-five shillings a week 'towards household expenses.' Neither party had much freedom in the matter. During this period, Gissing wrote openly about his broken marriage to both Morley Roberts and Henry Hick. 'I often wish I were out of the way', he told Hick at one point. 'Then someone or other would look after the two boys, & that mad-woman could be supported by her relatives.'[9] The 'someone or other' was Eliza Orme. She endured Edith as best she could, helped her as best she could. This included a fearsome episode that Gissing recorded in his diary: 'Miss Orme writes that E attacked her landlord and his wife with a stick, and a policeman had to be called.' There was another occasion when Edith tore up the bushes in the garden in a blind fury.

This is to anticipate a little. When he got back to England he was as anxious as could be to avoid confrontations with Edith and pretended for a while that he expected to settle in some remote, rural spot like Worcestershire! Gissing did not repeat the mistake he had made when he returned from Italy in 1890 – the mistake of dissipating the summer by spending it in Wakefield with his sisters. On the contrary, he immediately went into hiding. For years he had nursed the idea of living in the same manner as George Meredith, close enough to London to permit visits to his publishers, the British Museum and the London Library, but far enough in the country to be safe from intrusion. Not surprisingly Gissing chose Dorking, where early in May he found temporary lodgings at 7 Clifton Terrace, about three miles from Meredith's house at Box Hill. At least he called it a lodging in an off-hand way when he wrote to Bertz, but he in fact leased the house for a year and used a sizeable part of the £350 advance he received for *The Town Traveller* to establish himself in reasonable comfort. Though the rent of 7 Clifton Terrace was £42 a year and the wage of his housekeeper, Mrs. Broughton, £18 ('a most serious step, but I found there was no choice'), Gissing as usual exaggerated his problems, telling Henry Hick for example that the expense of setting up house had reduced him to 'beggary', whereas he had in fact established himself in a type of odmestic comfort not so very different from that described in *The Private Papers of Henry Ryecroft*.[10] He was determined to be alone, so much so that he asked Henry Hick to take his son, Walter, for the summer holidays: Walter stayed in New Romney for seven weeks and Gissing paid his friend, Hick, fifteen shillings a week for his son's board. This arrangement seems extraordinary and must be taken as a measure of Hick's understanding, shared with Clara Collett and Eliza Orme, of Gissing's desperate predicament. Things had gone too far, he was too hard pressed, for him to be expected to do anything other than what he had decided to do. Gissing himself, however, could not confess openly what his friends observed and his letters, in consequence, are sometimes disingenuous to say the least. 'My one fear', he told Bertz, 'is that some idiot may discover my address and make a newspaper paragraph of it.' His wife knew he would have to return to England, had tried to discover his whereabouts from the Wakefield Gissings, and was expected to be a nuisance. 'Of course I must hide myself,' said Gissing, 'in constant fear of attack by that savage.'

Such a situation could not continue. As usual when he was alone and not working, Gissing began to fret. His letters became querulous. He had treated himself to a home but lacked a life to live in it. Throughout the summer he continued to worry about his health, his wife, his money problems. 'Illness and toil and trouble!' he told Bertz in July; 'it is not my lungs that are now troubling me, but attacks of rheumatism, and the beginning of gout.' The old pattern of events was beginning to establish itself: he needed to work but had not yet started his new book. Eventually his wife found him early in September, turning up one day in Dorking with Alfred, and Gissing recorded in his diary that he had refused to listen to her pleading. In fact he sent her away so brusquely that he forgot to say a word to his son. This dreadful experience seems to have provided the release he needed to begin *The Crown of Life* over which he had been brooding throughout the summer. He knew that he had marred his reputation with *The Town Traveller* and that it was time to write a 'serious' book. With his wife out of the way, he set to work.

Long before this encounter, Gissing had persuaded himself that Edith's rebellious, hot-tongued, angry attitude towards him exonerated him from any need to behave responsibly towards her. He did not understand feelings that found expression mostly in anger. In the correspondence with other people which is so full of recrimination he never faced squarely the question of whether his wife had anything to be angry about. Uneducated, aggressive, too prone to treating him to home truths, too unsympathetic to his private irrationalities as a writer, Edith had become uncompliant and was expendable. He doggedly refused to search out any compromise.

Gissing's attitude to Edith, self-justification apart, was largely determined by the events of the late summer. His life had taken a new direction, one for which he had prepared, as it were, by working himself into a state of utter despondency. 'Medical examination goes on,' he had told H. G. Wells on 26 June. 'Latest report: decided phthisis (though not very active) – strong gouty tendency – uncertainty of heart – bad emphysema – liver at any moment to give serious trouble – disposition to eczema. It's all rather discouraging.'[11] Indeed it was. He wondered if it could be given out that he was dead so that 'with comfort of half a dozen intimates' he could work in peace for a year or two writing posthumous novels. His longstanding desire to secrete himself away now acquired a pathological intensity.

As usual with Gissing, profound turbulence in the depth of his being did not prevent his disporting himself on the surface of life. His doctor had ordered exercise and on the weekend of 30 June he went to stay with H. G. Wells (having with difficulty ensured that his housekeeper would have a relative to keep her company in 7 Clifton Terrace during his absence), Wells reporting that Gissing was very inexpert on the 'ironmongery' and that when he fell off, as he did frequently, he 'lay in the grass at the roadside, helpless with mirth'.[12] These extremes of elation and melancholy, accentuated by extreme ill-health and by an egotistical, non-informative type of introspection into which he relapsed when he was not doing the one thing that made him happy, were the same outward expressions of inner conflict that had manifested themselves throughout his life, particularly at moments of crisis. Now, once again, his crises was that he did not know what to do with himself. He who had done so much, had travelled freely to the places he had wanted to visit, had lived independently on his writing alone, as he had wished, and had published eighteen books, felt self-pityingly that he had not lived.

With Gissing in this state of mind, Gabrielle Fleury entered his life. She entered it and declined to leave. Born in Nevers on 21 November 1868 to Edouard Fleury, head cashier of the Docks and Warehouses Company at Marseilles, and his wife Anna, formerly Senly, Gabrielle Fleury was in fact of remote Italian origin. She knew English, Italian, and German, was a good pianist and is said to have had a 'passion' for classical music. Pierre Coustillas, in his edition of the correspondence between Gabrielle Fleury and Gissing, gathered together some contemporary opinions about her character and there seems to have been general agreement that, in the words of her cousin, Mme Le Mallier, she was 'highly strung and passionate' but was also 'given to depression and fits of hesitation, looking on the darker rather than on the brighter side of things, all the more when living alone'. She was not, in point of fact, living alone when Gissing met her. She lived with her mother and father in a flat in Paris. Like Gissing, she was a lonely person, despite her love of books, her vast interest in literature and a fairly wide circle of literary friends, including Madame Lardin de Musset, niece of the poet, and Sully-Prudhomme, to whom she had for a while been engaged.

Gabrielle Fleury discovered Gissing's whereabouts in the same way as Edith, that is, through his publishers. She wanted to translate *New Grub Street*, applied to Smith, Elder for permission to do so, and was directed to Gissing himself, perhaps through his agent, W. M. Colles. An exchange of notes failed to bring about a meeting in London and since Gissing had gone to Worcester Park, so that Wells could teach him to ride his bicycle, she was invited to meet him there. On 6 July 1898 they met in Wells' home. Because Smith, Elder and not Gissing owned the copyright of *New Grub Street*, there was little business for them to transact, though he assured her then and later that there would be no difficulty about making cuts. 'When all is decided,' that is, when she had made arrangements for the publication of a translation, 'you shall let me have your copy, and I will return it to you with the passages marked for omission.'[13] This was on 10 July. Gissing was so enthusiastic that he set to work immediately. He also returned to Dorking, cycling all the way with Wells and his wife and happily noting in his diary that he could 'descend hill with foot on rests.' Evidently something had occurred between them at Wells' house, for he said he would remain in Dorking until her visit. This visit could not occur immediately because she had gone to stay with friends in Suffolk but on 26 July she arrived in Dorking on the 10.30 from Victoria Station and their life together in a sense began.

Certainly Gissing was strongly affected. 'How often I shall see your beautiful hazel eyes', he wrote the following day, 'looking at me with kindness, with indulgence for my morbid weaknesses and all my wearisome peculiarities.'[14] She must have been affected, too, for she sent him in reply 'the kindest and sweetest letter' he had ever received. 'You say I ought not to feel alone here,' he replied, 'because your thoughts are with me – Dear, to be remembered by you is a great privilege; but more than ever I should have dared to hope; but I am of such a passionate nature, and imagination cannot satisfy me.'[15] An ardent correspondence followed until Gabrielle returned to Paris without seeing him again.

That their feeling for each other was mutual is amply demonstrated by the explicit and effusive nature of Gissing's letters. They had met twice and he had gone no further than to kiss her hand at Dorking Station, yet he wrote without inhibition.

> You and I, my love, what may we not make of life – if fate permits it! I see in you not only the beautiful girl whom I love ardently, whom I worship for her beauty's sake; not only the exquisite being, whose words are poetry, whose mind and heart are so nobly human; but the good, earnest, loyal woman whose companionship is the supreme desire of a man with intellectual and moral aims. What am I that you should give me your love? But my unspeakable gratitude will perhaps help to make me less ignoble compared with you. Put your hand in mine, dearest, and see what my life will become in the strength of such a union.

The friendship had begun that was to end only with Gissing's death a little more than five years later. With the naïve honesty of the egotist, Gissing told her that he had felt himself to be at a 'crisis', (did he not have in mind those earlier crises, like the one that resulted in his second marriage?) that he feared he would lose his 'power of creation', that it was only too likely that he would have sought 'the companionship of some woman' who would have involved him in new unhappiness, and that she had saved him from 'peril' by giving him 'security and worthiness'.[16] Gabrielle Fleury was undaunted. Indeed the correspondence could only have continued by her contributing to it with equal ardour. On her recommendation, he began to eat extract of cereal, sent her a large photograph and said he was intoxicated by the 'odour' of the hair she sent him.

In 1920, long after Gissing's death, Gabrielle Fleury told Clara Collett that she hesitated to allow her correspondence with Gissing to be published and that indeed she thought it might be better to destroy all the letters, because unsympathetic people who could not 'penetrate his feelings and nature' might easily tax him, unfairly, for 'playing on my sensibility and compassion.' She compromised by editing the letters to the state represented by Pierre Coustillas' edition. Since the letters as published are extremely effusive and extravagant, one imagines they must have been more so before Gabrielle Fleury went to work with the scissors. She erased or cut out bluntly sexual or physical passages. She also deleted remarks of Gissing's that assumed her early desire for a love affair. This was not so much because she wanted to misrepresent her part in the relationship at this early stage, though she saw Gissing's extravagance of phrase for what it was and reprimanded him accordingly, but because she was later criticised for having been responsible for separating him from his children. Thus when Gissing wrote in October, for example: 'I have no right to offer her my love, nor accept hers', she changed the words 'not accept hers' to 'or ask for hers'. When she erased the end of the sentence that began 'I have told you how highly I value physical beauty, and you know that . . .' she wrote over the erasure 'I love you with every kind of love'. If her feelings, however, had not been the same as his, she would not have replied at all to the fulsome letters he wrote in September. Nor would that most inhibited of men have continued to write in such an extravagant manner without encouragement.

From July, when they first met, to the end of September Gissing and Gabrielle Fleury, if the correspondence is to be trusted, consciously or unconsciously removed one by one the real and psychological obstacles to their knowing each other. Gissing did not tell her about his first marriage: she did not know about it until after he had died. But he did tell her about Edith, to whom he said he was legally but not morally bound and to whom he would only give the money she absolutely needed because to give more 'would be to encourage her in all manner of follies and even vices'; about his brother, 'an excellent naturalist, an admirable husband and father'; about his mother, whom he said he scarcely knew; about his children, saying he was devoted to Walter who was very 'intelligent but of difficult disposition' – though he would never 'bother' Gabrielle with them; and about two other very important matters, firstly that she would have to realise that he needed a lot of time by himself so that he could write (he knew the consequences of not making this clear) and secondly that there was little chance that Edith would agree to a divorce, since she demanded custody of both children. Embarrassingly, he tried to tell her more about himself than he had ever told anyone else. 'I am hungry for life – the true life, which I have never known. My nature is a strange compound of the bohemian and the bourgeois; I am passionate but at the same time I am very domestic. To the woman who loved me I should be absolutely faithful – .'[17] And so on. In August he wrote with considerable smugness: 'Is it not mere justice that I, who have lived twenty years, and more, hungering for love, idealizing woman, should at length be loved by a woman capable of understanding me?'[18] Gissing won the day. He persuaded her that his health was not an obstacle to their union. He persuaded her that Edith was such an objectionable person that he was morally free to live with her. And he persuaded her that, though he was willing to travel to Paris, she should visit him in England since he could not afford a break in his work routine.

Reading between the lines of Gissing's letters to Gabrielle Fleury during this period, one can see easily enough that like a young lover she tested him out on almost every subject under the sun. She did not know about the immense trouble he was having with Edith through his solicitor; that Edith had left or had been thrown out of her rooms during August; that the furniture had been stored and the fate of Edith and Alfred left undecided; that he had heard of fits of violence and that she had written 'an insulting and threatening post-card to Miss Orme, addressed "Bad Eliza Orme"'. Least of all did Gabrielle Fleury know that Gissing was resolved never to live with Edith however she behaved or, later, that he had turned her away from his door when she eventually found him in Dorking. It scarcely needs to be said that Gissing was not the first person to woo one woman by vilifying another. At all events she was satisfied and agreed to visit Gissing again in Dorking.

This she did in October, staying this time in the house for roughly the week beginning the 8th. During the visit they agreed to live with each other come what may and to wait only until the following spring, by which time Gissing hoped he would have sold some work. Afterwards he continued to say things in his letters that were not calculated to amuse emancipated women, for example when he said that Michelet was wrong to say in his novels that women could not live alone. 'Why, most women before their marriage are passionless. Of course it is the man who is maddened and tortured by loneliness.'[19] There is no record of how Gabrielle Fleury received this remark! But she did react when Gissing told her 'the foolish thing' he did one morning. 'Waking just after daybreak, I lay quite still and began in a low voice, to speak to *you* as if you were beside me . . .'[20] She deleted the rest of the sentence.

Just as Gissing had written the strongest part of *Workers in the Dawn* when he married Helen and had quickly written *New Grub Street* when he was waiting to marry Edith, in both cases after a period of acute depression, so now, between Gabrielle's visit to Dorking in October and Christmas, or at least mid-January 1899, he quickly completed *The Crown of Life*. He had given his new agent, Pinker, *carte blanche* to place the book as best he could, sending him the

novel to be typed as it was written. Consequently Gissing was correcting the typescript of the early part of the novel at the same time as he
was writing the concluding chapters. On 16 January 1899 he mailed
the last three chapters of the manuscript and two days later he wrote
to Pinker again: 'Today I post to you the whole of the typescript,
revised.'[21] Simultaneously, he was busy with his Dickens' prefaces.
During the summer of 1898, he had been invited to write introductions
to the volumes of the new Rochester edition of Dickens' work to be
published by Methuen. Between 18 August 1898 and 23 February
1899 he wrote six of them, specifically the prefaces to *David Copper-
field*, *Dombey and Son*, *The Pickwick Papers*, *Nicholas Nickleby*,
Bleak House, and *Oliver Twist*. Clearly the excitement of meeting
Gabrielle Fleury had released Gissing, as usual, for his work. The
depth or meaning of his relationship with her was still be be discovered, but at least he could work and when he worked he was happy.

So he continued until the end of February when he collapsed from
overwork. 'For six weeks I have been very ill', he told Bertz on 31
March; 'an attack of influenza, followed by lung congestion, pleurisy
and all sorts of things'.[22] Nonetheless he was not to be prevented from
packing up his things at the beginning of May, so that he could join
Gabrielle Fleury in France. They met in Rouen at the Hôtel de Paris
on 6 May 1899. People have been a little puzzled by Gissing's note in
his diary (for 7 May): 'In the evening, our ceremony. Dear Maman's
emotion, and G's sweet dignity.' In point of fact, however, they made
a perfectly simple arrangement. Gissing did not tell anyone that he
was going to live with Gabrielle Fleury, except Bertz and Wells. And
Gabrielle Fleury returned to Paris, after a honeymoon on the Normandy coast at St.-Pierre-en-Port, as 'Mrs. Gissing'.

9

Death in Exile

THROUGHOUT THE SPRING of 1899, including the period in which Gissing had been desperately ill in bed, he and Gabrielle Fleury had concerned themselves with practicalities. If, being English, he simply could not exist without frequent baths, could he take to Paris with him one of the new folding rubber hip-baths? Would he get for her a type of *sac-de-voyage* she had seen in London? Should he not buy himself some flannel shirts? (No, he had tried that and the shirts had shrunk.) More important, how would she sign business papers when they were living with each other? (She overcame this by handing over everything she owned to her mother.) And could not a detective provide grounds for a divorce? (Gissing employed 'a very respectable private enquiry agent' who failed to provide evidence against Edith.)

Left to himself, Gissing would barely have had energy for such matters. Either he wanted a study with his bureau, his revolving chair and his lamp (the only possessions he eventually took to Paris) or he was prepared to live out of a suitcase while travelling from place to place. Despite poor sales, he knew himself to be, by 1898, an established author who did not need to justify the style of life by which he had accomplished so much. Yet he responded to whatever Gabrielle Fleury said: his willingness to do so was positive proof, to him, that what he felt was special. Special it was for Gabrielle too, who simplified everything by deciding that they would live together whether he could get a divorce or not. 'Nous nous marions parce que nous nous aimons, parce que nous sommes sûrs l'un de l'autre, non par convenance mondaine.'[1] She had, after all, read, understood and appreciated his novels; she was ready for the emancipated life so many Gissing characters had desired; like many of her contemporaries she craved for the personal relationship that transcended social convention and social conformity; and like Gissing she already devoted her main energy to literature and art. Now she had found her ideal companion. From the beginning they called their life together a marriage and Gissing, from the beginning, called Gabrielle Fleury his wife. With hindsight one can see that Gabrielle Fleury needed the appearance of marriage for the sake of her parents, particularly her father who died only a few months before her union with Gissing, while in other respects she wanted a modern relationship outside the law, provided it was an equal one, not involving the idea of man and mistress but rather the rational decision of man and woman each committing themselves to a shared life; whereas Gissing, by contrast, while having no hesitation about living with Gabrielle Fleury while still married to Edith, actually wanted marriage more than emancipation. He craved – as he always had – the secure comforts of hearth and home and he retained (and could not by any stretch of the imagination bring himself to abandon) all those domestic sentiments, expectations and associations that made it necessary for him to call the woman he lived with his wife, even though the word was needed for the person to whom he was already married.

Late in April 1899 Gissing packed up his possessions in the Dorking house. As had been the case when he married Edith, the precise date was determined by the expiry of his lease. He said goodbye to his housekeeper, who was soon to provide the model for the ideal housekeeper in *The Private Papers of Henry Ryecroft*. Then, after a few uncomfortable nights in the White Hart Inn in Lewes, Gissing crossed to France from Newhaven on 6 May to meet Gabrielle Fleury and her mother in Rouen. For 7 May Gissing noted in his diary: 'In the evening, our ceremony. Dear Maman's emotion, and G's sweet dignity', but, as Pierre Coustillas has suggested, the ceremony no doubt was little more than the putting on of the rings Gissing had purchased in London. Gabrielle was to travel back to Paris as Mrs. Gissing and the Fleury family, including Gabrielle's brother, were not to be troubled by an open acknowledgment of the truth until after Gissing's death. Gissing was overcome with emotion. He had longed for companionship, had always desired the love and friendship of a woman who was his intellectual equal, had in his letters worshipped and idealized Gabrielle Fleury, and now was with her. She, too, was clearly motivated by the strongest of desires. In Rouen, they recovered the high rapture they had known in Dorking and were happy.

Had the middle-aged couple, as they prepared to embark upon what for both of them was a rather desperate adventure, wilfully deceived themselves about Gissing's health during the winter of 1898–9? Certainly Gabrielle Fleury had frequently expressed her concern, the concern of a lover, not yet the concern of a wife. Certainly Gissing told her, or implied that his ailments could be remedied. Whether in all those letters, the correspondence of lovers, they had faced steadily the real difficulties of the situation is more doubtful. Gissing himself adopted a cynical attitude to the matter. If he was going to die young, why refuse the opportunity to live with someone he liked and who liked him? He lacked self-knowledge in this as in other aspects of his own life, but in any case was without responsibility in the matter since Gabrielle Fleury desired the union so strongly. Thus the meeting in Rouen was a shock for her. Gissing was emaciated, only just beginning to recover from the serious illness of the winter months: he was underweight and Gabrielle quickly gathered the reality of it all from his bony ribs. She was surprised, too, by the amount of rest he needed; by his sleeplessness; by his erratic hours; by his cough and by the difficulty he had with his breathing. Obviously they tried to take the matter in hand. Had they not been separated? Would not Gissing now have someone to look after him? Was it surprising that he was run down after the heavy, solitary labours of the winter? Events show clearly how worried they quickly became. The rest of May they spent alone at Saint-Pierre-en-Port and nearby places in Normandy. Meredith had probably told Gissing about the Normandy coast and Saint-Pierre-en-Port would have been a much more isolated place than it is today. On the other hand, the huge and, in photographs, rather forbidding Hôtel des Terrasses (no longer standing), was designed for family holidays, not significant intellectual encounters, and the couple soon moved along the coast to Fécamp. As planned, they then went to the Fleury flat at 13 rue de Siam, in Paris, where they were to live for the next two years with Gabrielle's mother (though the plaque on the street wall states, deceptively, 'in 1900') and where Gissing immediately set to work on a novel to be called 'Among the Prophets' and, simultaneously, on the rest of the Dickens' prefaces. Whether chiefly for the sake of a summer holiday, or because of anxiety about Gissing's lungs, they then set off again, this time for Switzerland.

Whatever the reason for this expedition, the choice of destination was undoubtedly the consequence of Gissing's physical condition. He had tried the seaside resorts of England; he had tried Devon, Italy, Calabria, Siena. Now, perhaps on the advice of Gabrielle's Paris doctor, they went to the mountains. In point of fact, Gissing had no idea whatsoever which climate would best help his condition: he talked of cure but in fact moved restlessly from place to place in the hope that he would be able to breathe more easily.

On 23 July 1899 he told Bertz: 'I am writing to you from a place called Samoëns, in Haute Savoie, where we are passing a week to prepare ourselves for the higher altitude of Trient in Switzerland.'[2] The weather, he said, was very good but the heat made walking impossible. This was hardly surprising. Gissing had found Dorking in February too hot, partly because of his health, partly because he habitually wore a heavy suit, underwear, a waistcoat and two Jaeger sweaters. It's very unlikely that the three of them knew what to expect when they travelled up the narrow valleys and gorges from Lake Geneva by steam-tram. With the help of guide books, Gissing had once again picked out a place of outstanding natural beauty. Even by steam-tram the journey up to Taninges was a long one: the extra leg of the journey to Samoëns would have added, as it still does, an exciting, exhilarating sense of remoteness and peace – just the kind of place that the secretive Gissing always searched out. There appears to be no record of whether or not they enjoyed themselves. Mme. Fleury may well have longed for the calm of Passy. Gissing would have missed the historical associations that usually gave his stay in a place its meaning. Gabrielle Fleury later said that she preferred stability and could not live a suitcase existence with the same pleasure as Gissing. Nonetheless, they must have enjoyed the peace and quiet of Samoëns. Even if his health prevented his enjoying the deep ravines and gorges that make the approach to Samoëns so spectacular, he would have liked the serenity of the little village, so much so that it must have been the condition of his lungs and his determination to go as high as possible that made them travel on to Trient when Mme. Fleury returned to Paris.

After a week they travelled along the shore of the lake and then climbed again, reaching Trient 'by diligence from Martigny.' Gissing enjoyed himself during this holiday, though he remarked that he still had to 'shake off the results of that long wretchedness' and that perhaps he would never 'wholly attain to a cheerfulness like that of other men'.[3] Though he thought about himself all the time, he was not sensitively introspective – that is, he never really came to terms with himself – and in consequence he perpetually confused the physical and the psychological, giving things a psychological explanation when they had a physical cause, and refusing, openly at least, to accept the possibility that his state of mind might have been the result of his physical condition. As a matter of fact such a possibility was not entertained at all widely during the nineteenth century. Gissing was a man of the age in believing in the independence of mind. On this subject he had written to Gabrielle, cryptically, in April: 'My life (I know) is still greatly a mystery to you; it can only be made clear in long and intimate talk. Reassure yourself on *one* point; I have no mental disease, in the strict sense of the word. No, no! – But it will all be clear to you very soon. (I mean, the psychological trouble.)'[4] In the previous letter, the one dated 1 April 1899, he had written along similar lines and had explained why his abnormal tendency to unhappiness had such a hold on him.

It is impossible, my own love, *to describe* to you those fits of misery. One cannot *describe* a nightmare. It is a mental illness, resulting from a whole lifetime of wretchedness. Since I was a boy until the day you said you loved me, I had never known a tranquil mind. The reason? – Poverty, frustrated ambition, and above all vain desire of love. Combine these things with the imaginative temper, and *must* not mental suffering – the gravest mental suffering – result?[5]

All this, which was more a commentary on his past rather than his present life, Gissing forgot in Haute Savoie and Switzerland. Since he never again tried mountains to solve his breathing problems (except when he went up to Saint-Jean-Pied-de-Port for the last few months of his life), it seems likely that the extreme height of Trient did not provide the medical solution he sought. He was too ill for anything but alleviation of the symptoms. On the other hand, he and Gabrielle Fleury obviously needed the time together and the absence of letters from this period is reassuring. Furthermore, whatever his 'psychological trouble,' he quickly settled to work again once this extended holiday was over.

Free from Edith and highly excited by this idea of living with and being loved by Gabrielle, Gissing entered with an extraordinary determination into the last creative period of his life. From June 1899 to May 1901 he shared the Paris flat with Gabrielle and Mme. Fleury, with a number of brief breaks, notably the trip to Switzerland that has already been mentioned (late summer and autumn of 1899), to England (in March and April 1900) and to St. Honoré-les-Bains near Autun (August–October 1901).

In June 1899, after returning from Normandy and before going to Switzerland, he wrote three more Dickens' prefaces, those for *The Old Curiosity Shop* (16–19 June), *Martin Chuzzlewit* (20–23 June) and *Barnaby Rudge* (24–26 June). As soon as he had finished these, he turned his attention to *By the Ionian Sea* which he had been carrying around with him as a pile of notes, photographs, sketches and rough drafts. The book was completed by 9 August 1899. As on previous occasions, for he was a writer first and foremost, he made a major effort to earn enough money for his new life.

The greater part of the winter of 1899–1900 was devoted to the writing of 'Among the Prophets', the book he sent to Pinker when he had completed it and then ordered him to burn. March and April of 1900 were spent in Wakefield and other parts of England and then, back in France, Gissing continued to work hard, writing the whole of *Our Friend the Charlatan* between May and the end of August and, in September and October, in St. Honoré-les-Bains writing a first draft of *Ryecroft*. How reminiscent all this was of the years in Exeter when Gissing tried gallantly to support his second marriage by writing furiously. And how ironical that, despite the immense effort, he again experienced financial difficulties that such a prolific writer deserved, really, to escape.

Gissing had no financial resources on which to fall back. It is doubtful whether he ever saved a penny in his life. Consequently he was completely vulnerable to the fact that payment for a book did not always coincide with the acceptance of it. Since the sums of money involved were relatively small, and since Gissing's expenses had increased, delays could be extremely inconvenient and embarrassing.

Though unfortunate for Gissing the matter was really very simple. The strategy of trying to last from one book to the next by means of self-deprivation could no more work in Paris in 1900, when he had commitments which called for a steady income, than it had five years earlier when he had had to provide for his family. *The Town Traveller* had been published at the end of August 1898. For it he had received advances of £200 on the English and £100 on the American edition, enough to let him settle in Dorking in reasonable comfort. At that point he felt complacent about his fortunes – at least financially. Like Hardy and Meredith, the only English novelists he really respected, he had established himself independently on the basis of what he had earned with his pen. If he had also had the royalty income better luck and better management would have brought him, all would have been well. *The Crown of Life* was published a little more than a year later, on 23 October 1899, and for this novel he had received advances of £300 on the English and £100 on the American edition.

He no doubt felt, therefore, that he could afford his long stay in Haute Savoie and Switzerland. A man of affairs could easily have pointed out that Gissing might have made better use of his money. A hostile critic could have observed that his complaints about not having a settled domestic life were incompatible with long, indulgent trips in the Alps, however economical his life might have been in hotels. Such observations would be without meaning. There is a type of person who *must* follow periods of intense work with fallow periods away from the place where the work is done. The change of pace, the travel, the variety, the enforced relaxation were necessary if work of such intensity was to be achieved at all. Gissing simply had to be able to afford the things that went with his particular way of working.

Be that as it may, he did not publish another novel until May 1901, by which time he was desperately short of cash. For *Our Friend the Charlatan*, which was the novel published in May, he received a lump sum payment of £350 for a seven-year lease of the copyright and an advance of £100 from Holt for the American edition. In June, *By the Ionian Sea* was published; for this Gissing received £130 from Chapman and Hall and £120 for the serial rights. During the same period, roughly speaking, he received just over £100 for his Dickens' prefaces, after the deduction of the agent's fees. Put one way this does not sound too bad: during the last four and a half years of his life, which he lived with Gabrielle Fleury, Gissing's average annual income was between £300 and £350. Not much, but enough. Averages, however, are of very little help to people. There were, in fact, long periods of strain in which funds were low and future income uncertain. One of the worst of these periods was that long, eighteen-month gap between *The Crown of Life* and *Our Friend the Charlatan*.

To live in such straightened circumstances gives one no freedom of action at all. Gabrielle Fleury and her mother had been managing before Gissing joined them, so they obviously could still. It later became a matter of importance to her that she had contributed financially to *his* survival and had not taken money which might have been spent on the two children. Nonetheless the psychological strain was sometimes, during the Paris winters of 1899–1900 and 1900–1, considerable. Minor friction occurred. Mme. Fleury ruled the household and Gissing began to resent the French pattern of living and the food itself. She said he was unreasonable to want bacon and eggs for breakfast. He later said, in moments of pique, that he had been starved. He was not invariably good company when a book did not go well: his spending a whole winter on 'Among the Prophets' and then ordering it to be burned would have perplexed the two women. Why give a man all those hours by himself, day after day, if he then burns the result? Gissing's work methods were, and always had been, inexorable: there was little joy in it for anyone else. He did not, in any sense, settle in Passy, becoming familiar with shops, bakers, restaurants, cafés and so on as most, or at least many, people would do, gradually getting to know people who belonged to the place. Rather, he used the Passy flat in rue de Siam as a *pied-à-terre* for his work. Consequently minor domestic friction about food and food bills loomed large. Moreover, when Gabrielle Fleury and Gissing had been planning their life together they had looked forward to a home of their own. In this they had been frustrated, partly by Gissing's illness, partly by the poor health of Mme. Fleury, partly by lack of money, and partly by Gabrielle's clear-headed realization that it was pointless to give up the Paris flat until she could see how they would manage elsewhere. Domestic problems arise in every household and the ones that arose between Gissing and Mme. Fleury have been exaggerated. It is most unlikely that they touched the bond of feeling that existed between Gissing and Gabrielle – whatever her mother may have thought!

In May of 1901, Gissing and Gabrielle Fleury went to England 'on business' (two books were about to come out). They stayed first with the Pinkers at Worcester Park and then with H. G. Wells until Gabrielle returned to France as planned on 4 June.

It was only after she was safely back in Paris that Gissing's friends tackled him on the question of his health. They had not seen him for almost two years. Now he was persuaded to see Pye-Smith again, the doctor he had seen a few years before. After much argument, discussion, consultation and recrimination (Wells said it would be 'suicide' to return to France and starve), Gissing was admitted to Dr. Jane Walker's private lung sanatorium at Stoke-in-Nayland in Suffolk, where he spent the greater part of the summer.

Gissing wrote about all these matters to Bertz on 20 June.

You will wonder what has become of me. Things have been happening. Some three weeks ago, I decided to come to England, for a few days, on business. Gabrielle accompanied me, and we spent a delightful week here at Sandgate in the house of Wells. I benefited so much that it was decided I should prolong my visit; the poor girl was obliged to go back on account of her mother. Well, I was next persuaded to consult a London doctor, and he spoke of my health in the gravest way. He said that, evidently, in France I was being starved. Steadily I had been losing weight, and my lung was getting into a dangerous condition. To pass the summer in France would probably mean death next winter.

Well, what could I say. I knew only too well that the French food did not suit me – but of course it is a very delicate subject (complicated with the mother-in-law difficulty). My friends here opposed themselves, tooth and nail, to my return to France. I had to yield to reason – why should I die, if I can help it? – and I have now decided to enter an English Sanatorium for the next two months. [6]

Two days later he again wrote to Bertz: 'If you write to Gabrielle, try to impress upon her the (surely obvious) fact that nothing on earth could keep me away from her but fear of utter ruin to my health. I *must get well*, that I may face the hard life which is before us.' [7]

The Sanatorium at Stoke-by-Nayland still exists, though it is now used for the care of the mentally retarded. Its pleasant hilltop position amongst meadows and wheatfields appealed to Gissing. Despite his normal intolerance of other people, the intolerance of the egotist, he found that he could get on quite well with some of the other patients. There was even a cigarette-smoking Newnham don, Rachel White, with whom he could talk books. Moreover, the enforced rest and the heavy diet allowed him to build up his strength, at least a little, a difficult thing in itself since he had lost a further twenty to twenty-five pounds while in France.

There is no point in regarding Gissing, at this stage in his career, as anything but a very ill man, the strands of whose existence could not be unmuddled. His whole personal life had been governed by Victorian inhibitions which made it impossible to do simply what he wanted to do. Now it was too late. Life with Gabrielle Fleury might have rescued him from the inhibitions of his early years, and the dogmatism that went with them, or it might not. Now it was only a muddle. He longed for England but had to live in France because of

Edith. He longed for Gabrielle Fleury but had to be in England because of his health. He longed for pleasure, but was dying. One cannot help but remember Gissing's eulogy of English food in *The Private Papers of Henry Ryecroft*: the beef which is 'veritably beef'; the mutton which is 'mutton in its purest essence'; the vegetables each of which 'yields its separate and characteristic sweetness'; the cod which boiled has that 'special savour which heaven has bestowed on cod'; 'the boiled beef and new potatoes' that delight men of 'superior intellect' and Tennyson, and of course gravy. 'Only English folk know what is meant by *gravy*; consequently the English alone are competent to speak on the question of sauce.'[8] Nor can one forget his contempt for foreign cooking, least of all his hatred of lentils and haricots, 'those pretentious cheats of the appetite, those tabulated humbugs, those certified aridities calling themselves human food'. Poor Gissing. He lived with two women, one an elderly invalid, the other a sedentary person who cared little for domestic matters. He so much wanted to be looked after and he so lacked the ability to describe in simple, unemotional terms his own needs. In Stoke-by-Nayland he was in effect force-fed. The medical treatment was not sophisticated but his stay there may well have added a couple of years to his life.

Gabrielle Fleury was not amused. Only a few weeks before they had gone to England Gissing had had a thorough examination by Chauffard, their doctor in Paris, who, according to a letter to Hick, had prescribed 'burning with a red-hot point under right clavicle, subcutaneous injection of an arsenical preparation; high feeding (esp. eggs and milk); cod liver oil, if possible thrice a day; much sleep, absolute cessation of work, and the day in the open air, the window open all night.'[9] This may sound extraordinary but at least he had had advice! Indeed, it was on Chauffard's advice that they were to go away for the summer. What then was so superior about English medical attention and why had Gissing changed his mind? Gabrielle resented his staying in England. She resented his doing so on the advice of his 'friends' after she had returned to France. She resented his going into a sanatorium in England. And of course she resented the innuendo and criticism arising from other people's discussion of how she and George lived. Naturally the resentment was in large measure the expression of affection. It really was very difficult for her to accept his decision to be away from her. This is seen easily enough if one compares the letter from Gissing to Bertz, quoted at some length above, with her letter to Mrs. H. G. Wells dated 12 July 1901.

In this letter, Gabrielle defended herself as best she could against actual and implied charges, countering Gissing's complaint that he was not master of his own household. 'Good George has the faculty of getting strange fancies in his head and to be easily wrong in things of that kind. He has no idea whatever about the realities of domestic life, but thinks he has, and as his criterion in that as in everything is Wakefield, if something is different it is immediately condemned.' Gabrielle explained that in the Paris flat her mother had 'executive power' so that Gabrielle would have more time to work on her translations, but that Gissing had concluded that the mother managed their lives and complained about it ceaselessly, not accepting Gabrielle's assurances. Then comes the telling comment:

> He is too glad to have found out a shadow to embody his latent – always latent – complaints, disquietude, discontent. You may be sure that as long as he has not found any, he dreadfully suffers from want of giving an appearance of consistency to that tormenting unquietness of his soul. He *can't* be unreservedly happy; it is not in his nature; and that is what it makes it really hard to sacrifice without good reason someone to him: because you know it will be a useless sacrifice.[10]

Here in a nutshell is the explanation not only of the strain between Gissing and Gabrielle Fleury, a strain that would be lessened once they were together again, but also of his earlier matrimonial difficulties. Unwittingly perhaps, Gabrielle Fleury spoke for Edith Underwood as well as for herself. Gissing still wanted to be both bohemian and bourgeois. It was too early for him to have any hope of being satisfied. Not until well into the twentieth century did people hit upon ways of satisfying this need.

Gabrielle Fleury then came to what she called the 'capital part' of her letter, her concern to have him back. She was alarmed lest Gissing might not return to her immediately after leaving the sanatorium: and 'troubled by the fear of having our meeting indefinitely postponed, either by a relapse in his health occasioned by all that fatigue, rushing, heat, change of life, etc., or by the urging of his family.'[11] She knew, also, that Gissing had decided to tell the Wakefield family about her, that he was apprehensive about telling them he had been living with her for a couple of years, and that his hesitation – natural enough, one would have thought – somehow made their marriage a 'monstrosity'.

In the event, Gissing refused a number of friendly invitations when he left the sanatorium, spent a week in Wakefield, and then joined Gabrielle at the Châlet Feuillebois near Autun. Gissing told Hick that he and the Wells' had 'together picked him out of a very swampy place.'[12] He wanted to be back in France. The correspondence between them perhaps reveals a little of how Gissing and Gabrielle thought of each other under strain. Who has not had such feelings as these when tested by poverty, ill-health, or the turns of fortune? Gissing and Gabrielle Fleury had not had the chance to grow into happiness by living together without hardship, without the mother or mother-in-law, and without the vast illness which utterly prevented Gissing from escaping from his past. New sets of experience, new experiences shared with her over a longer period of time, might have allowed him to modify his attitudes. As it was, he had no strength left except for survival and she had been forced to decide that there was a limit to the help she could give him.

Gissing spent the autumn revising *Ryecroft* (still, at this stage, called 'An Author at Grass'), moved later from Couhans to Four-chambault near Nevers to stay with cousins of Gabrielle, and in November travelled south to Arcachon where he found a room for the winter in a boarding-house-cum-invalids' home. Gabrielle went with him but returned to Paris on 15 December. He settled down to what was to be a miserably lonely four months' stay in Arcachon, a place that he rapidly came to hate. Nonetheless, he managed to finish his abridgement of Forster's *Dickens*, began to plan *Will Warburton*, but postponed work on 'The Vanquished Roman' (*Veranilda*) be-cause he needed his books and because serious writing was impossible until he could sit up and work at his desk.

At Arcachon, too, he had what he called 'grave personal news'. Edith had been arrested for ill-treatment of Alfred and, after exami-nation, had been certified insane. It was said that she had assaulted her landlord with a stick, destroyed the garden by beating the bushes, accused Gissing – to her neighbours – of homosexuality (for behaving like Oscar Wilde, as she put it), and persistently ill-treated Alfred. For some time Gissing had been receiving sensational news of this kind from Miss Orme through his solicitor, Brewster, who was responsible for his payments to Edith. Now he heard that Edith had been com-mitted to Fisherton House, Salisbury, and Alfred sent by Miss Orme to a farm at Mabe in Cornwall, near the home of Eliza Orme's sister. Characteristically, Gissing commented: 'My mind, on *that* score, is enormously relieved. I always felt myself guilty of a crime in aban-doning the little fellow. He will how have his chance to grow up in healthy and decent circumstances.'[13]

Gissing had long ago ceased to regard his wife as a real flesh and blood person, with feelings and desires and anxieties which one might try to understand. The alienation had been so complete that he did not feel any association with her. Nor did he feel at all close to his children, whom he never saw again.[14] Because of the years in Exeter and Brixton, he remembered Walter as unruly and genuinely believed he would have the best possible life if he remained in Wakefield. Alfred, his second son, he did not know at all. He said he hoped he would be interested in turnips, meaning that he hoped he would be spared the turmoil and unhappiness of a literary existence. When Edith was committed, another man would have gathered his sons to him, whether in France or England. Gissing was too ill and had dissociated himself entirely from his second marriage, which had been a disaster in ways his first marriage had not. His family survived him. Walter died in the trenches in the Battle of the Somme. Edith died in Fisherton House in 1917 of 'congenital brain disease' – a euphemism used after a post-mortem that did not pretend to scientific accuracy. Alfred is alive still and lives in Switzerland. At Arcachon, during the miserable winter of 1901–2, Gissing lay on his back, helplessly, on a chaise-longue. There would have been no point in his family knowing the grave reality of his condition, and there was nothing anybody could have done for him.

To be alive at all, however, meant to be writing. Incredibly, Gissing maintained to the end of his life the style of living he had chosen for himself when he left school. For whatever cause, he carried with him a highly developed sense of what it meant to be a man of letters. Few Victorians manifested this more strongly than he did. Literature and life were mutually opposed; a man of letters was above those things which concerned the multitude. To keep one's mind clear and free of cant, to read continually, to be conversant with other languages and literatures, to travel to parts of the world where earlier civilizations had flourished, and to write, if one could, or in some way contribute to the arts; these were his ideals and in these he was typical of his age. He did not look forward, politically, as some of the writers of the nineties naturally did. Some of his characters looked forward but Gissing himself held to the principles that had given his difficult life its meaning. Consequently it is during the painful period between his leaving Arcachon in the spring of 1902 to his death in the early winter of 1903 that he wrote some of his most serene letters. He had what he wanted. He was reading, was writing – though only for one or two hours a day – was corresponding, though more infrequently, with his literary friends, and was living with Gabrielle Fleury. This was as much as he had ever desired and there is a sense in which the fact that he was dying made no difference to him. Had he known of the controversies that were to arise after his death he would surely have dismissed them as yet another example of people's failure to understand. His life in fact had had a consistency to it that few people, then or later, had been able to detect.

Gissing left Arcachon as soon as he could, went south and found a room for himself in Saint-Jean-de-Luz, or rather in Ciboure on the other side of the harbour, at 42 Quai de Ciboure, which is still much the same as it was when Gissing lived there. After much hesitation and deliberation, the normal talk of people searching for a new home, he and Gabrielle Fleury rented a house for one year, from 2 July 1902, with a rent of 1,500 francs a year. This was the Villa Lannes, Place de la Mairie in Ciboure. *The Private Papers of Henry Ryecroft* appeared in four instalments in the *Fortnightly Review* during 1902 and was immediately successful; Gissing did not enjoy the financial success since he did not live long enough, but the spontaneous and immediate acclaim was a delight. During the winter of 1902–3, he worked both at *Veranilda* and at *Will Warburton*, eventually putting the first aside, so that he could complete the easier one. He thus completed *Will Warburton* in March 1903, having worked at it throughout the winter. In June 1903, when the year's lease expired, they moved inland to the rarer air of Saint-Jean-Pied-de-Port and took a house, the 'Maison Elgué', on the outskirts in Ispoure. There Gissing devoted the whole of his attention to *Veranilda*, the Roman historical romance that he had had in mind for at least a decade. Unfortunately, the novel was not quite finished when Gissing died, partly because he gave a couple of weeks in December to the writing of a short story, 'Topham's Chance', for the *Daily Mail*. The labours of these years were published posthumously by Constable: *Veranilda*, lacking five chapters, in 1904 and *Will Warburton* in 1905. Gissing had kept writing to the very end.

Gissing died in Ispoure on 28 December 1903, the immediate cause of death being heart failure brought about by double pneumonia. H. G. Wells came from England, at Gissing's request, but arriving on Christmas Day was too late since Gissing, who had been ill since about 8 December and seriously in danger for more than a week, did not recover full consciousness. Wells was obliged to return to England before Gissing died. Morley Roberts went out from England and, with Gabrielle Fleury, was present when Gissing died, after several awful days of incoherent talk broken by fewer and fewer moments of lucidity. It is unlikely that Gissing would have cared one way or another about where he was to be buried, since he had been an atheist throughout his life: Gabrielle Fleury bought ground in perpetuity in the cemetery in Saint-Jean-de-Luz where his simple and dignified grave is still be be seen.

Gissing had not prepared for the event of his own death. For *him* everything was in order if, living and working with the person he loved, and writing as energetically as his strength would permit, which was the only thing he positively enjoyed, he was not bothered by other aspects of life by being made conscious of them. Had he known of the difficulties that were to arise after his death – that a controversy would arise over H. G. Wells' commissioned introduction to *Veranilda*, which was burned by the family, that Gabrielle Fleury's position would prove embarrassingly arduous because he had not told her about his early life or told people in England about her, so that even her right to be associated with him in name was cast in doubt, that there would be a dispute between the executors of his will, Clara Collett and his brother Algernon, and Morley Roberts over Roberts' claim to be the biographer designated by Gissing, and that the Wakefield Gissings would exert themselves, for the sake of the children and to protect his name, to prevent the full facts of his life being known, with the result that rumour and half-truth prospered where truth was denied – had he known of these difficulties, he would have regarded them not as things which, by prudent management, might have been avoided but as the inevitable pressures of existence which merely had to be accepted as they occurred. His life had had the strong cast of the late nineteenth-century determinist intellectual. Nothing had happened to him during his life to make him disavow the pessimistic type of humanism that had informed the years between leaving home and his death. Life was a hopeless muddle: that had to be accepted. Literacy, civilization, art and literature to some extent compensated for the muddle: they could be enjoyed. The intelligent, educated individual had little in common with the majority: he had to accept the difficulties that went with alienation if he wanted the pleasures. This nineteenth-century liberal creed seems hopelessly antiquated now. Gissing held to it steadfastly through his working years. Well might he have said that what happened after his death was no concern of his and, if he *had* said so, the remark would have demonstrated both the strength and the weakness of his whole thinking life. He had always placed the individual before the society and, being a person of immense courage, determination and strength of mind, had done so inexorably. He knew he had been misunderstood during his lifetime. Why should he be understood after his death?

In all probability the years Gissing spent with Gabrielle Fleury in the south of France, after the petty domestic bickerings of the Paris days had been resolved, were the happiest he had spent since the rapturous times with Helen twenty-five years earlier. For more than that he had no desire.

Notes

Abbreviations to the notes

ALS	Autograph letter script.
Beinecke	The Beinecke Rare Book Room and Manuscript Library, Yale University, New Haven, Connecticut.
Berg	The Berg Collection of the New York Public Library.
Bertz	*The Letters of George Gissing to Eduard Bertz, 1887–1903*, A. C. Young (ed.), Rutgers University Press and Constable 1961.
Commonplace Book	*George Gissing's Commonplace Book*, Jacob Korg (ed.), New York Public Library 1962.
Diary	Gissing's diary in the Berg Collection of the New York Public Library, currently being edited for publication by Pierre Coustillas.
Essays and Fiction	*George Gissing: Essays and Fiction*, Pierre Coustillas (ed.), The John Hopkins Press 1970.
Fleury	*The Letters of George Gissing to Gabrielle Fleury*, Pierre Coustillas (ed.), New York Public Library 1964.
Gettman	R. A. Gettman: *A Victorian Publisher*, Cambridge University Press 1960.
Hick	*Henry Hick's Recollections of George Gissing*, Pierre Coustillas (ed.), Enitharmon Press 1972.
Huntington	The Henry E. Huntington Library, San Marino, California.
Korg	Jacob Korg, *George Gissing: a Critical Biography*, Washington University Press 1963, and Methuen 1965.
Letters	*Letters of George Gissing to Members of his Family*, Collected and arranged by Algernon and Ellen Gissing, Constable 1927.
Maitland	Morley Roberts, *The Private Life of Henry Maitland*.
Pforzheimer	The Carl H. and Lily Pforzheimer Library, New York.
Ryecroft	George Gissing, *The Private Papers of Henry Ryecroft*, Constable 1903.
Wells	*George Gissing and H. G. Wells*, edited by R. A. Gettman, Hart Davis 1961.

Chapter 1 *The Bourgeois Bohemian*

1   *Athenaeum* 12 January 1895, p. 45; reprinted in *The Critical Heritage* (Coustillas and Partridge) pp. 233–4
2   *George Gissing: A Critical Study*, Martin Secker, London 1924, p. 18ff. (The first edition was published in 1912 but my reference is to the reset second edition)
3   R. West, introduction to an edition of *Workers in the Dawn* manufactured in 1930 by Bowling Green Press, but never issued. Beinecke Library.
4   W. M. Colles. 'George Gissing', *The Academy* LXVI (9 January 1904) p. 40.

Chapter 2 *Youth, Education, Prison and Exile*

1   *Commonplace Book*, p. 23.
2   *Ibid.*, pp. 23–4.
3   *Ibid.*, p. 23.
4   *Ryecroft*, p. 271.
5   *Commonplace Book*, p. 24.
6   *Ryecroft*, p. 288.
7   Ellen Gissing, 'George Gissing A Character Sketch', *The Nineteenth Century*, September 1927, p. 418.
8   Unpublished letter to Algernon Gissing: Beinecke.
9   *Ibid.*
10 *Fleury*, p. 54.
11 Ellen Gissing, 'George Gissing A Character Sketch', *The Nineteenth Century*, September 1927, p. 417.
12 Unpublished notebook in the Beinecke.
13 *George Gissing at Alderley Edge*, Pierre Coustillas (ed.), Enitharmon Press 1969, p. 13. T. T. Sykes wrote an obituary notice for the *Cheshire Daily Echo* and the *Alderley and Wilmslow Advertiser* which is reprinted in full in *George Gissing at Alderley Edge*.
14 Arthur Bowes, 'George Gissing's School Days', *TP's Weekly*, 22 January 1904, p. 100. See *George Gissing at Alderley Edge*, pp. 16–18 for further details of the obituary notice by Arthur Bowes.
15 Verbatim entry supplied by C. T. Latham, the City of Manchester Magistrates' Court.
16 *Bertz*, pp. xix–xx.
17 *Maitland*, p. 32.
18 *Ibid.*, p. 28.
19 This transcript from Owens College has been made available by Vincent Knowles, Registrar, Manchester University.
20 Pierre Coustillas, 'George Gissing à Manchester', *Etudes Anglaises*, T.XVI, No. 3, pp. 256–7.
21 *Ibid.*, pp. 258–9.
22 *Ibid.*, p. 259.
23 *Ibid.*, p. 259.
24 *Letters*, p. 19.
25 See Gissing's *Sins of the Fathers*, Chicago 1924 and *Brownie*, Columbia University Press 1931.

26 *Letters*, p. 16.
27 G. A. Stearns, 'George Gissing in America', *The Bookman*, LXIII, No. 6, August 1926.
28 *Korg*, p. 16.
29 See Michael Collie, 'The Revision of George Gissing's *New Grub Street*', *Yearbook of English Studies*, January 1974, pp. 212–24.
30 *New Grub Street*, III, Smith, Elder 1891, p. 110.
31 *Ibid.*, p. 110.

Chapter 3   *His First Marriage*

1 *Letters*, p. 28.
2 *Commonplace Book*, p. 25.
3 *Ryecroft*, p. 28.
4 *Ibid.*, pp. 28–9.
5 *Ibid.*, p. 21.
6 *Letters*, p. 31.
7 *Ibid.*, p. 31.
8 *Bertz*, p. xx.
9 'Diary'.
10 Beinecke, unpublished ALS to Algernon, September 1878.
11 *Letters*, pp. 45–6.
12 *Bertz*, p. xix.
13 *Letters*, p. 22.
14 *Maitland*, p. 40.
15 'George Gissing: A Character Sketch', *The Nineteenth Century*, September 1927, p. 413.
16 *Letters*, p. 52.
17 *Workers in the Dawn*, Doubleday Doran, II, p. 89.
18 *Maitland*, pp. 41–2.
19 *Ibid.*, p. 42.
20 Korg's *George Gissing A Critical Biography* was a splendid pioneer work and I intend no disparagement of Korg's scholarship in disagreeing with him, at times strongly, on questions of interpretation.
21 *Korg*, p. 12.
22 *Ibid.*, p. 12.
23 *Ibid.*, p. 22.
24 *Ibid.*, p. 26.
25 Pierre Coustillas, *Essays and Fiction*, p. 7.
26 See Michael Collie, *George Gissing: A Bibliography*, Dawson, 1975.
27 'The Lost Realist', *English Studies Today*, 1973, pp. 359–85.
28 *Workers in the Dawn*, II, p. 55.
29 *Ibid.*, II, pp. 58–9.
30 *Ibid.*, II, p. 105.
31 *Ibid.*, II, p. 109.
32 *Ibid.*, II, p. 110.
33 *Ibid.*, II, pp. 147–8.
34 *Essays and Fiction*, p. 7.
35 *Letters*, p. 64.
36 *Ibid.*, p. 73.

37 *Ibid.*, p. 72.
38 ALS, Beinecke, to Algernon, 23 April 1880.
39 ALS, Beinecke, to Algernon, 16 May 1880.
40 ALS, Beinecke, to Algernon, 3 November 1880.
41 Compare unpublished letter dated 8 August 1881, University of Virginia Library, 'Nell is back here now, & my leisure & ability for productive work consequently suffer diminution, but I absolutely *must* complete my novel this year.'
42 Unpublished letter to Algernon Gissing, January 1882, Beinecke Library.
43 18 January 1882 to Algernon, in Beinecke: 'I have just found a bottle of gin in one of her boxes. She vows it has been there since she went away. I do not know what to believe.'
44 Unpublished letter to Algernon dated 18 May 1882, in the McGregor Collection of the University of Virginia Library.
45 Unpublished letter to Algernon dated 2 November 1882, in the McGregor Collection of the University of Virginia Library.
46 Unpublished letter to Algernon dated 27 December 1882, in the McGregor Collection of the University of Virginia Library.
47 *Ryecroft*, p. 15.

Chapter 4 *Literary Apprenticeship*

1 *Commonplace Book*, p. 57.
2 *Gettman*, p. 231.
3 Austin Harrison, 'George Gissing', *The Nineteenth Century*, September 1906, pp. 453–63.
4 *Ryecroft*, p. 52.
5 This phase in Gissing's life is covered in his *Notes on Social Democracy*, Enitharmon Press 1968, which has a useful introduction by Jacob Korg.
6 *Commonplace Book*, p. 33.
7 *Letters*, pp. 73–4.
8 *Ibid.*, pp. 77–9.
9 Ellen Gissing, 'George Gissing A Character Sketch,' *The Nineteenth Century*, September 1927, pp. 420–1.
10 *Ibid.*, p. 420.
11 Austin Harrison, pp. 453–4.
12 *Gettman*, p. 220.
13 *Letters*, p. 142.
14 *Ibid.*, p. 141.
15 *Ibid.*, p. 140.
16 Unpublished letter to Frederic Harrison, Pforzheimer Library, 24 June 1884.
17 Unpublished letter to Mrs. Harrison, Pforzheimer Library, 6 June 1884.
18 *Letters*, p. 139.
19 Unpublished letter to Frederic Harrison, Pforzheimer Library, 17 August 1884.
20 Unpublished letter to Algernon, McGregor Collection, University of

Virginia Library, 23 December 1884: 'I am right gloriously established: if you could but see this study. Words are useless to describe it; you must come before long. How grand it was to hear the postman's knock this morning at my own front door! Really there is every convenience of a house, with none of the inconveniences . . . The independence and seclusion of the place is amazing.'

21 *Letters*, p. 152.
22 *Ibid.*, p. 159.
23 Unpublished letter to Algernon, 28 February 1885, in the McGregor Collection, University of Virginia Library.
24 *Letters*, p. 158.

Chapter 5 *Naturalism*

1   *Letters*, pp. 56–7.
2   *Ibid.*, pp. 128–9.
3   *Ibid.*, p. 140.
4   *Ibid.*, p. 211 (as edited).
5   *Ibid.*, p. 333.
6   *Letters*, p. 318.
7   *Bertz*, pp. 73–4.
8   Unpublished letter to Edith Sichel, 8 June 1891, Pforzheimer.
9   *Bertz*, p. 4.
10 *Letters*, p. 172.
11 *Ibid.*, p. 174.
12 *Ibid.*, p. 179.
13 *Ibid.*, p. 184.
14 *Ibid.*, p. 189.
15 *Ibid.*, p. 196.
16 Diary entry for 7 June 1888: 'I wrote it from February to May, immediately after finishing *Thyrza*. Then I took it to Bentley and offered it for [the magazine] *Temple Bar*. For that purpose he declined to use it but was willing to publish it in vols.'
17 Unpublished letter to Mrs. Harrison, 7 September 1887, Pforzheimer.
18 Diary entry, 3 June 1888.
19 *Diary*, p. 8.
20 *The Nether World*, 2nd edn, Ch. XXXI.
21 These and subsequent quotations are taken from Ch. XII 'Io Saturnalia'.
22 *Bertz.*, pp. 7–8.
23 *Diary*, 18 October 1888.
24 *Ryecroft*, p. 206.
25 *Bertz*, p. 13.
26 *Ibid.*, 13, 14, 18–19, 24.
27 *Commonplace Book*, p. 65.
28 *Ibid.*, p. 46.

Chapter 6 *The Second Marriage Disaster*

1   Unpublished letter to Ellen Gissing, 30 July 1889, McGregor Collection, University of Virginia Library.

2 Unpublished letter to Edith Sichel, 8 June 1889, Berg Collection.
3 'Diary', 9 November 1899.
4 *Bertz*, p. 89.
5 *Ibid.*, p. 81.
6 *Ibid.*, p. 91.
7 'A Lodger in Maze Pond', *The National Review*, February 1895; reprinted in *The House of Cobwebs*, Constable 1906.
8 *Bertz*, p. 110.
9 *Ibid.*, p. 112.
10 *Ryecroft*, p. 166.
11 *Commonplace Book*, p. 25.
12 Unpublished letter to Ellen Gissing, January 1891, Beinecke Library.
13 Unpublished letter to Ellen Gissing, 1 February 1891, Beinecke Library.
14 Unpublished letter to Ellen Gissing, 7 March 1891, Beinecke Library.
15 Unpublished letter to Algernon, 6 November 1891, Beinecke Library.
16 *Ryecroft*, p. 26.
17 Unpublished letter, 1 February 1891, Beinecke Library.
18 *Letters*, pp. 312–3.
19 *Ibid.*, p. 318.

Chapter 7 *Collapse*

1 *Letters*, p. 321.
2 *Ibid.*, p. 323.
3 *Bertz*, p. 137.
4 I cannot agree with Pierre Coustillas who said that 'Gissing's refusal to have his novel republished was . . . entirely due to circumstances', unless the circumstances were that Gissing so disliked the novel that he found revision an 'ordeal'. See, however, the introduction to the Harvester Press edition of *Isabel Clarendon*, p. xxxiii.
5 See Michael Collie, *George Gissing: A Bibliography*, Dawson 1975, pp. 26–9. Robert Shafer recorded Gissing's corrections to Vol I of the first edition in the two volume edition of the novel published by Doubleday Doran in 1935. These corrections immensely improve the book.
6 *Letters*, p. 323.
7 *Bertz*, p. 163.
8 *Letters*, p. 341.
9 *Bertz*, p. 98.
10 *Ibid.*, p. 171.
11 Unpublished letter to Morley Roberts, the Berg Collection.
12 *Fleury*, p. 29.
13 See Korg's account of this. 'During the winter he suffered from a serious cough.' *George Gissing: A Critical Biography*, p. 205. Although critics like Korg have noted Gissing's decline in health, few have accepted it as a principal cause of difficulty in his later years.
14 *Maitland*, p. 156.
15 'Diary'.
16 *Ibid.*
17 *Ibid.*

18 Ruth Adams, 'George Gissing and Clara Collet', *Nineteenth Century Fiction XI*, June 1956, p. 75.

Chapter 8 *The Crown of Life*

1   Unpublished letter to Morley Roberts dated 1 December 1893, Berg Collection.
2   *Bertz*, pp. 235–6.
3   *Ibid.*, p. 236.
4   *Ibid.*, p. 238.
5   *By the Ionian Sea*, 1905 Edition, p. 10.
6   *Ibid.*, pp. 109–10.
7   *Ibid.*, p. 235.
8   *Bertz*, p. 244.
9   Letter to Henry Hick, 17 June 1898, *Hick*, p. 52.
10 *Ryecroft*, pp. 6–9.
11 *Wells*, p. 102.
12 *Ibid.*, p. 104.
13 *Fleury*, pp. 24–5.
14 *Ibid.*, p. 27.
15 *Ibid.*, p. 28.
16 *Ibid.*, p. 34.
17 *Ibid.*, p. 32.
18 *Ibid.*, p. 38.
19 *Ibid.*, p. 91.
20 *Ibid.*, p. 79.
21 Unpublished letter in the Pforzheimer Library.
22 *Bertz*, p. 22.

Chapter 9 *Death in Exile*

1   Letter, dated 6 February 1899 from Gissing to Morley Roberts, quoted in *Fleury*, p. 105.
2   *Bertz*, p. 260.
3   *Ibid.*, p. 263.
4   *Fleury*, p. 126.
5   *Ibid.*, p. 125.
6   *Bertz*, p. 295.
7   *Ibid.*, p. 297.
8   *Ryecroft*, pp. 240ff.
9   *Hick*, p. 59.
10 *Wells*, p. 185.
11 *Ibid.*, p. 187.
12 *Hick*, p. 62.
13 *Bertz*, p. 306.
14 No simple account can be given of Gissing's attitude to his two sons. When he first told Gabrielle Fleury that he was married and had two children, he said that he regarded them both with 'infinite tenderness' (*Fleury*, p. 37). On the other hand, when she urged him to keep the boys with him and said she would help to care for them, he replied: 'I could not help feeling that there would be a certain *unkindness* in

taking him [Walter] away from my relations just now . . . the £40 which I pay for him . . . is a matter of considerable importance to my sisters; they would feel the loss rather seriously.' (*Fleury*, p. 121). Gissing knew that the situation had become hopeless in as far as Edith wanted custody of both boys as a condition of divorce. See also *Hick*, pp. 54–5.

Bibliography

George Gissing's Major Works

Workers in the Dawn, Remington, London 1880.
The Unclassed, Chapman & Hall, London 1884.
Isabel Clarendon, Chapman & Hall, London 1886.
Demos, Smith, Elder, London 1886.
Thyrza, Smith, Elder, London 1887.
A Life's Morning, Smith, Elder, London 1888.
The Nether World, Smith, Elder, London 1889.
The Emancipated, Richard Bentley & Son, London 1890.
New Grub Street, Smith, Elder, London 1891.
Denzil Quarrier, Lawrence & Bullen, London 1892.
Born in Exile, Adam & Charles Black, London 1892.
The Odd Women, Lawrence & Bullen, London 1893.
In the Year of Jubilee, Lawrence & Bullen, London 1894.
Eve's Ransom, Lawrence & Bullen, London 1895.
The Paying Guest, Cassell, London 1895.
Sleeping Fires, T. Fisher Unwin, London 1895.
The Whirlpool, Lawrence & Bullen, London 1897.
Human Odds and Ends, Lawrence & Bullen, London 1898.
Charles Dickens, Blackie & Son, London 1898.
The Town Traveller, Methuen, London 1898.
The Crown of Life, Methuen, London 1899.
Our Friend the Charlatan, Chapman & Hall, London 1901.
By the Ionian Sea, Chapman & Hall, London 1901.
The Private Papers of Henry Ryecroft, Archibald Constable, London 1903.
Will Warburton, Archibald Constable, London 1905.
Veranilda, Archibald Constable, London 1904.
The House of Cobwebs, Archibald Constable, London 1906.
The Immortal Dickens, Cecil Palmer, London 1924.

Sins of the Fathers, Pascal Covici, Chicago 1924.
A Victim of Circumstances, Constable, London 1927.
Brownie, Columbia University Press, New York 1931.
Notes on Social Democracy, Enitharmon Press, London 1968.

Letters

Letters of George Gissing to Members of his Family, Algernon and Ellen Gissing (eds.), Constable, London 1927.
George Gissing and H. G. Wells, Their Friendship and Correspondence, Royal A. Gettmann (ed.), University of Illinois Press, Urbana 1961.
The Letters of George Gissing to Eduard Bertz, 1887–1903, Arthur C. Young (ed.), Rutgers University Press, New Brunswick 1961.
The Letters of George Gissing to Gabrielle Fleury, Pierre Coustillas (ed.), New York Public Library, 1964.
The Letters of George Gissing to Edward Clodd, Pierre Coustillas (ed.), Enitharmon Press, London 1973.

Books

CLODD, Edward. *Memories*, Chapman & Hall, London 1916.
COLLIE, Michael. *George Gissing: A Bibliography*, University of Toronto Press, and Dawson, 1975.
COUSTILLAS, Pierre (ed.). *My First Rehearsal and My Clerical Rival*, Enitharmon Press, London 1970.
— (ed.). *George Gissing Essays and Fiction*, The Johns Hopkins Press, Baltimore 1970.
— (ed.) *Gissing's Writings on Dickens*, Enitharmon Press, London 1970.
— (ed.). *George Gissing at Alderley Edge*, Enitharmon Press, London 1970.
— and SPIERS, John. *The Rediscovery of George Gissing*, National Book League, 1971.
— and PARTRIDGE, Colin (eds.). *Gissing: The Critical Heritage*, Routledge & Kegan Paul, London 1972.
— (ed.). *Henry Hick's Recollections of George Gissing*, Enitharmon Press, London 1973.
DONNELLY, Mabel Collins. *George Gissing: Grave Comedian*, Harvard University Press, 1954.
GORDAN, John D. *George Gissing: 1857–1903* (Catalogue for an exhibition of materials from the Berg Collection of the New York Public Library), New York Public Library 1954.
HARRISON, Austin. *Frederic Harrison: Thoughts and Memories*, Heinemann, London 1926.

KORG, Jacob (ed.). *George Gissing's Commonplace Book*, New York Public Library 1962.

— *George Gissing: A Critical Biography*, Washington University Press, Seattle 1963; Methuen, London 1965.

ROBERTS, Morley. *The Private Life of Henry Maitland*, Eveleigh, Nash & Grayson, London 1923.

SWINNERTON, Frank. *George Gissing: A Critical Study*, M. Secker, London 1912.

TINDALL, Gillian. *The Born Exile, George Gissing*, London 1974.

WELLS, H. G. *Experiment in Autobiography*, Macmillan, New York 1934.

YATES, May, *George Gissing: An Appreciation* (Publications of the University of Manchester, English Series No. XII), The University Press, 1922.

Articles

ADAMS, George M. 'How and Why I Collect George Gissing', *The Colophon*, Part XVIII (1934), no pagination.

ADAMS, Ruth M. 'George Gissing and Clara Collet', *Nineteenth Century Fiction*, XI (June 1956), pp. 72–7.

BERGONZI, Bernard. 'The Novelist as Hero', *Twentieth Century*, CLXIV (November 1958), pp. 444–55.

BOWES, Arthur. 'George Gissing's School Days', *TP's Weekly* (22 January 1904), p. 100.

COLLES, W. M. 'George Gissing', *Academy*, LXVI (9 January 1904), p. 40.

COLLIE, Michael. 'The Lost Realist', *English Studies Today*, Istanbul 1973, pp. 359–85.

— 'Gissing's Revision of *New Grub Street*', *The Year Book of English Studies*, IV (1974), pp. 212–24.

— 'How George Gissing Disappeared', *English Studies in Canada*, I (Winter 1975), No. 4, pp. 434–49.

COUSTILLAS, Pierre. 'George Gissing à Manchester', *Etudes Anglaises*, XVI, pp. 255–61.

— 'George Gissing et Eduard Bertz: Une amitié littéraire', *Revue de littérature comparée*, XXVII, (July), pp. 394–405.

— 'George Gissing et H. G. Wells', *Etudes Anglaises*, XV, pp. 156–66.

— 'Gissing and Butler Clarke', *Gissing Newsletter* II (April 1966), pp. 6–7.

— 'Gissing: Some More Biographical Details', *Notes and Queries*, XIII, (1967), pp. 68–9.

— 'Gissing's Feminine Portraiture', *English Literature in Transition*, VI, pp. 130–41.

— and SPIERS, John. 'A George Gissing Bibliography', *The Book Collecting and Library Monthly*, (September, October, November 1969).

FARRAR, F. W. 'The Nether World', *Contemporary Review*, LVI (September 1889), pp. 370–80.

FRANCIS, C. J. 'Gissing and Schopenhauer', *Nineteenth Century Fiction*, XV, pp. 63.

GETTMANN, Royal A. 'Bentley and Gissing', *Nineteenth Century Fiction*, XI (March 1957), pp. 306–14.

GISSING, Alfred C. 'George Gissing—Some Aspects of His Life and Work', *National Review*, XCIII (August 1929), pp. 932–41.

— *London Times Literary Supplement*, (12 April 1933) p. 261, (27 April 1933), p. 295.

— 'Gissing's Unfinished Romance', *National Review*, CVII (January 1937), pp. 82–91.

GISSING, Ellen. 'George Gissing: A Character Sketch', *Nineteenth Century and After*, CII (September 1927), pp. 417–24.

— 'Some Personal Recollections of George Gissing', *Blackwood's Magazine*, CCXXV (May 1929), pp. 653–60.

HAIGHT, Gordon S. 'Gissing: Some Biographical Details', *Notes and Queries*, pp. 235–6.

HARRISON, Austin. 'George Gissing', *Nineteenth Century and After*, LX (September 1906), pp. 453–63.

KIRK, Russell. 'Who Knows George Gissing?', *Western Humanities Review*, IV, (Summer 1950), pp. 213–22.

KORG, Jacob. 'George Gissing's Outcast Intellectuals', *American Scholar*, XIX (Spring 1950), pp. 194–202.

— 'Division of Purpose in George Gissing', *PMLA*, LXX (June 1955), pp. 323–36.

— 'The Spiritual Theme of George Gissing's *Born in Exile*', in *From Jane Austen to Joseph Conrad*, Robert C. Rathburn and Martin Steinmann (eds.), University of Minnesota Press 1958

— 'George Moore (and) George Gissing', *Victorian Fiction*, 27, pp. 388.

LEAVIS, Q. D. 'Gissing and the English Novel', *Scrutiny*, VII (June 1938), pp. 73–81.

ORWELL, George. 'Not Enough Money', *Tribune*, London (2 April 1953), p. 12.

PURDY, Richard L. 'George Gissing at Max Gate 1895', *Yale University Library Gazette*, XVII, pp. 51–2.

ROBERTS, Morley. 'George Gissing', *Queen's Quarterly*, XXXVII (Autumn 1930), pp. 617–33.

— 'The Letters of George Gissing', *Virginia Quarterly Review*, (July 1931), pp. 409–26.

SHAFER, Robert. *Bookman*, LXXIV, pp. 674–7; *London Mercury*, XXIV, p. 462 (1932).

SICHEL, Edith. 'Two Philanthropic Novelists: Mr. Walter Besant and Mr. George Gissing', *Murray's Magazine*, III (April 1888), pp. 506–18.

STEINER, Jacqueline. 'George Gissing to His Sister: Letters of George Gissing', *More Books* (Bulletin of the Boston Public Library), XXII (November, December 1947), pp. 323–36, 376–86.

SWINNERTON, Frank. 'The Real Gissing', *The Bookman*, London, XLIII, pp. 173–4.

Times Literary Supplement (London), No. 2404 (14 February 1948), p. 92, 'The Permanent Stranger', No. 2861 (28 December 1956), p. 780.

— (London), 'Gissing's Academic Career', (20 May 1944), p. 252.

WELLS, H. G. 'The Novels of Mr. George Gissing', *Contemporary Review*, LXXII (August 1897), pp. 192–201.

— 'George Gissing, An Impression', *Monthly Review*, XVI (August 1904), pp. 160–72.

— 'The Truth about George Gissing', *Literary Supplement to Rhythm* (December 1912), pp. i–iii.

WOLFF, Joseph J. 'Gissing's Revision of *The Unclassed*', *Nineteenth Century Fiction*, VIII (June 1953), pp. 42–52.

— 'George Gissing: An Annotated Bibliography of Writings about Him', Northern Illinois University Press, 1971.

WOOLF, Virginia. 'George Gissing', in *The Common Reader, Second Series*, Hogarth Press, London 1932.

YOUNG, Arthur C. 'George Gissing's Friendship with Eduard Bertz', *Nineteenth Century Fiction*, XIII (December 1958), pp. 227–37.

— 'Gissing's *Veranilda*', *Notes and Queries*, IV, p. 359.

— 'The Death of Gissing: A Fourth Report', *Essays in Literary History*, XVI, pp. 217–8.

Index